READING THE APOCALYPSE IN BED
Selected Plays and Short Pieces

About the translators

Adam Czerniawski is a poet and has translated Różewicz's plays
and poetry. He lives in Norwich, England.

Barbara Plebanek is a Polish translator and interpreter. She
lives in London.

Tony Howard is a playwright and lectures on Polish theatre at
the University of Warwick.

READING THE APOCALYPSE IN BED
Selected Plays and Short Pieces

Tadeusz Różewicz

**Translated by Adam Czerniawski,
Barbara Plebanek and Tony Howard**

With an Introductory Essay by Tony Howard

MARION BOYARS
LONDON • NEW YORK

This volume first published in Great Britain and the United States
in 1998 by Marion Boyars Publishers
24 Lacy Road, London SW15 1NL
237 East 39th Street, New York NY 10016

Distributed in Australia and New Zealand by
Peribo Pty Ltd, 58 Beaumont Road, Mount Kuring-gai, NSW

The Card Index, The Interrupted Act and *Gone Out* first published in Great Britain 1969
by Calder & Boyars Publishers Ltd

The Witnesses, The Old Woman Broods and *The Funny Old Man* first published in Great
Britain 1970 by Calder & Boyars Publishers Ltd

All other plays first published in English in this edition

© Tadeusz Różewicz 1969, 1970, 1998

English translations and Introduction
© Marion Boyars Publishers 1998

British Library Cataloguing in Publication Data
Różewicz, Tadeusz, 1921–
    Reading the apocalypse in bed: selected plays and short pieces
    1. Różewicz, Tadeusz, 1921 – Translations into English
    I. Title
    891.8'527

Library of Congress Cataloging-in-Publication Data
Różewicz, Tadeusz.
    [Plays. English. Selections]
    Reading the apocalypse in bed: selected plays and short pieces/
Tadeusz Różewicz: translated by Adam Czerniawski, Barbara Plebanek
and Tony Howard: with an introductory essay by Tony Howard.
    Translated from Polish.
    1. Różewicz, Tadeusz – Translations into English. I. Czerniawski,
Adam, 1934–. II. Plebanek, Barbara. III. Howard, Tony.
    IV. Title.
    PG7158.R63A24 1998
    891.8'5273–dc21   98–25180

ISBN 0–7145–3037–9 Paperback

Typeset in 10½/12½ pt Cremona and Fujiyama by
Ann Buchan (Typesetters), Shepperton, Middlesex.
Printed by Athenaeum Press Ltd., Gateshead, Tyne & Wear, England.

CONTENTS

CHRONOLOGY OF THE PLAYS IN THIS COLLECTION

The Card Index (1957–9; Première Warsaw 1960. First published in *Dialog* Number 2; 1960; variations published 1971)

The Witnesses (1961–2; première Switzerland 1963. First published in *Dialog* Number 5, 1962)

The Interrupted Act (1963; première Germany 1965. First published in *Dialog* Number 1, 1964)

The Funny Old Man (1963; première Warsaw 1965. First published in *Dialog* Number 2, 1964)

Gone Out (1964; première Krakow 1965. First published in *Dialog* Number 10, 1964)

The Old Woman Broods (1968; première Wrocław 1969. First published in *Dialog* Number 2, 1968)

The following pieces have all been first published in this edition:

What You Got Here, The Little Garden of Eden (1960–65; première Kalisz 1971)

The Theatre of Inconsistency: 'Metamorphoses', 'Rubbing His Hands Together', 'Babybabba', 'Doppelgänger', 'A Discordant Drama', 'What's More What's Less' (première Warsaw 1979)

Birth Rate (1958–67; première Wrocław 1979)

The Order Squad (1964; première Wrocław 1979)

Note: The translations of *The Card Index, The Witnesses, The Interrupted Act, The Funny Old Man, Gone Out* and *The Old Woman Broods* in this volume are by Adam Czerniawski. The rest are by Barbara Plebanek and Tony Howard.

By far the fullest study of Różewicz's drama in English is Halina Filipowicz's *A Laboratory of Impure Forms: The Plays of Tadeusz Różewicz* (New York and London: Greenwood Press 1991), to which I am indebted. T.H.

FRAGMENTS FROM A PERSONAL FILE: THE INTERNAL THEATRE OF TADEUSZ RÓŻEWICZ

BY TONY HOWARD

1. Survivor

After the end of the world
after death
I found myself in the midst of life
creating myself
building life
people animals landscapes

—In the Midst of Life*

Tadeusz Różewicz is one of the most significant postwar playwrights. This isn't a casual definition, perhaps no other dramatist was so profoundly shaped by the Second World War. He was a partisan, his wife was a courier, his beloved elder brother was killed by the Gestapo; he witnessed the partial annihilation of his generation and the atrocity of the camps. But while Adorno spoke of the impossibility of creating art after Auschwitz, Różewicz set about doing it, deriving meaning from the rubble, and few poets have written with more modest restraint and power about Auschwitz itself. He was no longer confident that words or ideas possessed any validity at all — 'neither religion, nor science, nor art', he said, had managed to protect common humanity — but as a Polish writer in the aftermath of 'the most massive necropolis in human history', he felt compelled to reinvent everything. For him, writing is hard labour — Herculean? Sisyphian — and his plays involve us uniquely in the creative process.

Many of Różewicz's characters are afraid of the end of the world — but it has already happened and no-one seems to have noticed.

---

*All quotations of Różewicz's poetry are taken from Adam Czerniawski's translations, published in *They Came to See a Poet* (London: Anvil Press, 1991).

In his theatre, meaningful acts are hard to accomplish, but the concrete, indestructible consequences of half-forgotten deeds and past inertia surround everybody like debris. The image of the rubbish dump recurs throughout the plays, whether literally in *The Old Woman Broods*, where it grows till it swallows the Earth in an ethical-ecological disaster, or psychologically: in *The Funny Old Man* the 'hero' is a bemused and pathetic old toilet attendant on trial for interfering with children who believe that every outwardly moral citizen is actually 'full of refuse and all sorts of muck'. Meanwhile, around the obsessive tragi-comic protagonists, anonymous crowds work manically to update the garbage. Różewicz's technique matches his vision — many sequences in the plays are apparently random collages of visual and verbal quotations, from *fin de siècle* poets to Kafka to fragments from mass media and the scientific press; all the detritus that constitutes modern consciousness. The paradox, as readers and audiences of these amazingly inventive plays quickly learn, is that his theatre is nonetheless a repository of irony and wild humour, challenges and hope.

2. The Personal File

you are curious to learn
what a poet of today does
Indifferent
he talks to the indifferent

—Conversation with the Prince

Mingling bleakness and measured irony, Różewicz came to international prominence shortly after the war as a poet for whom rhetoric was anathema and the only truth was understatement. In some ways he matched the required profile for a public poet of reconstruction, but he kept himself off Party platforms and chose to live well away from literary circles — first in Gliwice, one of the most polluted conurbations in Europe, and then Wroclaw, which Grotowski too made his experimental base. Soon after de-Stalinization began, Różewicz started his first major play *The Card Index* (written 1958–

9, premièred 1960) and at a stroke he re-invented himself and shattered the idealistic assumptions that dominated postwar East European drama; 'theatre befitting our great age', to quote the play's Chorus. At the same time, he also demolished the messianic Romantic tradition that had been central to Polish culture for over a century.

The Card Index (whose title might also be translated as *Personal File*) is a welter of conscious contradictions. It's both Absurdist — exploring the existential crisis of the Hero, an apathetic modern Oblomov who hardly ever leaves his bed — and precisely factual, the collective biography of the whole war generation. Fragmented, non-sequential, demolishing the notion of Time, it is both a portrait of the constructed postwar community trying and failing to create Utopia and a perfect example of what Różewicz calls his 'internal' or 'poetico-realist' theatre, fusing theatre's capacity for ironic distancing with the intense subjectivity of poetry. It was Eastern Europe's *Waiting for Godot* and it continues, round the world, to shake up easy, reassuring preconceptions of the drama.

The contradictions are countless. The Hero is Różewicz (he has called the play 'autobiographical') and is not. He is specifically Polish and utterly universal. As well as being an Oblomov who doesn't seem bothered any more by his own bad faith and failures, he is also a parody of Prometheus visited by threatening and exhortatory figures from his past (but the parody vanishes when he throws himself against the wall of history with an anguished clarion call to the audience), as well as a socially cosseted philanderer in a bedroom farce. Indeed, he is virtually every protagonist who ever existed. His name is Henry and Victor and Franek, Felek and Bolek and Marek. There is no fixed time or place. The set is simultaneously a bedroom and a street — in the first production it was the street outside the theatre, with a fence posted with pictures of Romantic heroes and a poster for *The Card Index*; behind it all was a gigantic Chagall dream painting. As Jan Kott wrote after the première, Różewicz dismantles traditional dramatic forms instantly: 'The hero is five, twenty-five and forty years old. We accept the convention of *The Card Index* at once, from the very first line, without any resistance. The convention seems obvious, as if it were the only one, the natural form for the theatre.' Haunted by the past, he is simultaneously a child, a middle-aged man, and a corpse (his fingers must be unclenched by bureaucratic intruders before they can take his life story away in a briefcase as evidence). He disappears into a wardrobe to hang him-self, and then pops out again; he massacres the Chorus of old men who call on him to perform great patriotic deeds, but who also vet the play for signs of coded dissidence, yet they come back to life and steal his childhood. Originally Różewicz planned that the Hero would do nothing at all. Identity is constructed, and the selves that friends, family and strangers project on him are irreconcilable. There is, however, one final paradox: although the Hero seems the victim of his family, of history and of his own ennui, Różewicz demonstrates this inertia by creating an open dramatic form which is startlingly powerful because of its total freedom. *The Card Index* was published in the pioneering drama periodical *Dialog* in 1960 and then pro-duced at the Teatr Dramatyczny (the main stage in the Stalinist Palace of Culture, which dominates Warsaw), directed by Wanda Laskowska. The next year it reached New York with Peter Boyle in the lead and by 1967, when Adam Czerniawski's translation was premièred by the Experimental Theatre Company, Oxford, it had been seen in Germany, Sweden, Israel, Belgium, France, Yugoslavia, Holland and Denmark. In 1967, too, Konrad Swinarski's brilliant production for Polish TV won *The Card Index* a mass audience and as the Hero the great actor Tadeusz Łomnicki began a lifelong associa-tion with the play. Swinarski, a student of Brecht, emphasized the play's physical realities so that the surreal disruptions were all the funnier and more provocative. In 1979, Krzysztof Kieślowski di-rected a bleaker television version, starring another giant of modern Polish drama, Gustaw Hołubek. Kieślowski stressed the hero's public success and private alienation, prefiguring his *Decalogue* cycle by filming *The Card Index* in a Warsaw tower-block.

But its greatest popularity came after 1971, when Różewicz pub-lished 'variations' on the play. Sequences which he had originally suppressed gave it intensely controversial new life — six produc-tions followed within a year — because the assembled data in the original *Card Index* was incomplete: now it could be told that as an officer in the non-communist Home Army, the Hero had been forced to kill a fellow partisan, but that after the War he conformed and wrote Stalinist propaganda. We hear of political torture; a miner condemns the hero's lies. In a Hungarian café he looks at a merry-go-round but sees it as mass gallows with the leaders of the 1956 Uprising hanging from it. Like Wajda's later *Man of Marble*, Różewicz re-opened the file on the 1950s. There was no mistaking now the ways in which the domestic barracking, the petty self-accusations, the constant questioning, grotesquely parodied a show trial. But, crucially, the 'new' fragments did not replace the 'original'; they created new choices. *The Card Index* remains as political or as abstract as you wish it to be. Like all great plays, it demands involvement through re-interpretation and in 1989, as the Communist era came to its end Łomnicki worked on a production of *The Card Index* with no less than four young directors, and it emerged now as virtually an elegy for his and Różewicz's great, yet baffled, generation.

3. Unburied

I tread on a pane
on a mirror
that cracks
I tread on Yorick's
skull

—I Build

Then Różewicz looked around. *The Witnesses* (first performed in 1963) was subtitled 'Our Little Stabilization'. With Różewicz's help, this Polish term came to stand for the period of relative self-confidence and apparent prosperity from the mid-sixties to the upheavals of Solidarity. He pricked the bubble. He exposed a culture of neurotic unease and timeless hypocrisy, and like Pinter's and Albee's plays from the same period, *The Witnesses* and *Gone Out* (premièred in 1965) remain very disturbing. Różewicz's ruling dramatic principle was still bricolage, but the fragments looked larger and initially therefore more reassuring.

The unity of *The Witnesses* isn't a matter of plot or character, but of tone — tension and anxiety, voices subsiding into nervous whispers — and vision. It is auto-destructive theatre. Part One seems to be the safest of performances, a poetry recital, but the words are increasingly alarming. Part Two plays with the comforting comic familiarity of a married couple's domestic rituals, but again language splits it apart. The husband describes an idyllic scene outside the window — a little girl, a kitten playing — which turns to horror as a boy tortures the cat to death. The man sees, narrates, does not react; not only is there no communication, the bond between words and meanings has disintegrated: 'Our language is as imperfect as a ladder with broken rungs.' Różewicz can only offer such a world a theatre of disconnected tableaux; some spartan, some spectacular. The scene changes; sirens howl. Part Three replays Part Two simply with a change of set and new characters. At a street café (Różewicz's frequent signifier of false ease and hollow intimacy), two men try to confide in one another for the first time since the war while a bleeding, rotting half-dead creature — a run-over dog? a human being? — crawls towards them. They dare neither help nor escape, for fear of losing their place at the table. 'In the second half of the twentieth century in the very centre of the town there lies a dead beast and nobody cares.' Indeed, nobody cares: in our script a siren blares out at the end, but Różewicz later cut it to remove the implication that some external agency may relieve us of responsibility.

After the war, Różewicz studied art history. It's the unpredictable marriage of his prolific visual imagination — a gift to directors — and, of course, his language, as precise as a scalpel even when it seems nonsensical, that makes his comedies of menace so powerful. 'Drama,' he says, 'takes place in silence. In an ocean of silence. And words are only tiny (coral) islands scattered in this infinite space.' If *The Card Index*'s Hero drifts into silence, *Gone Out* begins as the heroine's distraught words emerge out of half-distinct cries and murmurs which seem clear on the page but which, in performance, must at first sound incoherent. The two plays are mirror-images in several ways: *Gone Out* is a scientific demonstration of the way any communal 'reality' disintegrates when even a single person declines to conform. It is also a good pointer to Różewicz's love-hate relationship with the literature of the past, an example of his intertextual strategies. Eve, the wife in this play, is Penelope yearning for her husband to return. Her house fills at one point with manic Suitors vying for attention.

But his absence reduces her to existential panic, her need for his love is a humiliating perversion of religious ecstasy, and her Odysseus is actually just an office worker who's an hour late for dinner. Except that he is also Hamlet, dropping off on the way home to chat with the gravediggers who, in the first production, looked like Beckett's tramps. Although this world is saturated with cultural echoes, the old generic rules no longer work, and causality is unpredictable: the gravedigger eats a banana, *ergo* someone must slip on the skin. But it's the Hero who does so and it happens between scenes. In Różewicz, comedy has no punchlines, and tragedy no cathartic closure. The husband is brought home with a totally bandaged head, looking like a lightbulb. In a perfect reversal of *The Card Index*, where the Hero has too many memories, the husband has lost all of his. And so the self-policing family must try to 'reconstruct him'. The fine set for the Warsaw production showed them dwarfed by their constructed reality — a prismatic, tiered environment built of skeletal doors and windows. A 1976 revival, directed and designed by the artist Franciszek Starowieyski, tapped into other primal aspects: the cast frantically huddled and pressed together inside a kinetic, billowing cloth painted with sexual-cum-sacred emblems, part sail, part hiding place, part-womb. Sexual instinct and libido are the hidden dynamo of many of Różewicz's plays.

4. Persistence

I like old women . . . .
Hamlet rages in the net
Faust's role is comic and base
Raskolnikov strikes with his axe
old women are
indestructible
they smile indulgently
a god dies
old women get up as usual
buy fish and wine

—A Tale of Old Women

Różewicz is very conscious of his predecessors and contemporaries. In these plays he discusses Chekhov and Buñuel, Witkacy and Gombrowicz, for example, and attacks what he sees as the twin superficialities of naturalism and theatrical journalism (documentary theatre). But he has a very particular debate with Beckett, 'the Shakespeare of our times.' Half-way through *The Card Index* Pozzo and Lucky walk into the play. Różewicz localizes and politicizes them; his (nameless) Lucky is neat and well-behaved, he is a doglike tamed intellectual: another version of the Hero, and presumably of Różewicz himself. Wryly challenging fashionable opinion, Różewicz praised Beckett in *The Interrupted Act* as a supremely comic writer and imagined a production of *Happy Days* where Winnie is up to her waist in a sandpit full of children playing. This became the nucleus of *The Old Woman Broods* (1969), his redrafting of Beckett's vision in which a bag lady gives birth in the rubbish dump we are making of the planet. Buildings are swept aside, garbage falls like snow, but sunbathers still come out to bask in it, hairdressers set up shop, wars break out, and the authorities suppress the androgynous young. This is crucial. For Różewicz, decay itself teems with life. Humanity adapts, and although, as a satirist, he must expose the dishonesty involved in this process, as a poet he must also celebrate courage. He is — as the short play *Doppelgänger* admits — a schizophrenic writer, and the end of *The Old Woman Broods* exemplifies this. While life seems to die out finally, the bag lady is still there — Różewicz's Mother Courage, Mother Earth, digging for children in the garbage, the gravedigger scrabbling to find the forceps. Różewicz has said that he cuts some three-quarters of the text out in the process of preparing his scripts, and like Beckett he began to write increasingly brief pieces, several of which are included in this volume and many of which were performed as *The Theatre of Inconsistency*. Yet they show no trace of exhaustion. They are packed with characters, plot, events, terrors and farce: 'a reduced world/is always/more concentrated,' Różewicz noted in 'Autistic Poem'. Inevitably, in *What's More, What's Less*, a debate about despair, Beckett appears as himself — or is it a part of Różewicz?

5. Creation

From the crack
between me and the world
between me and the object
from the distance
between noun and pronoun
poetry
struggles to emerge

—In the Theatre of Shades

'This is my hand. I am moving my hand. My hand,' says the Hero. In a world of perpetual catastrophe and perpetual stasis, solipsism is his only refuge — control over one's body is at least minimal proof of the existence of cause and effect. Paralleling this physical self-observation, Różewicz now began to put his own mind under the microscope. For him drama is a 'living organism', so it was logical to redefine the form to take in the very processes of literary creation and make a stage out of the author's mind. He detected a tension in himself between an 'artist-writer' and an 'artist-theoretician'. He became ruthlessly experimental.

Halina Filipowicz has usefully described *The Interrupted Act, Birth Rate* and *The Order Squad* as a 'postmodern trilogy', and they certainly defy classification in standard dramaturgical terms. They affirm that, given our history, the new drama must be a question of form, not the discovery of sensational new topics. *The Interrupted Act* cannot get past the first scene; most of the text is a meandering set of stage directions, digressions (for example, a long note about Saint Michael), confessions, meditations, literary theorizing and gossip. Dissatisfied with himself and with the genres, irritated by the self-taming of the *avant-garde*, Różewicz keeps rewriting it as a hyper-naturalism (he describes a hair on the set, a buzzing fly, a character's fillings), Surrealism, and Symbolism. The characters and events, however, refuse to submit themselves to the dictates of any known dramatic form. *The Order Squad* sketches out a grotesque new formula for theatre where the audience themselves will experience the conflict between authoritarianism, chaos and freedom. *Birth Rate* grapples with the author's inability to write at all. How long is it — about ten pages? The half an hour it takes to read? Or the ten years (1958–1967) which it took to write?

The debt which modern theatre — especially physical theatre — owes to Poland is incalculable, from Grotowski and Kantor to Gardzienice. However, while it was natural for iconoclastic directors and actors to challenge the authority of the writer and the word, Różewicz, extraordinarily, did it as a writer. New Polish plays were usually published, most notably in *Dialog*, well before being taken up and produced, so many dramatists wrote first — and often only — for a highly sophisticated reading public. This allowed Różewicz to develop a unique quasi-literary form, an embryonic drama as it were, where the reader participated in the writing process while the author, words and ideas all became characters; themselves the victims, it often seemed, of alienation and energy loss, unsure of how to realize their potential. But they are performance texts too. The 'non-scenic' *Interrupted Act* was premièred in Germany in 1965, and, in 1979, Różewicz collaborated with the director Kazimirz Braun on a realization of *Birth Rate* which incorporated *The Order Squad*, extracts from *The Old Woman Broods* and *The Funny Old Man*, and several short plays, poems and fragments, as well as bits of Chekhov and Conrad. Just as *Birth Rate*'s text ponders the theatrical relationship between isolated writing and group creation, this important production explored that relationship through months of improvisation and is a pointer to the physical possibilities of the theatre of Różewicz.

Mimicking the evolution of a production, the audience were taken to the rehearsal room for a discussion with the director, and then to the scenic workshop for a chance to examine chastity belts, observe genetic experiments and to see a striptease — at which point they suddenly found themselves the subjects of research into the connection between visual stimuli and erotic arousal. Their dehumanization intensified when they found themselves taking part in *The Order Squad*, watched and controlled by armed attendants who arbitrarily divided them into groups and controlled what they could see, and when. When the audience were finally allowed into the auditorium, they found the stage totally hidden by a curtain. They were allowed to squeeze singly onto the stage through openings designed for persons of three different heights and sizes. The climax was a performance of Różewicz's first embryonic idea for *Birth Rate*; the farcical-apocalyptic spectacle of a crowd of people squeezing themselves into a railway compartment as 'human' conventions collapse in the scrabble for space and air. Suddenly, above the human mass, two lovers appeared on a trapeze in a world, a system, of their own. The execution was Braun and the company's, but the deeply personal quality of Tadeusz Różewicz's theatre was stressed as the spectators left and the actors spoke to them individually, using words from his poem 'Faces'. Różewicz has spoken of his desire to control his texts, to keep them in the study in the one-man ideal theatre of his mind. Equally he has called many of them 'dialogues' with the theatre world.

In the 1970s and 1980s, Różewicz's plays astonishingly changed course. He produced a series of full-length masterpieces which are as free and disconcerting as any of his works — a barbershop turns into a place of torture, a respectable father becomes a rampant Picasso satyr, a war 'hero' dies sitting on a latrine — but they deal with the strange evolution of our century and to do so they focus on powerful historic characters and situations. *Dead and Buried* demythologizes World War Two with savage bitter comedy; *Mariage Blanc* is a carnivalesque study of the awakening of sexuality and draws heavily on fairly recondite turn-of-the-century texts; *The Trap* is a magnificent journey into the mind of Kafka, who becomes a man unable to understand the prophetic nature of his own fragmented visions. *The Hunger Artist Departs* brings a Kafka story to life, re-imagining it with the hindsight of our century. These plays still possess all Różewicz's inventiveness, they still use fragmentation and collage to mirror our own fractured consciousness, but they also represented a quiet decision to see the stage as a public arena and workplace. To an extent he worked through calm provocation. In different ways, they were all controversial — *Dead and Buried* sensationally so, because it attacked so many deeply-felt beliefs about modern history and nationalism — but most of them reached huge audiences on stage and TV. *Mariage Blanc* has been filmed, and Braun's production alone ran over 500 nights. Wajda's *Mariage Blanc* at Yale was highly successful but all these plays demand to be better known in the English-speaking world. In 1992, in his seventies, Różewicz directed the première of his latest full-length drama, another deconstruction and reinvestigation of a great writer and a twentieth-century classic; *The Card Index Scattered* . . . .

Fragments. Split selves. The loss of childhood 'innocence'. The inconvenient survival of the old. Betrayals. Spaces packed with strangers. A wardrobeful of fears. A writer nailing himself inside his study. Two writers in the park. A bedroom at the crossroads of the world. And the ceaseless labour — heroic? ludicrous? — of forcing back meaning into words, of giving life some form of coherence. Tadeusz Różewicz: b. 1921, Radomsko, Poland. Fought as a partisan with the Home Army — codename 'Satyr'.

THE CARD INDEX

(I am not offering a list of characters. The play's 'Hero' is of indeterminate age, occupation and appearance. On various occasions our 'Hero' ceases to be the hero of our tale and is replaced by other 'heroes'. Many of those who take part in this chronicle do not have significant roles, while others, who might have played the lead, are often not allowed to express themselves or have little to say. The place of the action doesn't change. The stage setting doesn't change. A chair moved once during the whole performance will be enough. And the time . . . .

The play is realistic and takes place in the present. The chair is real, all the objects and pieces of furniture are real. Their measurements are slightly larger than normal. An ordinary average room.

Table. Bookcase. Two chairs. A sink. A bed on high legs. The room has no windows. There are doors at the opposite ends. Both doors remain open all the time. The bed stands against the wall. The light in the room, ordinary daylight, remains constant throughout. The lights are not switched off even when the tale is ended. The curtain doesn't fall. Perhaps the tale is only interrupted. For an hour, for a year . . . .

One further remark. People appear in their ordinary everyday clothes. They mustn't be dressed up in any striking apparel, gaudy rags or other similar accessories. The stage design is of no consequence. The less stage effects the better.

Various people pass through the doors: some move quickly, others slowly. From time to time we hear snatches of conversation. Some stop to read a newspaper. It appears as though there is a street passing through the Hero's room. Some stop to eavesdrop on the conversation in the Hero's room. They may add a few words and then move on. The action is continuous throughout.)

HERO: (*lying on the bed, his arms supporting the back of his head. He stretches out one hand and holds it up to his face*)

This is my hand. I am moving my hand. My hand.

(*Moving his fingers*)

My fingers. My hand is so obedient. It does everything I tell it to.

(*Turns towards the wall. Falls asleep perhaps. The* HERO'S PARENTS *enter. They look worried.* FATHER *glances at his watch.*)

MOTHER: Don't keep your hands under the bedclothes. It isn't nice and it isn't healthy.

FATHER: What will become of him if he lolls in bed like this? Up you get, my boy!

MOTHER: At forty he's only a music-hall manager!

FATHER: He's playing a nasty game under those bedclothes. I'm sure of it. All by himself.

MOTHER: Nonsense! Can't you see there's someone else under there? I think it's a woman.

FATHER: You're mad! A seven-year old boy. . . . Pinched a shilling from me yesterday . . . I'll flog him for that! And he scrounges sugar from the sugar bowl.

MOTHER: But he is due at a board meeting, with speeches for and against.

FATHER: He stole a shilling from me. If he's only said, 'Daddy, please give me a shilling, I want to buy something,' I would have given him one. He must be punished!

MOTHER: Quiet! He's asleep.

FATHER: Who is he taking after?

Enter CHORUS OF ELDERS: *There are three of them. Dressed in creased, rather shabby suits. One is wearing a hat. They sit by the wall in folding chairs which they bring with them. They move about despondently but recite their scripts very clearly in ringing tones and without undue mimicry. The* CHORUS OF ELDERS *takes advantage of breaks in the action; it imparts lessons, issues warnings, creates confidence.*

CHORUS OF ELDERS:
> He who in childhood cut off Hydra's head,
> Will in his youth the blood of Centaurs shed,
> Will rescue victims of the Demon,
> Will gather laurels up in Heaven.*

FATHER: (*leaning over the bed, takes the* HERO's *ear between two fingers and pulls it*) Don't pretend you are asleep. Get up when your father is talking to you.

HERO: Stop! Stop! Who goes there? Stop, or I'll shoot! Halt!

MOTHER: He's talking in his sleep. Ah, that terrible war.

FATHER: I want to talk to you, you little monkey.

HERO: (*sitting up in bed*) I'm listening.

FATHER: Why did you eat all the sugar in the sugar bowl?

HERO: That was Bolek.

FATHER: Don't tell lies, tell me exactly how it was.

HERO: Something tempted me, Daddy, some devil, Daddy. . . .

FATHER: If you had said: 'Daddy, may I have some sugar. . . .'

HERO: But Daddy, you were picking your nose. I spied on you. . . .

FATHER: Viper! What will you grow up into? God is my witness. . . .

MOTHER: How dare you talk to your Father like that . . . I don't recognize you, my child.

FEMALE VOICE UNDER THE BED CLOTHES: It's time for the meeting, sir.

HERO: Mum and Dad; after thirty years I have realized the enormity of my sins. Yes, it was I who ate the sausage on Good Friday, the fifteenth of April 1926. I am ashamed of my act. Olek and Teofilek and I schemed for days to eat that

---

*This is a quotation from a famous Polish classic, 'Ode to Youth' by Adam Mickiewicz. (A.C.)

sausage. My dastardly act, my dearest Dad, can't be excused. I ate the sausage out of greed. I wasn't hungry. Thanks to your care, Dad. I had enough bread in my childhood. I also had pocket money for sweets. Nevertheless, I erred.

MOTHER: But your father is asking you about the sugar, not the sausage.

HERO: Mum, don't defend me. Renounce your son. I ate both the sugar and the sausage. I remember that we began eating the sausage at about 15.05 hrs. I had the biggest share. I also planned the removal of our dearest Granny.

MOTHER: But Granny died a natural death. . . .

HERO: My poor parents! You've spawned a monster. For ten years I had, with malice aforethought, been adding strychnine to Granny's sponge cake. I also well remember my despicable practices with matches. I now recollect with revulsion that I planned to remove Dad as well.

FATHER: This is a nice thing to hear!

HERO: These thoughts and plans were hatched in my head when I was five. I remember the five little candles that were glowing on the little birthday cake.

FEMALE VOICE UNDER THE BED CLOTHES: (*impatiently*) It's time you went, sir.

HERO: I would also like to confess that. . . .

FEMALE VOICE UNDER THE BED CLOTHES: It really is time you went, sir.

HERO: As you can hear, a board meeting awaits me.

    (Parents leave)

FEMALE VOICE UNDER THE BED CLOTHES: The meeting is not for another two hours, but you ought to be prepared. I will prepare you for everything.

CHORUS OF ELDERS:
    Hush-a-bye, baby, on the tree top,
    When the wind blows the cradle will rock;
    When the bough breaks the cradle will fall,
    Down will come baby, cradle, and all.

(HERO falls asleep. He is woken up by a gun explosion. The bang ought to be colossal, so as to frighten the audience as well!)

HERO: The idiots! War again?

FEMALE VOICE UNDER THE BED CLOTHES: No sir, the Princess of Monaco has given birth to octuplets! In this connection follies and drolleries and such like are being organised throughout the country. From the peaks of the Tatra Mountains to the blue Baltic.

HERO: But why in Poland? The Princess resides in Monaco!

FEMALE VOICE UNDER THE BED CLOTHES: This makes no difference. A hundred of our young activists will pay homage by travelling on scooters to the Congo. Others are making vows of chastity.

HERO: *(looking at the ceiling)* Buffoons. *(Pause)* Idiots. *(Pause)* Cretins, baboons, dungheaps, thieves, swindlers, pederasts, astronauts, onanists, sportsmen, feature writers, moralists, critics, bigamists.

(Pause. Lights a cigarette and looks at the ceiling.)

I am in bed. The chiefs of state and the chiefs of staff are allowing me to lie and look at the ceiling. The ceiling. The beautiful, clean, white ceiling. The bosses are so nice. I shall have a quiet Sunday.

(OLGA comes into the room. She is a middle-aged woman. She stops at the foot of the bed. Takes off her coat. Places her coat, bag and scarf on the bed.)

OLGA: I was passing by and heard you calling me. . . .

HERO: I calling you?

OLGA: It's fifteen years since you left home. You haven't given me a sign of life since.

HERO: That's true.

OLGA: You left no address.

HERO: I had none.

OLGA: You said you were going to get some cigarettes.

HERO: I got them.

OLGA: It's fifteen years since you went. How are you? Speak. Say something.

HERO: I'll tell you a joke.

OLGA: A joke at a moment like this? This is awful. He wants to tell me a joke after fifteen years. . . .

HERO: I'd like a cup of tea.

OLGA: Tea, when I want an account of what you've been doing all this time. You've been a disappointment to me, Henryk.

HERO: My name is Victor.

OLGA: Victor, you've been a disappointment to me. You are a swine and a fraud.

HERO: (*yawns*) I don't want to talk any more.

CHORUS OF ELDERS: (*each* ELDER *talking to himself*) He doesn't want to talk. . . . But he is the chief hero. . . . Who else is there to talk?

OLGA: (*stamping her foot at the* CHORUS) Shut up, you over there. . . . If only you had said a word. . . . But you didn't. . . . Nothing!

HERO: I shall not achieve anything in these circumstances.

OLGA: You stroked my breasts, you fawned upon me like a snake, you seduced me with beautiful words.

HERO: Beautiful words?

OLGA: You said we would have a house with a garden, a couple of children, a son and a daughter. . . . The world was coming to an end and you were lying! You broke. . . .

HERO: The world didn't come to an end. We've come through. Oh, you can't imagine how glad I am to be lying down. I can lie down, pare my nails, listen to music. The bosses have given me the whole of Sunday. Why don't you come to bed? We'll talk.

OLGA: I mustn't be late for the music show. I've already got my
        ticket. . . . I will never forgive you.

        (She leaves)

HERO: Leave me your newspaper. I thought we would all die, so I
        talked to you about children, flowers, life. It's quite simple.

        (Opens the newspaper, looks through it and reads aloud.)

        'Before pouring beer into them, bottles ought to be care-
        fully washed. The workers employed in this job often do
        not trouble themselves sufficiently to check whether the
        bottles are clean. The result is that, when filled, bottles ap-
        pear to contain various foreign bodies. There are also cases
        of flies swimming in the beer. In our previous article on
        beer we wrote about the almost barbarous attitude to this
        beverage on the part of the retail workers. The beer trade
        provides criminals with opportunities. For example, how
        can one turn a 100 litre barrel into a 120 litre barrel?'

CHORUS OF ELDERS: Very simply.

HERO: 'All one has to do is to apply more froth to every glass of
        beer consumed. Instead of a full glass of beer, the customer
        receives a glass only half or a third full.'

        (His voice grows more powerful and tragic)

        'We agree that beer ought to possess the so-called head of
        froth, but we are concerned with the fact that the contents
        of a glass should relate to the norm. That is why all glasses
        ought to be marked showing where 250 or 500 cubic cen-
        timetres of drink come up to. Alas, the beer mugs are not
        even rinsed properly. The inside of the glass is covered
        with a film of grease, and grease is enemy number one of
        the golden drink. There is a culpable absence of responsi-
        bility in the beer trade. We must end this once and for all.
        We must punish. . . .'

        (The CHORUS splits up)

FIRST ELDER: *(putting his hand to his ear)* What is he talking about?

SECOND ELDER: About beer!

THIRD ELDER: Does this beer contain allusions to the government, has it got hidden meanings, symbols, allegories, is our Hero an ideological watchdog?

FIRST ELDER: He is talking about beer.

SECOND ELDER: There must be something hidden in that beer!

THIRD ELDER: He says flies are swimming in the beer.

SECOND ELDER: Flies? Well, that's something.

FIRST ELDER: Rubbish! In his case beer means beer and a fly means a fly and nothing else.

THIRD ELDER: For heaven's sake, this is no hero. He is just a nonentity. Where are all the heroes of old, the bards, knights in armour and the prophets. A fly in 'small beer'! Not just beer, but small beer. What does it all mean?

SECOND ELDER: (*twisting his face ironically*) It is the theatre befitting our great age.

THIRD ELDER: The age appears great but the people are rather small.

FIRST ELDER: As always, as always.

THIRD ELDER: Flies swimming in small beer. There is something hidden in that.

(*CHORUS nods in agreement. There is dead silence, during which we hear the song of a canary. After a while, an old man with a moustache and an old hat enters the room.*)

HERO: Uncle!

UNCLE: I've joined a pilgrimage to a monastery. . . . I am calling on you on the way: 'He descended into Hell, because it was on his way.' And how are things with you, Franek?

HERO: So-so, so-so, uncle. So many years. We haven't seen each other for 25 years, uncle!

(*HERO sits up on the bed and pulls up his socks.*)

I'm sure your feet ache, uncle. Must be a hundred kilometres. Do sit down, uncle. How nice that you've called on me, uncle. I'll prepare some water so you can soak your feet in it and I'll make some tea! Lie down, uncle! Put your feet in the water.

(HERO pulls a washbasin from under the bed and pours water into it. He is pouring real water into a real basin from a real jug.)

Please uncle.... In a minute I will....

(overjoyed he fusses around UNCLE.)

Uncle, to uncle ... of uncle ... with uncle ... oh, uncle! ... in uncle ....

UNCLE: What a kind-hearted boy. Thank you, child, for this ceremonious welcome.

(UNCLE takes off his leggings and his socks. Soaks his feet in the basin.)

And how are things with you, Stefan?

HERO: Well, you see, uncle, I was going to write to you, but Sophie said you were ill, so I thought you had died.

(Places his hands on UNCLE's shoulders.)

I'm terribly glad to see you, uncle. You have no idea, uncle. How are things with you, uncle?

UNCLE: Ah well, one has to push this barrow of life somehow. Nothing to get excited about.

HERO: But you are real, uncle, and your hat is real.

(Takes UNCLE's hat off.)

And your moustache is real, your feet are real, your trousers are real, your heart is real and your feelings and thoughts are real. A whole real uncle. Even your leggings are real, and the buttons and your words. Real words!

(He is talking with mounting emotion and rapture.)

UNCLE: Well, and how are you, Stefan? Helenka told me you've been to Paris.

HERO: Yes, I have.

UNCLE: Well, let's hear something about that Paris of yours. I will never get a chance to see it. . . . Auntie is also curious.

HERO: With pleasure, uncle.

UNCLE: Wasn't a waste of time, was it?

HERO: Of course not.

UNCLE: And how do people manage over there?

HERO: Oh, they manage somehow. . . .

(Takes out his cigarettes.)

Would you like one? They're French.

UNCLE: If they are French, I'll take two.

HERO: I bought some matches in Paris, I bought toilet soap in Paris, a toothbrush, razor blades, shirts, perfumes, slippers, paper clips, pins, needles.

(The CHORUS OF ELDERS is examining some photographs. They laugh, tell each other stories; we can hear snatches of them.)

UNCLE: And what about the arts and literature . . . ? And politics?

HERO: Well, it's so-so. You can't take it all in. You know something, uncle, I've seen Napoleon, the Pope, the Queen, all life-size. All pink and made of wax. They eat a lot of salads, they eat cheese and drink wine. Of course the cooking is French.

UNCLE: So you've had a change of scene and you bought a thing or two.

HERO: You know, uncle, this city lies in a blueish mist — like pure alcohol.

UNCLE: *(after a pause)* But . . . well, you appear a little downcast. Oh, Romek, Romek, why do you worry so much?

HERO: Well, you see, uncle . . . . Ah, it's not worth talking about . . . . I clapped. I cheered.

UNCLE: What do you mean 'clapped'?

HERO: Just simply clapped.

UNCLE: Everybody clapped.

HERO: I am not interested in everybody. I am thinking of myself. I
clapped.

UNCLE: You are a baby, Piotrysh. Picasso also clapped.

HERO: Oh, uncle, uncle . . . .

UNCLE: What is it, then, Romek?

HERO: I know a lot of people clapped, but they have forgotten it by
now. They now occupy themselves with the latest cars or
enjoy themselves at masked balls, but I still put my hands
together and that clapping still claps inside me. Sometimes
there is such a colossal clapping in me. I am empty like a
cathedral at night. Clapping, uncle, clapping . . . .

(Silence)

UNCLE: Well, anyway, you are a miserable, weak, lifeless lot. Bald
and splitting hairs. What am I to say? All this clapping you
people had to do is nothing in comparison. I remember
during the disturbances we threw our commander into the
tomato soup. Let's see, what was his name?

HERO: Into the soup?

UNCLE: It so happened there was some tomato soup bubbling in
the cauldron. Times were uneasy. There were various incidents. Rebellions. In other words, things were on the boil
. . . . He was making an inspection of the kitchen. Soup was
being cooked for the whole company. We threw him in. We
covered the cauldron with the lid and he got cooked together with his moustache. The spurs got cooked and the
medals as well. Even now, I can't help laughing when I
remember it.

(UNCLE pats HERO on the shoulders.)

You have a delicate conscience. I absolve you!

HERO: I am sad, uncle. You know, uncle, when I was a little boy, I
played at being horses. I would turn into a horse and rush
through the courtyard and the streets, my mane flying. But
now, uncle, I can't change into a human being though I am
a director of an institute. I'd like to dig up the earth, pick

out a potato or two and roast them for you, uncle. Potatoes have a grey, coarse skin. Inside they are white, soft and hot. In my life, I would like to own an apple tree with little branches, leaves, blossoms and apples . . . . Such a long time since I've sat in the shade. Apples are covered with a transparent film of wax, finger prints are clearly showing on such apples. Apples are hanging on branches. They are awaiting my hand. Just like girls.

UNCLE: Well, Romek, will you come home? We are all waiting for you: Mum and your sisters.

HERO: I can't, uncle.

UNCLE: Don't you want to turn your back on the great big world?

HERO: No.

UNCLE: Haven't you eaten your fill?

HERO: My appetite is still growing, uncle. Whenever I open my mouth I would gulp whole cities, people, buildings and paintings and breasts, TV sets, motors, stars, odalisques, socks, watches, titles, medals, pears, pills, newspapers, bananas, masterpieces.

UNCLE: Why not pack and come with me? Tomorrow you will be home.

HERO: No, uncle, I can't go back.

UNCLE: Come, come, the birds are singing, spring's coming.

HERO: I have a lot of things to do, various matters to settle, I can't tear myself away from all this, I can't make head or tail of it. Later perhaps.

UNCLE: (*is drying his feet on the blanket, puts on his shoes, pushes the basinful of water under the bed*) Well, Henryk, I think I'll go now. God be with you.

(*He goes out. HERO is silent. He lies with his eyes closed. TWO MEN enter the room. One is wearing a cyclist's cap, the other a hat. They wear long, old-fashioned jackets. One of them draws some papers out of a briefcase; the other pulls out a metal measuring tape. They begin to measure the HERO's room. They do this with great meticulousness.)*

MAN IN CAP: 3 m 48 cm.

(MAN IN HAT writes. MAN IN CAP measures the door and the bed and calls out the figures. MAN IN HAT writes them down, adds, multiplies and divides. MAN IN CAP comes over to the HERO, measures his length and breadth, his feet, the circumference of his head and neck, the width of his shoulders, etc. MAN IN CAP leans over the HERO.)

MAN IN CAP: What is he clutching in his hand?

MAN IN HAT: Papers.

MAN IN CAP: We will have to unclench his fingers.

(Pulls back HERO's fingers one by one and removes the papers from his hand.)

MAN IN HAT: What is it?

MAN IN CAP: Some sort of papers. Memoirs . . . . *(reads aloud)* 'I was born in 1920; after finishing at the village school . . . I forgot to add that I had a friend in the village school who used to give me cheese, this friend came from the village. When I finished school . . . . When I received my school certificate I applied for a job with the Town Hall. In 1938 in a hotel room I polished my shoes with the bedspread. After completing my elementary schooling I went to a secondary school and after finishing at the secondary school I tried to . . . .'

(MAN IN CAP shakes his head, reads on)

'Come to me all you people.'

MAN IN HAT: What is he doing? Is he asleep? Maybe he is pretending?

MAN IN CAP: *(reads on)* 'In 1938 in a hotel room I polished my shoes with the edge of a carpet and I slashed the towel when I was wiping my razor blade. Then, when I was 18, I faced my final exams but I had no time to sit for them because on the first of September 1939 the World War broke out. That terrible cataclysm which swallowed . . . .'

(MAN IN CAP puts the papers away in his briefcase and they both leave.

A smartly dressed middle-aged MAN crawls into the room on all fours. He is impeccably turned out and perfectly groomed with a knife-edge parting in his hair. As if his hair has been combed from the inside. He walks around the whole room on all fours, sniffs the table legs, the chair, peers under the bed, then begins to talk, raising his muzzle towards the HERO.)

MAN WITH PARTING: Do you know who I am? Do you know who you are? Who is he? What he is? I have my pride. No, sir, you are too insignificant to talk to me like this. I didn't want to know, had I known I couldn't have cheated. But I am suffering. I am . . . I am . . . .

(HERO shifts and sniffs. MAN WITH PARTING is quiet.)

HERO: I smell a stranger. I smell varnish and whitewash, farting and literature. Who is there?

(MAN WITH PARTING adjusts his hair and tie with his paw.)

Oh, it's you, Bobby.

(FAT MAN in glasses walks through the room. He is reading a newspaper and looks round. He is standing in the middle of the pavement. He calls MAN WITH PARTING.)

FAT MAN: Bobby, heel!

(MAN WITH PARTING rubs his muzzle against the FAT MAN's trouser leg.)

Bobby, down.

(MAN WITH PARTING lies down.)

Dead dog.

(MAN WITH PARTING pretends to be dead. FAT MAN, smiling, takes a bone out of his pocket and throws it under the table. MAN WITH PARTING fetches the bone back.)

Bobby, beg. Good dog . . . .

(MAN WITH PARTING begs beautifully, cocking his head to the left, then to the right and smiles. FAT MAN draws out his hand.)

Paw, Bobby.

(MAN WITH PARTING offers his left paw and has it smacked.)

Right paw.

(MAN WITH PARTING corrects his mistake and offers right paw.)

(to HERO):   He is well trained, isn't he?

HERO: *(sitting up on the bed)* I don't know.

FAT MAN: Tell him to suffer and he suffers. Tell him 'jump' and he jumps. He can even read and write. Got a medal at a dog exhibition in Paris. He is intelligent and well-trained . . . training isn't difficult . . . all you need is a skilful approach and a little patience . . . . There are four elements which affect a dog's efficiency: his hunting instinct, the winds, his feet, and his intelligence. Bobby's got feet and he is good at sniffing the winds . . . . Will you take him?

HERO: I have no money . . . doesn't he bite?

FAT MAN: *(laughs)* He has no teeth, he's only got a tongue. He licks.

HERO: I'll give you a pair of socks in exchange.

FAT MAN: All right.

(HERO takes off his socks and hands them to the FAT MAN who puts them away in his pocket. He walks away reading a newspaper and has quite forgotten about Bobby. HERO stretches out his hands and strokes MAN WITH PARTING's head.)

HERO: Want a drink?

MAN WITH PARTING: *(still on his four feet)* An espresso and a brandy, please.

HERO: You drank black coffee at the previous political phase and what good did it do you? You better have some water.

(Pulls the basin full of water from under the bed.)

An honest simple man soaked his feet in this water. Drink. It's medicine for the likes of you. For the likes of me . . . .

(MAN WITH PARTING draws out his tongue like a dog and is about to drink the water from the basin. HERO laughs.)

Enough! You are civil! Stop being a fool and sit down. We'll have some coffee in a minute. Admittedly I haven't got any coffee or cups or money, but then, what are surrealism, metaphysics and the poetry of dreams for! (*Calls*) Two large coffees!

(*WAITRESS comes into the room. She is wearing a cap and an apron. She places a silver tray on the table.*)

WAITRESS: Shall I undress?

HERO: That's not necessary. I hate cabaret.

(*WAITRESS runs out.*)

CHORUS OF ELDERS:

Tramp
trash
trainer
training
Tripolis
trollop
truism
trumpeter

(*HERO and MAN WITH PARTING are absorbed in drinking their coffee. They stop drinking to examine their hands carefully, then they show their hands to each other: the right and the left. They examine them closely.*)

HERO: (*holding the MAN WITH PARTING's left hand*) Oh, there is a stain here! It's black.

MAN WITH PARTING: That's ink.

HERO: Ink? You could lick that off.

MAN WITH PARTING: Oh, you've got a stain too! Two stains! Two red stains!

HERO: That's blood.

MAN WITH PARTING: Real blood?

HERO: Enemy blood.

MAN WITH PARTING: I only know the taste of water, vodka, saliva and ink. What does blood taste like?

HERO: (*takes out a pin and pricks the finger of the* MAN WITH PARTING, *who sucks it*) A drop of blood. How did you survive the war, the occupation? Did you ever hold a gun?

MAN WITH PARTING: Thanks to the wife! The wife, to the wife, in the wife, with the wife, oh, the wife ... on the wife ... under the wife.

HERO: (*shouting*) Get lost!

(MAN WITH PARTING drops on his four paws, reaches for the cup with his paw and drinks up the coffee. Enter two well-preserved middle-aged WOMEN. They carry on a lively conversation interspersed with bursts of laughter.)

WOMAN: I him, he me, he to you, she to him, you know what he's like, when you to him, to himmmmm.

(She roars and neighs and laughs. She looks around.)

Oh, darling, there you are!

(MAN WITH PARTING stands on two feet.)

My husband, my dear. This is my friend, darling.

(MAN WITH PARTING kisses the other WOMAN's hand. Smiling, full of the joys of life, he leaves with the WOMEN. The WOMEN have varnish on their finger nails.)

CHORUS OF ELDERS: Corps de ballet, correspondence, cosmetics, cosmic, copulation, marmalade, marble, martyrology ....

(HERO is looking for something feverishly. Crawls under the bed. Opens drawers. Looks in all the corners. CHORUS leaves. HERO is alone. He is searching his pockets. At last he pulls out a length of rope and ties it round his neck. He tests the rope. Looks around the room. Searches for a nail. Goes to a hat stand. Finally he opens the wardrobe and gets inside, shutting the door behind him. The wardrobe is closed. It opens after a long pause.)

HERO: Why don't you hang yourselves? I prefer the little toe of my left foot to the lot of you taken together. What? Go and hang yourselves! No! You love yourselves too much. That hag loves her little dog more than me, a man. Because it is her doggie. She loves her appendix more than the whole of humanity.

(HERO sits on the bed, pulls a bag of sandwiches out of his pocket, unwraps the paper and begins to eat. FAT WOMAN enters.)

FAT WOMAN: Shame! So young and already a Peeping Tom!

HERO: *(stops eating)* What are you doing here, madam? This is a private apartment. Who let you in?

FAT WOMAN: Ha ha ha ha ha ha! *(laughs herself silly)* Private apartment!

HERO: I don't know who you are.

FAT WOMAN: Victor, you spied on me in my bath.

HERO: A quarter of a century has passed since then! Yes, I remember. But I see, madam, that you have now come out of the water. You can go your way now. I am busy just now, I have to read my correspondence.

FAT WOMAN: I'll wait.

(Sits down in the chair. She may start knitting a pullover.)

HERO: *(takes some envelopes from the table. Opens a pink envelope. Reads in a clear voice)* 'My dear Felek, I am touched by this proof that you haven't forgotten me. Do come, so that with my own little fingers I can drop in your mouth the sweetest chocolate from the box you've sent me. Yours, Bronia.' *(Opens another envelope and reads)* 'Dear Henio, I hear very unwelcome news about you and about your exceedingly reckless acts. Is this how you repay me for my solicitude, for my efforts and expense which I contributed to your education and upbringing? You were seen in a billiard room, a party to an incident with a common fellow. You don't go to lectures, you are absorbed by games, gambling and love affairs. So this is what I have to endure in my old age. You must pull yourself up, my dear Henio, because one more bad

piece of news and I will cut you off and not only will I stop
your allowance, but I shall also disown you as my son. I
send you my fatherly blessing, may it give you the strength
to direct you in the right path. Your Mother is weeping.
Your heartily disappointed father.'

(Daunted, the HERO *crumples the envelope and puts it in his
pocket. Takes out another envelope and reads.)*

'Dear Cousins, the celebration on the occasion of your Silver Wedding Anniversary causes me great joy. As a witness
of your wedding 25 years ago, I cannot now believe that a
quarter of a century has already passed since that moment
when you pledged each other to push forward together the
wheelbarrow of life beneath the lofty emblem of love. 25
years have passed like a brief moment. May life continue
for you full of roses, so that, reborn in your children, grandchildren and great grandchildren, you may become for them
the patriarchs of those principles which you yourselves have
so worthily embraced. Your old friend, N.N. Warsaw, the
24th January, 1902.'

(After reading the last letter HERO *puts on his slippers and leaves
the room. He is followed a moment later by the* FAT WOMAN.
*Now there is nothing happening on the stage. A 5–10 minute
break is suggested. The curtain may be lowered, or left hanging.)*

HERO *returns after the interval. Pulls out his sandwiches from
his pocket, unwraps the paper and begins to eat.* FAT WOMAN
enters a moment later. She looks around.)

FAT WOMAN: Shame on you! Such a young boy peeping at women.

HERO: *(interrupting his meal)* Who let you in here? This is a private
apartment.

FAT WOMAN: *(laughs)* Private apartment? A private apartment!

HERO: I don't know who you are.

FAT WOMAN: Mr Romek, you spied on me in my bath.

HERO: That was ages ago . . . . Yes, I do remember. I see, madam, you have now come out of your bath.

FAT WOMAN: Mr Bolek, I remember you as a little boy in a sailor suit with a collar.

(HERO lies down on the bed. His back turned to the audience, his back towards the FAT WOMAN. She sits on the bed.)

HERO: Ages ago.

FAT WOMAN: So what? So what, my precious?

HERO: *(jumps up)* You old cow, you flitch of bacon, you barrel of lard. I do remember. I was fifteen. It was July. The light of the setting sun in the water. A red river under the crowns of black alders. You were white and fat. You were a young bosomy wench. White as snow. Emerging slowly from the dark water. Black alders stood over the water. A red sun in their crowns. I would have given half my life, my whole life, a whole city, the whole world, to touch your breasts. If I could put my hand on your thigh, on your mons veneris.

FAT WOMAN: On what?

HERO: On your mons veneris. You idiot, you cow, you could have been my queen. You could have been music, a garden, a fruit, you could have been the Milky Way, you cow. But you kept it for some wise guy, twister, cynic, buffoon, thief. Now you're blubbering. You could have been my flame, a spring and a joy. How I suffered then. I wanted to jump out of my skin.

(FAT WOMAN is knitting a pullover!)

Because of you I nearly ended up a Sodomite. Your belly was a greater revelation to me than America was for Uncle Kowalski. Your rump was a star. You idiot, you barrel of pickled meat. Run away before I crush you on the spot!

(HERO falls silent. A very lively middle-aged WOMAN enters the room. She runs to the FAT WOMAN, kisses her rapturously and starts her patter.)

LIVELY WOMAN: Just imagine, my dear. Sleek fitted cloque, shoestring straps for a low square bodice and a built-in bra. The back view shows a plunge line and there is a bow trim on a horizontal strap. Black and rhinestone earrings cylindrical in shape. Gilt highlights the pastel terylene georgette and there is a braiding round the cutaway bodice and hem. Or a swoosh of silk organza over a taffeta slip. Rich gold braid round a mandarin collar, a curved bodice and sleeves. (*Jumping up from the bed and kissing* FAT WOMAN) Bye, bye, you must 'phone, you really must . . . . Bye, bye, do 'phone . . . remember . . . bye, bye!

(She goes out)

FAT WOMAN: (*folding up her knitting*) So you wash your hands of me, Mr Bolek!

HERO: I do.

FAT WOMAN: I placed so many hopes on a visit to you. I thought that for the sake of an old friendship you would give a hand to a lonely woman. But you couldn't care less. What is it to you that the secretion of my gonad is increasing. Yes, Mr Marek . . . .

HERO: I told you so many times, my name is Stefan.

FAT WOMAN: Yes, Mr Stefan. Now I often suffer from headaches, hot flushes, dizziness and pains in the joints. I noticed that lately I have undergone slight digestive disturbances and changes in my electro-cardiogram. The doctor thinks the oral use of Estradiol will be sufficient, and that Duoetylostybestrol is equally effective. But this drug gives me nausea and stomach pains, so what do you suggest in the circumstances? If it hadn't been for the fact that I have known you since you were so little (*shows how little*) I wouldn't have turned to a stranger over such an intimate matter.

HERO: (*reading from the newspaper*) 'The number five sugar refinery in the Hrubieszow Region was the first off the mark in this year's campaign.'

FAT WOMAN: How the world has changed. People are quite indifferent to the sufferings of their fellow-beings.

(Children's voices are heard: 'Mummy, mummy'. FAT WOMAN

leaves. HERO stretched on his bed goes on reading. Enter CHO-RUS. They sit in their places.)

CHORUS OF ELDERS:

Do something, get a move on, think.
There he lies while time flies.

(HERO covers his face with the newspaper.)

Say something, do something,
Push the action forward,
At least scratch your ear!

(HERO is silent.)

There is nothing happening.
What is the meaning of this?

HERO: Leave me in peace.

CHORUS OF ELDERS:

Thank God, he is not asleep.

HERO: Are you saying I must do something? I don't know . . . (*yawns*)
. . . perhaps . . . .

CHORUS OF ELDERS:

He's falling asleep, the gods will rage!
There can be no bread without flour.
There must be action on the stage,
Something should be happening at this hour!

HERO: Isn't it enough when the hero scratches his head and stares
at the wall?

CHORUS OF ELDERS:

That already is something.

HERO: I don't feel like doing anything.

CHORUS OF ELDERS:

But even in a Beckett play
somebody talks, waits, suffers, dreams,
somebody weeps, dies, falls, farts.
If you don't move the theatre is in ruins.

HERO:

> Today a flea circus is performing 'Hamlet'
> leave me alone
> I am going away.

CHORUS OF ELDERS: Stop!

HERO: I am going away.

CHORUS OF ELDERS: Where?

HERO: I want to be excused.

CHORUS OF ELDERS: He is drunk.

HERO: Stupid bunch, let me sleep.

CHORUS OF ELDERS:

> You are falling asleep again
> What does it mean?

HERO: I'll finish the lot of them!

> *(HERO takes a sharp kitchen knife from the table and approaches the ELDERS who are sitting still. He pierces through two of the ELDERS and cuts off the third ELDER's head. Now he lays out the CHORUS on the floor. Sits on the bed. He smiles at the audience. Washes his hands. Visibly shaken, he walks around the room. Even starts to run. Stops. Hits himself first on the right then on his left cheek. Walks up to the wall. Presses his hands against the wall.)*

HERO: There, you see, you fool. Go on, crack it with your head. Batter it. Where do you think you are going? Where? To that stupid woman? To the hospital, to humanity, to the fridge, to the salmon, to the vodka, to a pair of thighs, to a teenage leg, to the nipple. Ah, there you are! Go on, bite your own fingers. It's good nourishment. Everything dies under your hand because you don't believe. Where do you think you are crawling, you ass? You have been crawling for the last 38 years. To the sun? To truth? To the wall. I stand against the wall. My brothers, my generation, it's to you I am talking. They can't understand us, neither the young nor the old! *(Turns to the audience)* How did it happen? I can't understand it. There were so many different things in me and I was so many different things and now there is nothing. Here. Here! There is no need! No need to cover up my eyes. (*Pause*) I want to see right to the end.

(*A pretty* GIRL *enters the room. Jumper. Tight fitting trousers. Handbag, magazine, book, apple.* GIRL *walks there and back once or twice. She is what is known as 'a smashing bit'. She sits at the table. Looks at the newspaper. Combs her hair. Takes out a mirror, etc, etc. Turns to* HERO.)

GIRL: I'd like a cream bun.

HERO: (*as though ashamed, talking to himself*) Well, yes, after all, why not.

GIRL: I'd like a cream bun, please.

HERO: (*to the audience*) When I was still alive ... well, really ... I think you will be shocked ... you will be bored and amused by this tale.

GIRL: I'd like a cream bun and a small coffee.

HERO: Why small?

GIRL: Don't you understand my language?

HERO: Are you a foreigner?

GIRL: Meine Hobbies: Reisen, Bücher, Theater, Kunstgewerbe ... ich suche auf diesem Wege einen frohmütigen und charakterfesten Lebensgefährten ... ich bin vollschlank, keine Modepuppe ....

HERO: You are German.

GIRL: Yes.

HERO: I am delighted. You see, I must explain that there has been a misunderstanding.

GIRL: Ah, so?!

HERO: You see, this is a private apartment. I live here .... Naturally I am very pleased ... make yourself at home. I must tell you ... du bist wie eine Blume ....

GIRL: So this isn't the 'Crocodile'?

HERO: You young ones have no idea . . . how old are you?

GIRL: Eighteen . . . but the door was open . . . . I saw various ladies and gentlemen, they chatted and drank coffee . . . .

HERO: (*sits at the table beside the* GIRL. *Takes her hands, stares at her face. The* GIRL *smiles.*) There you are, you young ones poke fun at everything . . . . Though maybe that is how moronic journalists see you . . . I have faith in you people . . . please do not laugh. I have a request to make. Allow me a few minutes. I want to tell you . . . I heard you speak German. Are you German? Yes. Actually, I have nothing interesting to tell you. Please don't think I want to seduce you, to push you into bed . . . .

GIRL: Oh yes, there is a bed here. Do forgive me, I hadn't noticed.

HERO: God! If only you could understand me. It's all so simple. I will only take a few minutes and then go away, but I have a duty to tell you something and you have a duty to listen right through. I wish to say that it is good that you exist. That you are in this world of ours, just like this, that you are eighteen, that you have such eyes, lips and hair, that you are smiling. That's how it should be. Young, with a clear bright face, with eyes that have not seen . . . have not seen. I just want to say one thing: I do not feel hatred towards you and I wish you happiness. I wish you would go on smiling like this and be happy. You see, I am covered in dirt and blood . . . your father and I hunted in the forests . . . .

GIRL: Hunted? Hunted what?

HERO: Each other. With rifles, with guns . . . no, no I shan't go into that . . . now the forests are quiet, aren't they? It is quiet in the forests. Please, do smile. In you lies all the hope and joy of the world. You must be good, pure and gay. You must love us. We were all in a terrible darkness beneath the earth. I want to say it again: I, an old freedom fighter, wish you happiness. I wish happiness to the youth of your country as well as ours. Let's say our farewells. We shall not see each other again. I've expressed myself rather clumsily. How silly, how terribly silly. Isn't it possible to say anything, to explain to another person? It's impossible to convey what's most important . . . . Oh, God!

(A moment's silence. Again there is silence. An inarticulate cry emerges from the LOUDSPEAKER. Then more clearly, the words:)

LOUDSPEAKER: Aufstehen! Aufstehen!

(HERO rises. Stands to attention by his chair. GIRL looks at him with surprise as if she hadn't heard the din.)

Raus! Alles raus!
Maul halten, Klappe zu, Schnabel halten!
Willst du noch quatschen? Du hast aber Mist gemacht!
Du Arschloch, Schweinehund, du Drecksack!

(HERO stands against the wall. Presses his face against it. LOUD-SPEAKER grows silent. Silence. GIRL gets up and tiptoes out of the room. She leaves behind a red apple. A minute's silence.)

CHORUS OF ELDERS: *(recites)*
Don't be afraid
this is your room
see there's the table there's the wardrobe
an apple's on the table
furniture frightens you
you silly thing
that man won't come back

You are frightened of the chair
of an old newspaper of a knock
of voices behind walls
perhaps you wish to draw attention
by your eccentric behaviour

Smile
that man won't come back
look in our eyes
don't hide in corners
don't stand against the wall
no one compels you
to stand against the wall

Speak

(Enter TEACHER *carrying a briefcase. He sits at the table. He takes various papers out of his briefcase. Puts on his glasses. Pays no attention to anything or anyone. He talks, he poses questions. The* TEACHER *may be played by the actor who played* UNCLE. *He has glasses instead of a moustache.)*

TEACHER: Please don't be nervous. Please think.

FIRST ELDER: What are you doing here?

TEACHER: He is sitting for his school leaving certificate. His matriculation exam.

FIRST ELDER: Yes, all right, but why today?

TEACHER: He is already 20 years late. I can't wait any longer.

FIRST ELDER: What questions have you got for him?

TEACHER: *(all the while keeps looking at his papers)* Oh, various. Please sit down and get ready.

FIRST ELDER: You really have chosen the time badly.

TEACHER: What can you tell me about Poland's annexation of Ruthenia?

*(*SECOND ELDER *hands* HERO *a cup of coffee. Leads him to his bed, helps him to lie down and covers him with a blanket.)*

FIRST ELDER: With the death of King Daniel, Ruthenia passed through a period of decline. Although one of his sons, Szwarno, being Mendog's son-in-law, did briefly occupy the Lithuanian throne, the chronicles provide an unflattering account of the other son Lion I. His reign was followed by that of his son, Jerzy I, who united under his rule the principalities of Wlodzimierz and Halicz. His sons, Andrzej of Wlodzimierz and Lion II of Halicz, lost Podlasie and Polesie in favour of Giedymin, but subsequently entered into friendly relations with him and one of Giedymin's sons, Lubart, married Busza, the daughter of Andrzej. Boleslaw, the son of Trojden, the prince of Mazowsze, married one of Giedymin's daughters, that is the sister of Aldona, the wife of Kazimierz the Great . . . .

TEACHER: *(looking at his papers)* Excellent, brilliant. Well done, young man, you are splendidly prepared for life. As a matter of fact, you've passed your matriculation exam but, to make absolutely sure, I must put a few more questions to you. You will understand that this is pure formality . . . . Do tell me, what have you been reading recently?

FIRST ELDER: The newspapers.

TEACHER: But what in particular?

FIRST ELDER: The personal advice column.

TEACHER: Please describe in your own words.

FIRST ELDER: During her holidays a certain Anka fell in love with Bolek. They used to go out together, but earlier on, Bolek who was Anka's first passionate love, used to go out with Halina, which fact he disguised from Anka and was sent to the army. When I sent a letter to Bolek that I was expecting a baby which was conceived earlier, Bolek did not reply but wrote to me later that he was expecting a baby from Halina who used to go out with Tadek. My parents wouldn't allow me to go out with Marek because Bolek was fifty years younger than me. And now, dear Aunt Mary, I am 16 and when I first knew Victor I was eight and I trusted people. Now I have lost faith in Bolek and people point at me in our little town. Please advise me, my dear Aunt Mary, what am I to do. My situation is the worse because my Mummy, who for seventy years was barren, has now been cured and is also expecting a baby. What sort of life can I look forward to?

TEACHER: All the same, you young ones are all set to enjoy life. Fact, a sad fact . . . and who is to do the suffering in this world?

FIRST ELDER: This is just the problem, professor.

TEACHER: What are your plans for the future?

FIRST ELDER: I am taking up Chinese.

TEACHER: Splendid . . . and how old are you?

FIRST ELDER: Eighty . . . .

TEACHER: Splendid, young man, remember that 'The child is father of the man.' Thank you, I have no more questions.

   (FIRST ELDER takes up his place next to his colleagues. The CHORUS is now sitting against the wall.)

   Ah, but *(recollecting)* tell me one more thing: why do you love Chopin?

FIRST ELDER: Chopin, sir, hid guns amid flowers and has popularised Poland's name all over the world.

TEACHER: Yes, but what do you feel when you listen to his music the whole year through?

FIRST ELDER: I experience a deep gratitude to the composer.

TEACHER: *(shakes his head)* How can they say our youth is cynical and indifferent.

HERO: *(sitting up and gesturing to the TEACHER to come over to him)* Professor, come over here.

   (TEACHER sits on the bed next to the HERO, HERO stretching his hand, fingers apart, towards the TEACHER.)

   What is this, professor?

TEACHER: A hand.

HERO: *(clenching his fingers)* And this?

TEACHER: A fist.

HERO: *(clenching and opening his fist)* Hand, fist, hand, fist, hand, fist. One can use a hand to kill, strangle, write a poem or a prescription, or to fondle.

   (Strokes the TEACHER's cheek, takes the apple in his hand.)

   What is this?

TEACHER: An apple.

HERO: *(showing him a button)* And this?

TEACHER: A button.

CHORUS OF ELDERS:

Guano	gun	glucose
Guatemala	goodies	glue
goulash	goose	glum
guzzle	gooseberry	glutton

(CHORUS stops suddenly . . . is silent as though 'thunder-struck'. The SECRETARY enters the room. It is the same little person who had earlier played FEMALE VOICE UNDER THE BED CLOTHES. We behold rounded buttocks encased in a dress or trousers. The CHORUS gapes. SECRETARY sits on the bed and opens her documents file.)

SECRETARY: These are for signature, sir.

(Silently the HERO signs a series of documents with his index finger.)

CHORUS OF ELDERS:

Give what, tho' thou giv'st it often, is yours still,
Give, what later thou wilt vainly strive to fill
When wrinkles plough this face, and at last
The glass show thy gaze that youth is past . . . .

SECRETARY: *(laughing)* I adore Kochanowski.

CHORUS OF ELDERS:

Be not shy, dear, thou knowest well the tale:
When the cat grows older, the stiffer is his tail;
An oak, too, when withered, parched and dry —
If its root hath life — will stand up high.*

SECRETARY: There is a journalist outside under the window, he would like an interview.

HERO: Tomorrow.

SECRETARY: He's been waiting a whole year; you see, sir, in our time speed of information takes precedence, agencies await the latest news, developments and gossip . . . .

HERO: *(to TEACHER)* You will excuse me, I am very busy.

(The TEACHER gets up but turns back in the doorway.)

---

*Two fragments from Jan Kochanowski (1530–1584). (Tr.)

TEACHER: One last small question. Could you lend me loo zlotys? No . . . ? Ciao, bambina!

(Goes out with his briefcase and beard.)

SECRETARY: *(yawning and stretching)* I am so tired and sleepy. I'll get into bed.

(Gets into bed and settles down to sleep.

The room becomes a pavement and there are people walking along the pavement. A gentleman with a briefcase, then a young couple who stop, look around and kiss long and passionately. Two middle-aged women speak quickly while walking: 'Meat, of meat, to meat, from meat, oh meat, with meat, meatless'. They pass. Enter HERO'S PARENTS. MOTHER puts her finger to her lips. They stop over the bed. FATHER glances at his watch.)

FATHER: Yes, it certainly is time!

(MOTHER looks knowingly at FATHER.)

You see, Franek . . . we must have a chat about certain . . . .

MOTHER: Tadek . . . .

FATHER: You see, Tadek, today I want to have a man-to-man talk with you. As you know, time passes . . . I'm sure you've noted certain disturbing changes in your organism. Your beard is getting coarser and thicker, hair is falling out of your head, your voice is growing deeper . . . . I am sure you sometimes have dreams, then you wake up and think about various things . . . .

MOTHER: *(with feeling)* Do you remember, Kornel, not so long ago you were showing him the little window through which the stork had dropped him into our flat . . . we mothers are a wretched lot . . . .

FATHER: You see, my child, the purpose of life is to maintain life. The most primitive type of life is sexless reproduction. Reproduction comes about through division or blossoming. An individual normally splits into two parts or he develops a kind of blossom which after a while drops off to form a new individual.

MOTHER: You never told me about this.

FATHER: The virgin conception among plant life is notorious. No less interesting is the parthenogenesis of vorticels.

CHORUS OF ELDERS:
King
kink
kiosk
kipper
kiss
kirk
kitchen

FATHER: (*looking at his watch*) Well, you can't expect me here and now to produce a detailed description of the external mechanism of love in all the species of animals. It would take too long and in any event would be tiresome and uninteresting. Among crickets the male possesses a musical apparatus, while the female is endowed with an auditory organ which is located on her back feet. Similarly, in the case of grasshoppers, except that only the male can emit sounds. Are these sounds love-calls?

MOTHER: I have no idea.

FATHER: (*looking at his watch*) 'Don't put off till tomorrow what you can do today . . . .' The best you can do is not to think about silly things.

(*FATHER bends over the sleeping HERO, kisses him on the forehead. PARENTS leave.*)

HERO: Pity you were asleep. Father was saying interesting things.

SECRETARY: So you've got a father? How strange.

HERO: And a mother.

SECRETARY: Ha ha ha ha ha ha ha (*laughs*).

HERO: What are you laughing at?

SECRETARY: I can't imagine you as an embryo. So you were as small as my little finger?!

HERO: Yes, just as small . . . .

SECRETARY: And then you were breast-fed?

HERO: I was bottle-fed.

SECRETARY: And you dropped little golden lumps into the pottie . . . ? And what about your moustache? When did you start growing a moustache and a beard?

HERO: On Monday.

SECRETARY: What a deep voice my little cockerel has . . . .

HERO: Poor father . . . .

SECRETARY: Poor? Tell me about your old man.

HERO:

Had my father
been a captain of a ship
a bishop
if he had a sabre a star a ribbon a stool a crown
had he discovered America
conquered a peak
in a word
had he differed at least a little
from ordinary average people

SECRETARY: My dearest, people are not average!

HERO:

. . . had he been different
from these ordinary average people
had he been a cannibal
a Lollobrigida
an astronaut

But he was an insignificant clerk
in a small provincial town
he was like me
like you
like all of us
Such people depart quickly. One forgets them. You will leave here and you will forget me. Isn't that so? You are already forgetting.

(*SECRETARY takes the apple in her hand.*)

HERO: When I was a little boy I dreamt of being a fireman. I wanted
to have a shining helmet, a belt and a hatchet. I imagined
carrying a little girl I knew out of a burning house with
everybody admiring me, thanking me and pinning a medal
on me. I ran around the courtyard with my arms outstretched
(*opens out his arms and imitates engine noises*) and then it
seemed to me that I was an aeroplane and a pilot. I was
also a tiny foal .... When I started school my dreams
changed, I wanted to be a traveller, a millionaire, a poet or
a saint.

SECRETARY: And now?

HERO: Now I am always myself. I travelled a long way before I
reached myself.

SECRETARY: Yourself? And how are things over there? What is there?

HERO: Nothing. Everything is on the outside. And there are faces,
trees, clouds, the dead . . . but all this merely flows through
me. The horizon narrows down constantly. I see best when
I close my eyes. With eyes closed I can see love, faith,
truth ....

SECRETARY: I know nothing about that.

HERO: Yes, that is how it is ....

SECRETARY: (*giving him the apple*) Eat it . . . tempt yourself .... He is
asleep .... Men are terribly childish. They are always pur-
suing something, and when they at last arrive at their goal,
they despair. They are in a hurry, they murder. A seed
would never have grown inside them. They are careless.
None of them is capable of protecting a fruit for nine months.
It's lucky it's we who carry and give birth to life .... They
are born abstractionists. There is death in that.

(*Sits on the bed and, smiling, begins to eat the apple.*)

CHORUS OF ELDERS: (*loudly*)
He who in childhood cut off Hydra's head ....

SECRETARY: Shhhhh ... quieter ....

CHORUS OF ELDERS: *(declaiming in a whisper)*
Will in his youth the blood of Centaurs shed,
Will rescue victims of the Demon,
Will gather laurels up in Heaven.

SECRETARY: Leave him!

(CHORUS fold up their chairs and leave the room on tiptoe. SEC-RETARY looks at herself in a mirror. Various people pass through the room. Some are in a hurry, some walk slowly. They talk excitedly, they read newspapers, call their children, exchange greetings. A young couple kiss and walk on. A JOURNALIST enters. He walks through the room, returns, looks around as though he were looking for an apartment or an unfamiliar house. He moves upstage to the centre of the room and stops by the bed in which the HERO is sleeping. The SECRETARY pays no attention to the JOURNALIST. She takes the arm of the first available passerby and leaves the room.)

JOURNALIST: *(lights a cigarette. Walks about the room. Stubs the cigarette. Grips the HERO by the arm.)* I say! I say, sir!

(HERO utters inarticulate sounds.)

Please wake up, it's me.

HERO: *(sits up in bed)* What? Who?

JOURNALIST: It's me, I must put a few questions to you.

HERO: You? To me?

JOURNALIST: *(takes a notebook out of his pocket)* Your secretary has doubtless mentioned . . . .

HERO: You from the press? Haven't you seen an apple here?

JOURNALIST: No.

HERO: Perhaps you've eaten this apple . . . from the tree of knowledge of good and evil?

JOURNALIST: *(laughing)* No, I haven't eaten it.

HERO: *(thinks)* These aren't the only tricks you people are capable of . . . .

JOURNALIST: I want to talk seriously. With the approach of the New

Year, our Agency wishes to conduct interviews with various celebrities and with ordinary . . . .

HERO: Simple . . . .

JOURNALIST: . . . exactly, with simple citizens.

HERO: Well?

JOURNALIST: Could you tell me your aim in life?

HERO: I have already achieved it and now it's rather difficult to say . . . .

JOURNALIST: And are you glad to be alive?

HERO: Yes . . . no . . . yes . . . in fact, yes.

JOURNALIST: And why?

HERO: How should I know . . . ?

JOURNALIST: Then who should know?

HERO: I have no idea.

JOURNALIST: And is there anything you still wish to achieve?

HERO: Well . . . . I have various plans, I would naturally wish . . . although . . . .

JOURNALIST: (*writes it down – thinks – suddenly asks*) What are your political views?

HERO: Who's got political views at five in the morning? The chap's mad. He wants me to have views at dawn! One has to wash, dress, relieve oneself, brush teeth, change a shirt, put on a tie and pull up one's trousers, and only then it is time to have opinions . . . .

JOURNALIST: I see . . . . Do you believe in salvation?

HERO: Yes . . . no . . . that is . . . up to a certain point . . . funny question.

JOURNALIST: If I'm not mistaken, you are an ordinary person?

HERO: Yes.

JOURNALIST: Do you know that you hold the fate of the world in your hands?

HERO: Up to a point.

JOURNALIST: What do you intend to do to maintain peace in the world?

HERO: I don't know.

JOURNALIST: Do you realise that in the event of nuclear warfare humanity will perish?

HERO: (*almost gaily*) Naturally, naturally.

JOURNALIST: And what are you doing to prevent the explosion?

HERO: (*laughs*) Nothing.

JOURNALIST: But surely, you love humanity?

HERO: Naturally.

JOURNALIST: But why?

HERO: I don't know yet. It's difficult to say, it's only five in the morning. Perhaps if you drop in around midday I might know.

JOURNALIST: (*puts his notebook away*) I haven't learnt much here.

HERO: You've come too late.

JOURNALIST: Goodbye.

(*HERO is silent.*)

THE WITNESSES

or Our Little Stabilization

CHARACTERS

HE	poetry readers
SHE	
A WOMAN	
HER HUSBAND	
A STRANGER	a waiter or perhaps a servant
SECOND	middle-aged men
THIRD	

PART I

The two READERS *step forward in front of the Curtain. They recite a poem called: 'Things are Almost Back to Normal.'*

SHE: stupidity is evolving
normally

HE: infinity is shorter
than the leg
of Sophia Loren

SHE: the demands of love and hate
have diminished

HE: whiteness is no longer so white
so dazzlingly white

SHE: blackness is no longer so black
so really black

HE: temperature is average

SHE: winds moderate

HE: Van Gogh's ear
looks almost comic

SHE: like the green ear of a herring

HE: metaphysics has the legs
of a dachshund

SHE: rocks dissolve
and recount anecdotes

HE: we again have something
resembling poetry

BOTH: you cross your legs

HE: at a meeting at a concert
in the theatre in an aeroplane

SHE: dogs are wearing quilted jackets
teenagers have an air of mystery
best to forget
writes Aunt Lavinia

HE: a pimple on the nose creates
an alienation problem

BOTH: you cross your legs

HE: you read the apocalypse
in bed

SHE: have it quoted in magazines

HE: the Establishment fights
contraceptives instead of

SHE: fighting to raise their quality

HE: we talk indulgently
about the end of the world

BOTH: we cross our legs

SHE: houses are standing

HE: cars drive around

SHE: gentlemen have ladies

HE: ladies have furs

SHE: furs have collars

HE: and so on

BOTH: we cross our legs

HE: in churches they speak of hell
with circumspection

SHE: funeral establishments
are sumptuously stocked

HE: with a great variety
of coffins and wreaths

SHE: here too abuses occur

HE: but the customers are always right

SHE: one can drop in

HE: one can drop out

SHE: one can be shocked

HE: but not too deeply

SHE: one can drink coffee

BOTH: and cross one's legs

        (Pause)

HE: you know I am a bit afraid
        I'm afraid I may lose it

SHE: what

HE: well nothing really
        I'm afraid I may lose
        that something

BOTH: and things will not get back to normal

HE: that I may lose getting out of
        bed in the morning

SHE: going to bed at night

HE: and lying in bed

SHE: and my job and my attitude
        to my job and the boss's
        attitude to me

HE: and our attitudes to each other

SHE: which are
        none too good

HE: but surely this is better
        than not at all

SHE: I'm a bit afraid
        that I may lose this flat

HE: and the lunches which are sometimes better
        and sometimes worse and you

BOTH: and your and mine and our

HE: views so to speak

SHE: I'm a bit worried about the wardrobe

HE: and the trousers in the wardrobe
and the art of poetry

SHE: and the china and aesthetics
and glasses and ethics

HE: and about our last words
before sleeping

SHE: before yawning

HE: and about the ceiling over our heads

BOTH: it may only be a dream
that things are almost back to normal

HE: but deep inside I honestly
believe everything will
turn out all right

SHE: and we shall be able
to relax

HE: on the other hand
something worries me

SHE: all day long

HE: that things are almost back to normal . . .
may be but a dream . . . .

PART II

A room with a table, chairs and an armchair. There are cups and a jug on the table. Through the open window there flows a stream of sunlight and a pastoral, elegant quiet melody . . . Rameau's 'Le rappel des oiseaux'. The WOMAN is sitting in a light-coloured spring dress. She has black leaves stuck over her eyelids. There is light on her face. A distinct male voice is heard from the adjoining room through an open door or curtain. The music grows faint, almost inaudible.

WOMAN: Are you asleep, my pussy cat?

MAN: I'm not, my pet.

WOMAN: What are you doing?

MAN: I'm dead, my pet.

WOMAN: You're joking, my pussy cat.

MAN: I am joking, my pet.

WOMAN: And what did you dream in the night?

MAN: Can't remember . . . a wardrobe. I was opening a wardrobe. And you?

WOMAN: I dreamt of a wardrobe too.

MAN: *(to himself)* I must get out of bed. One, two, three, get up, old horse!

WOMAN: If somebody were eavesdropping he would think we were two children, playing at being a married couple.

MAN: Eavesdropping?

WOMAN: What are you doing?

MAN: Nothing, and you?

WOMAN: I'm thinking.

MAN: What about?

WOMAN: What you were saying before you fell asleep.

MAN: Don't remember.

WOMAN: You were saying that from today you want to turn over a new leaf and then you dropped; off to sleep like a log.

MAN: The things we say before falling asleep! Everything gets lumped together for no apparent reason.

WOMAN: (*drinking coffee*) What are you up to now?

MAN: My morning exercises .... (*MAN enters. He is still young, he is wearing black trousers and a white shirt*) I feel like a little bird.

WOMAN: Wait, I'll close the window.

MAN: Why?

WOMAN: So you won't fly away, my eagle.

MAN: (*laughs*) Do you write down your witticisms?

(*Kisses the WOMAN on the cheek.*)

WOMAN: Kiss me again.

MAN: Now I remember what I said last night. That wasn't a joke.

WOMAN: Leave it until tomorrow.

MAN: I can't.

WOMAN: Please.

MAN: (*approaching the window, stretching his arms. Gazes into the distance*) What a lovely day!

WOMAN: This view from the window alone is worth a hundred a month.

MAN: A thousand.

WOMAN: Sometimes I just stand here and watch the clouds go by. They float and float on and on.

MAN: What do you think of then ... ? Oh, look down there what a funny kitten! Where did he spring from?

WOMAN: I think of you and of me and that our life too floats away.

MAN: You know, that is an interesting observation. It never struck me before. I just never have the time.

WOMAN: Clouds change their shapes ... sometimes they remind you of something. Yesterday I saw a cloud like a steam engine and then it turned into a Cossack on horseback.

MAN: Really .... Have you ever seen a Cossack on horseback?

WOMAN: (*laughing*) No.

MAN: (*still at the window*) What are you laughing at?

WOMAN: You — you have no imagination at all.

MAN: Wait, do you know I can now see a cloud like ... like ....

WOMAN: Like what?

MAN: Like a refrigerator ... but it's changing already ... come quickly.

WOMAN: I have already looked out of the window this morning. About three or four minutes.

MAN: And now it is like a pillow ... this is fantastic.

WOMAN: Reminds me of the time we were engaged. We used to have such mad conversations from morning till night: full of high spirits, wit, nonsense and poetry ... do you remember?

MAN: (*surprised*) Poetry?

WOMAN: Yes, yes my little pet, poetry. You know I'd almost forgotten one could spend the time in this delightful carefree way. I used to long for such a conversation with you.

MAN: (*lighting a cigarette*) Why didn't you tell me? What a funny little chap that kitten is. Chasing his own shadow. Jumping about ....

WOMAN: It rolled on to the meadow this morning like a ball of white wool.

MAN: This one is black.

WOMAN: What's the difference ... it's probably his little brother.

MAN: (*after a pause*) He's funny. Like clockwork. He's determined to catch his own tail.

WOMAN: Shall I pour you some coffee?

MAN: No thanks, I'll have milk.

WOMAN: Mummy's written to say she is coming.

MAN: Poor Mummy . . . you didn't tell me anything.

WOMAN: The letter only came this morning.

MAN: We'll have to put the bed up for the night.

WOMAN: It's in the hall.

MAN: And where shall we put it?

WOMAN: Here or in the kitchen.

MAN: Last time I put it up I couldn't fold it up again.

WOMAN: Maybe you did something wrong . . . these beds aren't as practical as they say.

MAN: For two or three nights it doesn't really matter. In any case Mummy can sleep with you and I will sleep in the armchair.

WOMAN: It isn't as simple as that. (*MAN sits at table and crosses his legs*) Mummy wrote to say she wants to stay with us for good, so it's no good you just sitting there with your legs crossed.

MAN: Oh, that's different . . . . We can divide the kitchen with a screen and put the bed up each night and keep it in the hall during the day. Have you seen my razor blades? You were cutting the seams in my old trousers yesterday.

WOMAN: Poor Mummy, she hasn't had an easy life.

MAN: She'll be able to have a rest here. The atmosphere here will do her good.

WOMAN: She'll water the plants and keep an eye on the flat.

MAN: Feed the white mice.

WOMAN: Give them milk.

MAN: I'm sure she will love it here.

WOMAN: She's always been longing for a real home.

MAN: When I get back I'll check whether the bed works. In any case she can sleep on the sofa.

WOMAN: When you are going past the market see whether they have any chicken.

MAN: All right.

WOMAN: (*gets up goes to the window and stands facing the* MAN) Life is so beautiful.

MAN: In spite of everything life is so beautiful.

WOMAN: Only people are horrid ... though not everyone.

MAN: They are fundamentally good ... though not everyone.

WOMAN: Have you drunk your milk?

MAN: No.

WOMAN: It's in the mug in the kitchen.

MAN: Have you taken the skin off?

WOMAN: (*about to go*) I forgot.

MAN: Oh, never mind.

   (*Goes out. Again pastoral music flows in through the window . . . . A musical portrait by Couperin or Rameau.*)

WOMAN: (*after a pause*) What are you doing out there, my pet?

MAN: (*his voice heard through the door*) Drinking milk.

WOMAN: Milk is definitely very good for you.

   (MAN *is silent or hums a tune.*)

WOMAN: Have you taken the skin off the milk?

MAN: Yes, pussy.

WOMAN: Now eat it, the skin is the best part.

MAN: I can't stand the skin − I've been telling you so these last ten years.

WOMAN: I forgot.

(MAN *hisses and smacks his lips.*)

WOMAN: What's happened?

MAN: I've burnt my tongue.

WOMAN: You should have blown on it . . . . Is it very bad?

MAN: Very.

WOMAN: There, you see.

(*Sound of breaking crockery*)

WOMAN: What are you doing?

MAN: I broke the mug and saucer.

WOMAN: Put some cream on. I'm coming in a second.

MAN: No need to.

WOMAN: Have you done it?

MAN: (*mumbling*) I have.

WOMAN: Does it hurt less now?

MAN: (*mumbling*) Yes.

WOMAN: You mumble so, I can't tell whether you mean less or more.

MAN: (*more clearly*) Less.

WOMAN: I'm glad. I'd rather have burnt my own tongue. To see someone you love suffer hurts more than any other pain. Don't you agree?

(MAN *is silent.* WOMAN *turns to face the window and even leans over as if she has just seen something. Her back is turned towards us. It is not just a specific shape, but a stylistic one as well. This turning back not only affects the spectator's perception, it is also a kind of archetype, an embodiment of an idea slumbering in men's subconscious.*)

WOMAN: Look — that lovely little girl out there playing on the lawn amid the grasses, flowers and herbs. A little angel. She has a small red bucket with white roses painted on it. In her other hand she is holding a little shovel. She has a garland of daisies on her head. Now she has got down to work. She is digging a hole in the ground and throwing out the sand with her shovel and she's so absorbed in her work that she's biting her little tongue. The hole is getting bigger and bigger and the pile of golden sand is growing. Such a tiny thing and playing all by herself so beautifully. Now she's pouring the sand into the little bucket, pats it with her shovel, turns the bucket upside down onto the lawn, lifts it up and . . . there! What a wonderful sand-pie! (*Claps her hands, turns away from the window and sits down in the armchair.*)

MAN: (*through the door*) I'm ready at last.

WOMAN: Don't go without a tie today!

MAN: Which one do you want me to wear?

WOMAN: The white one with black stripes.

MAN: Where is it?

WOMAN: Surely, it's hanging up . . . you hung it up yourself yesterday.

MAN: There is a black one with white stripes here. I can't see the other one.

WOMAN: Then put on the black one with white stripes.

MAN: (*enters room carrying a tie*) But darling, my beard will cover it up anyway.

WOMAN: That is not the point. It's just that it should be there.

MAN: No one will see it and I will feel uncomfortable with the knot round my neck.

WOMAN: That is just it: you should feel you are wearing a tie.

MAN: But if nobody sees it, it is just as if I hadn't got one on.

WOMAN: Bend down . . . . (*She ties the tie*) There are things which you can't see and yet are more important than others. Love, honour, faith.

MAN: Yes, yes, of course.

WOMAN: And, for heaven's sake, don't forget the chicken: it will do Mummy good to have chicken broth after her journey.

MAN: (*going up to the mirror*) These folding beds are quite practical in their way. In the last resort I can sleep on the bed and you and Mummy can sleep on the divan. We'll manage somehow for these few days.

WOMAN: Mummy's written that she wants to stay with us for the rest of her days.

MAN: Then it's better to do as I said. We'll put up the bed for Mummy at night and fold it up during the day. The chairs can be moved to the hall.

WOMAN: And the table?

MAN: We'll move the table towards the window. We can put a screen up in the dining room and move the sideboard in such a way that Mummy can have a niche of her own. Or it can stand by the window and be folded up for the night.

WOMAN: You are a darling but you need a shave.

MAN: That goes without saying — you know how much I respect her.

WOMAN: She hasn't had an easy life. Perhaps we should move the chairs now?

MAN: There is plenty of time, but if you insist . . . .

WOMAN: I'm glad everything's turned out all right. And I was beginning to get apprehensive . . . . Have you noticed the table doesn't wobble any more? Yesterday I put a book under there.

MAN: Which book?

WOMAN: Have a look, I don't remember.

MAN: (*kneels by the table*) *The Decline of the West* by Oswald Spengler.

WOMAN: It's out of date.

MAN: (*gets up, brushes his trousers and sits at the table, crossing his legs*) I like to sit for a while after a meal. You know, just now when I was kneeling by the table, it struck me that faiths and ideologies should be like pills. They shouldn't tear and wound. They should have a mild, laxative effect. For God's sake, this is the second half of the twentieth century! We are slowly getting back to normal and all at once you get new clouds gathering overhead .... We have acquired a certain number of possessions.

WOMAN: We have put something by.

MAN: We've saved a little.

WOMAN: We are quite settled down .... Surely we have a right to know what to expect.

MAN: You're terribly funny. Don't you know the end of the world was to come last Wednesday?

WOMAN: You can't go out like that — have a shave.

MAN: It's no mere joke, millions came to believe that the world was to end last Wednesday. Hindu astrologers had predicted it all accurately. The horrible snake Rachu was to swallow the sun and the earth. An ambassador apparently sold his pictures and his cow, others were giving away their possessions. Amina, that Hindu princess who performs the belly-dance in Milan night clubs, said at a press conference that for several nights running she was performing dances of propitiation to avert the holocaust threatening the world.

WOMAN: I've seen her on a newsreel. I'm not surprised the gods allowed themselves to be propitiated by the gyrations of her belly. It's difficult to imagine such a belly being destroyed by blind forces.

MAN: You are wonderful! (*Laughs*)

WOMAN: When I was a child I could never say 'propitiatory' and even now I think I've made a slip.

MAN: You are so childish.

WOMAN: But I too have my secrets. Small dark crevices.

MAN: Don't I know it! (*Laughs. Indulgently*) Go on, tell me.

WOMAN: I'd like to die.

MAN: Come, come.

WOMAN: You laugh at me, but I sometimes like to go away somewhere, fly away.

MAN: Surely, that could be arranged.

WOMAN: (*suddenly serious, harsh*) I can't live like this, I can't live like this any longer.

MAN: You can't? But my little bird ....

WOMAN: (*almost brutally*) I can't (*tears the leaves from her eyelids*).

MAN: Well, if you can't live ....

WOMAN: (*with growing anger*) Then what?

MAN: Nothing.

WOMAN: I know what you wanted to say.

MAN: By what?

WOMAN: You said 'Nothing'. That means I can die.

MAN: Nonsense.

WOMAN: It isn't nonsense. You wanted to say: If you can't live, then you can die.

MAN: I didn't wish to say anything.

WOMAN: But you did.

MAN: I won't say anything.

WOMAN: (*with mounting irritation*) You don't want anything.
How can you speak to me like that
Don't you see I am suffering
I know you don't see it
why have you suddenly gone blind
you don't see me
but I see you

(*The WOMAN's voice becomes a scream.*)
oh how well I see
if you knew
how clearly I see
how remote you are

(The voice is now a whisper.)

how remote
how terribly remote you are

MAN: Please, always tell me everything.

WOMAN: *(cheerfully)* Of course . . . .

MAN: But . . . . But . . . . You can't. How can you . . . . *(Helpless)* Here, drink this. *(Hands her a cup. She drinks)* Do you feel better now?

WOMAN: *(nods)* I am sorry.

MAN: What happened so suddenly, out of the blue . . . .

WOMAN: *(smiling)* It's nothing. Sometimes I am very unhappy.

MAN: But sometimes you are happy?

WOMAN: Of course.

(MAN lights a cigarette. WOMAN goes to the mirror, wipes her face with a handkerchief . . . etc.)

MAN: *(looks out of the window)* Look, there's that kitten again. He's chasing a feather. He's chasing the shadow of a cloud and his little black tail. Now the little girl has seen him. She's thrown down the bucket and is running after him. She has got him in her arms. She's cuddling and kissing him. Kissing his little eyes and nose. Stroking his head. The kitten's closing his eyes and purring. There is a drop of milk on his nose. His whiskers are gleaming in the sun like tiny black wires. He is licking himself with a rosy little tongue. The girl is rocking him in her arms and saying something to him.

(Now the MAN is walking up and down the room.)

WOMAN: There is little advantage in keeping cats — they are kept chiefly for pleasure.

MAN: The only useful thing about cats is they catch mice.

WOMAN: Their sense of smell is not as good as that of dogs but they hear and see remarkably well.

MAN: This helps them to track down their prey.

WOMAN: Once they spot it they lie in wait for it.

MAN: Whereupon they leap and sink their claws into it . . . .

WOMAN: Cats belong to the order carnivora.

MAN: Just like dogs.

WOMAN: We mustn't let dogs lick our face and hands.

MAN: For a dog may sometimes infect man with worms.

WOMAN: The cat gives birth to a litter of blind, small, helpless kittens.

MAN: The kittens live on their mother's milk.

WOMAN: She looks after them — she licks them clean and warms them with her own body.

MAN: When the young have grown a little, she plays with them . . . .

(Sound of Rococo-pastoral music. The wave of music comes and fades. Silence. MAN and WOMAN sit next to each other. They hold hands. Her eyes are half shut. His are open.)

WOMAN: Do you love me?

(MAN is silent)

Say if you love me.

MAN: Listen, my dear . . . .

WOMAN: Do you love me?

MAN: You can't ask me just like that.

WOMAN: Tell me.

MAN: Of course.

WOMAN: Say 'I love you', not 'of course'.

MAN: I love you.

WOMAN: Have something to eat before you go.

MAN: No, thank you. I feel rotten. What have I eaten?

WOMAN: But you haven't eaten anything.

MAN: Yesterday.

WOMAN: Perhaps those sausages were stale.

MAN: Perhaps.

WOMAN: So many times I've asked you not to eat at bedtime. I've been asking you for years and for years it's the same old story. I ask I explain I tell you and what's the use.

MAN: Revolting beast! A revolting beast.

WOMAN: What?

MAN: I was thinking of a fellow I know. Beast! A thorough beast!

WOMAN: Forget about it. If I could be born again I'd live in a totally different way . . . quite different. Sometimes I think man is capable of the greatest sacrifices. And sometimes that he is capable of the vilest deeds.

MAN: The world is a strangely constructed machine and man is both the oil and the sand in the cogs of this machine.

WOMAN: I could never understand Tolstoy's running away from his home and family. This was quite childish: from a warm comfortable mansion to a railway station — merely to spite his wife!

MAN: Genius is often childlike. Besides, he was obsessed by an idea.

WOMAN: What a good thing obsessions are not so demanding nowadays.

MAN: True . . . I've spilled some gravy on my trousers. We'll have to take them to the cleaners . . . . When is Mummy coming?

WOMAN: In the evening. So you will have to . . . .

MAN: The first plan I suggested.

WOMAN: Only small changes . . . .

MAN: You know how I respect her . . . .

WOMAN: When you come back, we'll move the furniture . . . .

MAN: Everything'll be all right.

WOMAN: Do shave, for heaven's sake.

(WOMAN goes to the mirror. Examines her face carefully. Touches her face with her fingertips. She smiles. The MAN is sitting at the table turned towards the window but not looking through it. A wave of soft music.)

MAN: Now pay attention: I will be brief. A sky speckled with clouds reflected in the water. The clouds float along. A little girl running across the meadow. Scooping up water in her hands and carrying it here and there. The kitten is lying peacefully. Now a boy comes running on to the meadow. He is twelve or perhaps thirteen. Smiling. Soft luminous down on his upper lip. (*WOMAN is at the mirror. She touches her neck with her fingers. Then she sticks her tongue out several times. Some sort of exercise to prevent atrophy of the neck muscles and skin. During the course of the MAN's narration she repeats the exercise two or three times.*) He sits by the water-side looking at his reflection. Now he's jumped up. He is turning somersaults, shouting, laughing. He is walking on his hands. He is plucking flowers and scattering them about. He has broken a twig and torn off the leaves and sharpened it with a penknife. It is now as sharp and pointed as an arrow. Now the boy has thrown the stick away. He has spotted the kitten. He is moving towards it on tiptoe. (*He breaks off, then resumes*) The boy has caught the kitten and is carrying it to the water which reflects the sky and clouds. He has thrown the kitten into the water. The kitten is struggling with its little paws. The boy is pushing it away with a stick. He is smiling. The kitten has come ashore and is shaking itself. The boy is pushing it back into the water with his foot. The little girl has abandoned her bucket and the sand. She is watching the kitten. The boy is pressing the kitten's head down with his foot so that it cannot breathe. Now he smiles again. Now he has raised his foot. The kitten has struggled out of the water again. Looks like a wet rag. It tries to escape but the boy has caught up with it, grasped it by its tail, spun it round and round and thrown it into the air like a ball. (*Pulls out his wallet, looks through his papers. Speaks*) Now the boy's got the kitten again. He has pulled a string round its neck, he is dragging it to the hold the little girl has dug. He is putting it in the hole. He's burying it. Now only the head is visible. The boy has moved back a step and looks. He isn't smiling any more. The kitten's head moves. The boy has taken the red bucket from the little girl and covered the kitten. Now the boy and the girl watch the bucket which moves slightly. The boy has taken the bucket off and is sitting beside the kitten. The kitten's head now looks like a lump of mud only now and again its pink tongue is visible. Now the boy takes the shovel and throws it away. He is squashing the kitten with his foot — harder and harder. Its eyes flow out: two white balls on red threads. Now he pours sand over the kitten. Golden sand, the heap grows and glistens in the sun. Now he is treading down the earth. His eyes are shining. He isn't smiling anymore. Now he has run off, he's disappeared. The little girl is wiping her face with her hand, she appears to be crying. She takes her little spade and bucket and walks away. A pigeon's flying by, it's lost a feather. The white feather is slowly falling to the ground . . . .

The WOMAN *is performing her 'exercise'. She is flicking her tongue faster and faster. She examines her face carefully in the mirror. The* MAN *kisses the* WOMAN *and leaves. Inarticulate conversation and laughter heard through open door, then the* WOMAN's *voice 'Bye, bye, darling'. Silence. A stranger enters the empty room. He is dressed like a waiter with a cloth in his hand. As he passes the table, he automatically begins to wipe and rearrange things as if he were wiping out traces of the married couple's conversation and presence. He stops in front of the window and then shuts it slowly. When the window is closed the curtain falls.*

PART III

Darkness. A muffled prolonged wail of a siren. A light comes on in the darkness. A café verandah. Almost deserted. A few tables but no chairs. Two MEN *of unspecified age sit in armchairs. Dressed almost smartly. One has his back to the audience, the other is facing the audience. In the background a curtain through which a light filters. The armchairs stand next to each other but at such distance that the outstretched hands of the sitters would be unable to meet. A muffled prolonged wail of a siren. As though an ambulance had arrived. Then silence.*

SECOND *shifts about. Places himself in a more comfortable position. Crosses his legs. Sits motionless. Stares at the people. Does nothing. Perhaps he is thinking intensively, but who can tell?*

Only the top of THIRD's *bald head visible above the back of the armchair. A hand is visible on the arm rest. He breathes 'a deep sigh of relief'. He must have been on a long tiring journey before reaching this place.*

SECOND *shifts again. Now we can see both his hands, fingers gripping the arm rests.*

THIRD: Yes. (*Sighs*)

SECOND: Are you sitting?

(THIRD *is silent.*)

At last.

(THIRD *is silent — * SECOND *animated.*)

Comfortable?

THIRD: And you?

SECOND: One gets used to it. It isn't standing quite firmly.

THIRD: You won't fall out?

SECOND: I am holding on with hands and feet.

THIRD: And your teeth.

SECOND: With teeth and claws. (*Smiles*)

THIRD: Not too tight?

SECOND: Damned tight.

THIRD: What's the view on your side? Any interesting landscapes or people?

SECOND: There is a shimmering grey mass. But it's very far away. It's probably the air shimmering like that.

THIRD: Aren't you bored?

SECOND: No. I have to be careful.

THIRD: Can you change your position? Turn around?

SECOND: There is no need.

THIRD: You are right .... Have you got water over there?

SECOND: No.

THIRD: Fire?

SECOND: No.

THIRD: Pity.

SECOND: No.

THIRD: I have bits of meat stuck between my teeth. It's irritating.

SECOND: You will get used to it.

THIRD: It is very irritating — you haven't got a match?

SECOND: No.

THIRD: Then look for one!

SECOND: No.

THIRD: No what?

       (*SECOND is silent.*)

       But you are there?

SECOND: Yes.

THIRD: (*sighs with relief*) That's good.

SECOND: Yes, yes, I am here — don't worry.

THIRD: I hate being alone.

SECOND: I too .... (*aside*) *That* thing has moved again.

THIRD: Did you say anything?

SECOND: No.

THIRD: What did you say?

SECOND: Nothing ....

THIRD: But what is it?

SECOND: I don't know.

THIRD: An object, an animal, a cloud?

SECOND: A small dark lump.

THIRD: You said it is moving.

SECOND: I think it's coming closer.

THIRD: Perhaps you should go and see?

SECOND: (*almost frightened*) No, no.

(*THIRD is silent.*)

I can't.

THIRD: So what are you doing?

SECOND: I am busy. I have got masses of things to do. I have been putting off everything. I can't move. Quite impossible.

THIRD: Tear yourself away from your duties for a moment and go and see what it is that is lying out there.

SECOND: I can't.

(*THIRD is silent.*)

I must come to grips with and clarify certain matters for myself.

THIRD: You are not speaking clearly.

SECOND: I am saying that I must decide certain problems within myself.

THIRD: Well, I too have an inner life.

SECOND: There is a storm raging in me at the moment. I love and I hate. Pity you can't see it. I love and I hate. Does that sound funny?

THIRD: And what is it you love so much?

SECOND: For instance — our home town.

THIRD: Really? My home town? I don't understand.

SECOND: I love it.

THIRD: What? Houses, bridges, people, trams?

SECOND: Houses, people, buses, the past, the future, the young.

THIRD: Beer stalls, waste-bins, benches . . . .

SECOND: What benches? (*After a pause*) Them too, naturally.

THIRD: Monuments.

SECOND: Yes, monuments as well.

THIRD: Lavatories.

SECOND: These too I love in a special way. I love the whole town.

THIRD: And I don't.

SECOND: Our language is as imperfect as a ladder with broken rungs . . . .

THIRD: (*sighs*) Yes . . . .

SECOND: Quiet. (*After a pause*) I think *that* thing's made a sound. (*Listens*)

THIRD: The thing that was lying out there?

SECOND: I think it is crawling towards us.

THIRD: It has probably got itself run over by a car.

SECOND: I think it is moving away now.

THIRD: Well, my time is up.

SECOND: (*apprehensively*) What do you mean, your time is up?

THIRD: I'll be going.

SECOND: That is impossible. (THIRD stretching his hand towards SECOND) You can't go away now.

THIRD: There are lots of things I have to do.

SECOND: I — my — me — to me . . . .

THIRD: What do you mean 'I — my — me'?

SECOND: Surely you won't leave me like this.

THIRD: Why not?

(*SECOND is silent.*)

(*Laughs*) I was only joking.

SECOND: (*smiles*) Thank you. I was beginning to think I would have to talk to myself.

THIRD: Talking means a lot to you, but you have told me everything now.

SECOND: No, I have told you nothing. You know nothing about me. You do not know me. Me.

THIRD: And when I do get to know you, what then?

SECOND: It *is* a dog, that's what it is . . . .

THIRD: D'you think so?

SECOND: He is holding flowers in his mouth.

THIRD: In his paw.

SECOND: He is holding them between his teeth.

THIRD: Is he still moving?

SECOND: No, but why should that be any concern of yours?

THIRD: Is he showing any signs?

SECOND: I don't know . . . . Listen . . . . You must get to know me, you must get to know me properly. I am sure you think I am different. Naturally I know that I am but you too must know. I must be present in you. Like a maggot in cheese, like a violin in its case, like darkness in a room. If you don't confirm what I shall tell you about myself, then . . . . You must be my witness.

THIRD: (*appearing amused*) Well, well.

SECOND: Something binds us together. I don't want to call it friendship — but still. After all, I can't unveil my secrets to a stranger.

THIRD: Why not? It is an excellent idea. Your best bet is to tell everything to the first Chinaman you meet round the corner . . . .

SECOND: I can't. (*Thinks, listens*) And what are you doing at this moment?

(*THIRD is silent.*)

Can you hear me?

THIRD: No.

SECOND: I asked what you were doing.

THIRD: I was listening to what you were saying.

SECOND: But are you listening attentively? This is very important for me. It is almost decisive for my existence.

THIRD: I am listening. Go on.

SECOND: But please, stop thinking about your own affairs.

THIRD: That I can't promise.

SECOND: I know.

THIRD: I am always involved in my own affairs, but that doesn't prevent me from listening to others.

SECOND: If you don't listen carefully to me, you won't know what I am like. But please don't look at the newspaper now. I heard paper rustling.

THIRD: You were imagining things. It's the wind rustling the branches of the trees or maybe birds flying past.

SECOND: There aren't any trees here. If you don't listen carefully, you will get a false impression of me. I will throw light on all the aspects of this event. You must see me in a proper light. The things people say about me! I really am quite different.

THIRD: And what *are* you like?

SECOND: I am just about to tell you about myself. About myself, myself, myself. I will reveal to you . . . .

(THIRD gets up and walks away straight ahead warily on tiptoe. Disappears behind the curtain. His armchair is empty. SECOND speaks without interruption.)

SECOND: Actually, I hate confessions. It is probably the first time in my life I am opening myself up like this before another man. You must be patient with me today. You must hear everything. In fact, a man can tell the truth about himself only to another man. Last time I spoke like that was to a friend of mine — twenty years ago. Today there are no friends and in fact one can't unburden oneself like that any more. You feel as if you suddenly noticed lice on the other's head. Or one yellow louse on the collar of his dinner jacket. That friend of mine has perished. People used to perish in those days. That's of no consequence. We used to talk about the most important things in life. Whether man has a soul, whether he will rise from the dead, whether life has any sense. That sort of nonsense. Naturally all this philosophy would go overboard as soon as a member of the female sex appeared on the horizon. A wiggling behind would bring us to a state bordering on enthusiasm. We gaped at it as if . . . anyway, you know how it is. I'll quote a little piece of verse by a certain poet. You are laughing, eh? Listen:

I feel desire
he said
unfortunately he has no soul
the soul has gone
burst out laughing
the young waitress
her shape was such
one could soulless

with her create
a new man

Honestly her ass
is more finely moulded
than
the dome of that famous
cathedral — he thought —
a splendid vessel
temporarily closed.

You don't say anything? And yet, you like it! A poem does
sometimes have something to say. There was no soul. And
now again something is stirring, being born in that heap of
rubbish. It is moving. Only the midwives aren't up to much.
Some provincial females from the glossies recommending
this and that, some primitive and simple shepherds, while
what we need is a cross between Oppenheimer and Freud,
Schweitzer and Tom, Dick or Harry. Oh! What rubbish! I
am getting away from the subject. True confessions are not
easy. In a way we wait all our lives to confide and confess.
And suddenly we make a general confession in a completely
unsuitable place: in a railway compartment, in the dentist's
waiting room or a third class restaurant. In a way, every
place is suitable. Women naturally always confide — in every
one at every moment. But they confide on a superficial
level. Yesterday on the train a woman was telling me about
her first husband, that he had been to university. A daughter by her second marriage. That she is frigid that she likes
walking barefoot on the grass but can't do so in town. She
gave me details of a certain complaint. She had to get off
just as she was in the middle of it all at the moment when
she started on matters of faith and morality. You are laughing, eh?

I don't find it easy to talk of this problem of mine, because
it's revolting and funny. Sometimes I think it is only funny,
sometimes that it's only revolting. I have to spit it out, get it
out of my system. But please, don't pass judgment now. You
can pass sentence. I will submit to any verdict. I won't tell
you about my youth. My face resembles an omelette that's

fallen on a dirty floor. Enough. That was when that great world crisis began. Then the crisis passed and a great world war began, back to normal, things are almost back to normal. This business happened during a certain journey. I stopped at a residential hotel, small but clean. I was in certain difficulties at the time. Sometimes I would eat at the hotel. Once I found a hair in the soup. Actually it wasn't soup, it was broth.

(THIRD has returned to his seat. He is again sitting in the armchair. We can see the top of his bald egglike head.)

SECOND: Ever since I was a child I adored broth but the boys tried to make me loathe it by calling it dead man's brew . . . .

THIRD: Children! Children are so innocent . . . .

SECOND: Please don't interrupt now. I am just about to . . . .

THIRD: Sorry.

(Silence, which is gradually being filled with sounds and voices − fragments of conversations − speeches. Sounds of a great city: increasing stream of noise − occasionally single words by SECOND can be heard: 'soup . . . broth . . . father . . . I loved . . . terrible . . . broth . . . hair'. Noise increases. We can see SECOND's lips moving. He now seems to talk with great effort. Sometimes he purses his lips. Then a slight movement of the lips. A smile, Among the street noises a distant muffled sound of a hooter. Suddenly silence.)

SECOND: And that's really all. I shan't tell you about the occupation − you know all that from your own experience. I now have quite a high and responsible post. I remember I swore to myself that I'd never − you understand − never again . . . and yet I broke it. That is all.

(THIRD is silent.)

You are silent.

THIRD: Time is the best healer.

SECOND: Yes.

THIRD: Listen old boy, you shouldn't split hairs when you find them in your own broth. *(Laughs)* That is a good one, eh?

SECOND: Is it? Oh, excellent, excellent, old man. You know, I think you have the right approach to life. When I listen to you I feel — I know I must have blown the whole thing up. (*Pause*) I've been carrying it about with me for twenty years. For twenty-three even . . . . Thank you.

THIRD: Not at all.

SECOND: You weren't even surprised. I thought you would not want to listen. So you are not disgusted by me, you do not show contempt?

THIRD: My dear chap, there is really nothing to talk about. Let's forget it. You are making a mountain out of a molehill. Broth. It certainly can affect the liver. I like cream cakes. In Greek mythology they roast their own children. And in Dante's hell a father eats up the brains of his children . . . .

SECOND: You always say things to make me laugh. (*Does not laugh*) You know . . . . Look, this thing is still crawling towards us.

THIRD: What can you see now?

SECOND: Nothing interesting. (*Crosses his legs*)

THIRD: That mound.

SECOND: What mound?

THIRD: That dark object you told me about once.

SECOND: Just so, just so. I think it is coming closer.

THIRD: Is it saying anything?

SECOND: No, I can't hear anything.

THIRD: What a pity we are so busy. Perhaps you could find a moment to nip across?

SECOND: (*filing his nails*) I can't now — out of the question. I'll try when I've finished.

THIRD: And is there no one in the neighbourhood who could . . . .

SECOND: I don't know.

THIRD: Pity, I can't see it.

SECOND: Turn round. Surely you can turn round.

THIRD: I can't. I must look this way now.

SECOND: What are you looking at? What do you mean by 'must'?

THIRD: That's not my business.

SECOND: You are right — best to mind your own business.

THIRD: Everything is in its place. At last. After such a long break. After all, we are living in a civilized world.

SECOND: There is a municipal garbage disposal unit.

THIRD: We could ask them to come round and clear it away.

SECOND: I'd like a drink.

THIRD: What are you doing over there? I don't think you are listening to what I am saying to you.

SECOND: No.

THIRD: What?

SECOND: It just struck me that I have told you everything about myself but you haven't breathed a word about yourself.

THIRD: I have nothing to say. Just an ordinary man.

SECOND: Man?

THIRD: Man.

SECOND: My God!

THIRD: Why 'my God'?

SECOND: A man.

THIRD: What's so surprising?

SECOND: Nothing.

THIRD: Nothing?

SECOND: Tell me what you are like. First tell me what you look like.

THIRD: Outward appearance? All right, if that interests you.

SECOND: It does very much, perhaps more than your interior.

THIRD: I will begin at the feet. I have a black bowler on my head.

SECOND: I thought it raised its muzzle.

THIRD: Muzzle?

SECOND: Don't stop. So you've got a black bowler on your head.

THIRD: Yes. Now I will describe my character.

SECOND: It seems to me you are witty.

THIRD: Hasn't that one over there rotted away yet?

SECOND: What do you mean 'rotted away'? What's rotted away?

THIRD: That dog that's been run over.

SECOND: To start with we don't know whether it is a dog. It may be a seal.

THIRD: A seal?

SECOND: Or a tree trunk.

THIRD: Listen — why don't you go over there and look? You won't risk anything. I'll wait here.

SECOND: I can't move. I've already told you I can't now.

THIRD: In fact you have already told me three times but I still don't understand why you can't move. Are you tied down?

SECOND: I used to try. Sometimes I'd get away. But I haven't even tried these last ten years.

THIRD: I've got a knife here.

SECOND: A knife?

THIRD: Not a real knife — just a little fruit knife. I'll hand it to you in a minute.

SECOND: Don't bother.

THIRD: Then you'll be able to cut those fetters.

SECOND: I don't want to cut anything.

THIRD: Pity.

SECOND: No.

THIRD: At last! I am free to move. I can get up and go away.

SECOND: Come to me, then.

THIRD: I can only go straight ahead without looking sideways.

SECOND: You've told us about the bowler.

THIRD: There is really nothing to add.

SECOND: Describe everything in detail. Sometimes a tiny detail has a bearing on the whole.

THIRD: Today I am dressed in the uniform of the Guards: stripes, epaulettes, silver collar, gold sleeves, tabs, buttons. In a word, the ceremonial uniform for officers on gala days and parades.

SECOND: You are being funny again.

THIRD: Yes. In fact I want to cover up an open wound with words.

SECOND: You are suffering.

THIRD: Indescribably.

SECOND: Try to forget.

THIRD: I will.

SECOND: Don't joke about your outward appearance. If you had to leave now you would stay in my mind in a musical comedy uniform. Jokes aren't safe. Have you got a hobby?

THIRD: Yes, I catch flies. I often get up at dawn. You can't imagine what pleasure it is in our shattered world to catch flies. I spend hours looking at the window pane or a wall. Got it! I pop them into the bottle and then count them.

SECOND: Quite. And what is your dream?

THIRD: To catch a fly the size of a sparrow. I was already catching flies when I was a boy and I even composed a little poem about it.

One day naughty little Jim
Caught some flies inside a tin
And lest of hunger they should die
Fed them well on jam and pie.

SECOND: You haven't changed at all.

THIRD: Neither have you.

SECOND: My yellow shoes are horribly tight.

THIRD: So are mine.

SECOND: Can you feel how tight mine are?

THIRD: I can feel how tight mine are.

SECOND: Don't let's drift away from the heart of the matter. You
           stopped at the description of your head. But you haven't
           said a word about dandruff . . . . What's that moaning? Some-
           one's groaning here . . . .

THIRD: I wanted to give this problem a wider context, to examine
           its various aspects.

SECOND: Now I have some idea of the whole. About your person
           and personality. If you were to go away now, I could recon-
           struct you. (*Pause*) Was that you groaning?

           (*THIRD is silent.*)

           It must be that unfortunate seal.

THIRD: A seal in the street?

SECOND: Could have come out of a pond. In any case it isn't a seal.
           It's a dog. Now I can see better.

THIRD: A dog?

SECOND: Yes.

THIRD: A setter?

SECOND: Pointer.

THIRD: Shorthaired?

SECOND: Coarsehaired.

THIRD: Dachshund?

SECOND: Soft-haired.

THIRD: Long-haired?

SECOND: The beast certainly's got a howl.

THIRD: I told you it's a Doberman pinscher.

SECOND: Newfoundland.

THIRD: Poodle.

SECOND: St Bernard.

THIRD: Can you see him clearly?

SECOND: No, I must go to an optician tomorrow.

THIRD: And I've got to see a dentist.

SECOND: Just imagine, he's getting up.

THIRD: Can you see him clearly?

SECOND: Yes . . . it's quite interesting . . . . (*Pause*) The skin has several shades of white.

THIRD: From pinkish white to yellowish.

SECOND: Body very hairy, hair on the head slightly wavy.

THIRD: In some places almost straight, eyes and hair light in colour.

SECOND: Black fuzzy hair.

THIRD: Comparatively short.

SECOND: Eyes very dark.

THIRD: There, I told you.

SECOND: Now he is standing on two paws.

THIRD: Probably ran away from a circus.

SECOND: He is not moving.

THIRD: Then pop over and have a look!

SECOND: I can't, you know I can't leave my place.

THIRD: I forgot.

SECOND: You are quick to forget what you've been told. You know what a struggle I had to win this chair. I went hungry, I didn't gamble, I didn't hunt, I didn't love, and now you are trying to persuade me to leave my place.

THIRD: You are very excited. Calm down.

SECOND: Quiet!

THIRD: You know what I have just thought?

SECOND: Wait, it seemed to me that . . . .

THIRD: Of course it only seemed to you. Leave that dog alone . . . I wonder what you will say about my idea.

SECOND: It's a dog.

THIRD: Throw him a bone and you will get some peace.

SECOND: I haven't got a bone. I think we are not going to get any peace now either.

THIRD: Throw him a stone then. A brute like that won't notice the difference.

SECOND: No (*Pause*) no, that's impossible. I must have misheard.

THIRD: There, you see.

SECOND: I don't see anything.

THIRD: He is calling us.

SECOND: Barking?

THIRD: Funny business.

SECOND: Bloody funny — just imagine, he's got a tie round his neck.

THIRD: A tie?

SECOND: A tie.

THIRD: Get closer to him.

SECOND: I can't move — I thought I'd explained that to you. Stupid business that it should happen to us.

THIRD: There's not a moment's peace.

SECOND: Do you believe?

THIRD: I do.

SECOND: What in?

THIRD: The resurrection of the body.

SECOND: You are a believer, then.

THIRD: Yes. And you?

SECOND: No. (*Pause*) He's raising his head. I can see his eyes and lips. He's raising his eyes to the sky. He is crawling again.

THIRD: Throw him a piece of meat or a cigarette.

SECOND: He is looking at me.

THIRD: You are imagining things. You are over-sensitive.

SECOND: He has fallen down. He is lying down. He is lying down in his own dung. Digging with his paws.

THIRD: Let me know when he's dug himself out.

SECOND: What will you do now?

THIRD: I've got business to attend to. I must go.

SECOND: Now?

THIRD: My path isn't roses all the way either.

SECOND: (*wiping his face with a handkerchief*) I don't understand.

THIRD: I tell you we all have our worries. I'm going.

SECOND: What do you mean 'I'm going'? You want to go away? Now?

THIRD: Don't take it too seriously.

SECOND: (*smiling, relieved*) Take my advice: don't move. Don't move. Better stay. Don't move. You've said yourself you are settled down quite comfortably. You have a comparatively comfortable place, wide horizons, clothes for all occasions, a garage. You've still got a few ideals left.

   (*THIRD sniffs.*)

SECOND: What did you say?

THIRD: Nothing, go on.

SECOND: What about?

THIRD: (*sniffs*) What's that? There's an unpleasant smell.

SECOND: I can't smell anything.

THIRD: How is it you can't smell it if I can? (*SECOND shrugs his shoulders*) I can smell it perfectly. There is something giving off an unpleasant smell. Very close by.

SECOND: Perhaps you've trodden in excrements?

THIRD: No . . . . What a nasty smell!

SECOND: Then stop sniffing.

THIRD: I've got to breathe somehow.

SECOND: Breathe through the mouth not the nose. (*Pulls out a handkerchief and holds it against his mouth and nose.*)

THIRD: Nothing smelling over at your side? Be honest!

SECOND: (*mumbling*) I give you my word of honour I can't smell anything.

THIRD: What kind of honour?

SECOND: Well, honour.

THIRD: Honour?

SECOND: Honour.

THIRD: Yes, that is the only value that is left to us.

SECOND: Yes, this one thing we still have.

THIRD: What?

SECOND: (*puts his handkerchief away*) What did you say?

THIRD: What a stench. There is something rotting here.

SECOND: You are right.

THIRD: Don't sniff.

SECOND: The air is full of it.

THIRD: Then move somewhere else.

SECOND: No, that is out of the question.

THIRD: You say the stench is suffocating you.

SECOND: Maybe I'll get used to it.

THIRD: I admire you.

SECOND: I'll try to get used to it.

THIRD: (*ironically*) I admire your courage.

SECOND: Listen, let's sing something. That will cheer us up. One, two, three ... all together ....

   (*THIRD is silent.*)

   There must be a carcass here somewhere.

THIRD: And what are the authorities doing? Where is public opinion?

SECOND: What?

THIRD: Public opinion.

SECOND: Quite.

THIRD: In the second half of the twentieth century in the very centre of the town there lies a dead beast and nobody cares.

SECOND: Quite.

THIRD: A dog? What dog do you mean?

SECOND: The one that was crawling towards you.

THIRD: Towards me? I don't know anything about it.

SECOND: (*as if terrified*) Oh God!

THIRD: I beg your pardon?

SECOND: (*laughs uncertainly*) Poor John!

THIRD: Were you talking to me?

SECOND: No .... He's dived muzzle first into the dung.

THIRD: Poor creature.

SECOND: He's still moving.

THIRD: And where is he now?

SECOND: Someone should finish him off.

THIRD: I am asking you how far is he from us.

SECOND: He is lying at my feet.

THIRD: What?

SECOND: He is lying a step away from my foot.

THIRD: And what is it?

SECOND: I don't know.

THIRD: Surely you can move now.

SECOND: I can't.

THIRD: (*raising his voice*) What do you mean you can't? What does that mean? Can't you move a step?

SECOND: I can't move away from my seat.

THIRD: No one will take it now. Get a move on!

SECOND: My dear chap, I see you are getting excited. (*Smiles*) I hear a new tone in your voice ... an emotional one. You are indignant, you command, you shout.

(*THIRD is silent.*)

I do hope you won't start improving me. Only a step divides you. 'Get a move on'! What nerve! Or perhaps you will start reminding me of my duties towards my neighbour. Shout a sermon, let yourself go. 'Get a move on'! I've already explained to you I can't move from this place.

THIRD: (*calmly*) And can you bend down?

SECOND: I can't.

THIRD: What?

SECOND: I don't feel like it. (*Pulls out his handkerchief and covers his mouth.*)

THIRD: Break those fetters!

SECOND: (*calmly, almost jovially*) What fetters? That was just pure talk. There aren't any 'fetters' here to cut. I just don't feel like moving from my place. Is that clear, admiral?

THIRD: Is he still breathing?

SECOND: I don't know.

THIRD: If you lean over a bit, you might hear something.

SECOND: I can't.

THIRD: What does he look like?

SECOND: It's difficult to tell. He is decomposing pretty quickly.

THIRD: Surely, he still has a shape.

SECOND: He looks like a sack full of rotting meat and rags.

THIRD: Can't you tell the breed?

SECOND: No.

THIRD: Hasn't he got any mark, ring, identity card?

SECOND: I don't know what you are talking about. It's a scandal that no one has cleared away this carcass.

THIRD: You speak of him as if he were a dog.

SECOND: It was a dog.

THIRD: Are you sure?

SECOND: Naturally. (*Crosses his legs, replaces the folded handkerchief in his breast pocket.*)

THIRD: Thank God!

SECOND: What did you say?

THIRD: Nothing.

SECOND: I'm glad you are regaining your composure. You know, I never suspected you would commit yourself to such an extent. You've almost been shouting at me.

THIRD: They should be here by now.

SECOND: They don't seem to be in a hurry.

Growing bustle of a big city. Distant siren. Silence.

THE INTERRUPTED ACT

CHARACTERS

CIVIL ENGINEER	
NURSE	
BEAUTIFUL GIRL	the Engineer's daughter
ROBUST WOMAN	housekeeper in the Engineer's house
THE COMMISSIONER	
STRANGER	
FIRST DEPUTY	the Engineer's deputy
FIRST WORKER	
SECOND WORKER	from the bridge building crew

THE AUTHOR'S CONFESSION

I spent July and August in town. I did not succumb to the holiday mania. I spent the summer of the century working at the bench. The thermometer was climbing to 40°, 45°, 46° Centigrade. The town was white with heat, quiet and deserted. In such an atmosphere I began to write my first comedy. I intended it to be a bedroom farce. Contemporary. Even at times modern. With the aid of various pseudo-avantgarde tricks the classics are being murdered on the stages of our theatres. This will not do as a substitute for a contemporary theatre. Still, this is not the place to criticize the shortcomings of our theatre. Let me get back to home ground. And the fact is that my work on *The Interrupted Act* did not result in the fulfilment of my idea. Only the first and second scene were written according to the original conception. The succeeding two scenes were an act of capitulation. Although in the stage directions I explain the role of the Stranger I have not been able to work this scene into the plot. Perhaps there was a place for pantomime in this scene. While, when writing the first two scenes I was 'decided', when I cam to write the third and fourth I lost my self-confidence, my enthusiasm and sense of well-being. In its present form my play is not destined either for the theatre or television or radio. The great number of remarks, intrusions, theoretical deliberations and polemics (with possible opponents) tend to turn this comedy into a narrative script. It may be that dramatists happier than I will be able to make use of the ideas contained in the stage directions (and the polemical remarks) of this play. They mustn't be misled by the playful form in which I present certain formulations concerning the role upon the stage of dialogue, or words, of silence, gesture and time. It may be that our critics and theorists of the theatre (drama) may wish one day to take up the work which was begun before the War by Witkiewicz and Chwistek*. Our theatre, or rather Polish contemporary plays, are based on the 'dramaturgy' of the so-called drawing room flirtation. Various characters tied by all sorts of knots exchange opinions regarding their various experiences, feelings and so on. It's enough to read Chwistek's 'Theatre of the Future', an essay which appeared in *Zwrotnica* in 1922(!) Anyway, I am only addressing myself to the few 'just men'. Our theatre (our drama) is not bad because it is 'modern', it is bad because it's faceless. It is a theatre lacking both purpose and ideas. It will not be long before we shall see *Pan Tadeusz, Pan Balcer in Brazil, The Peasants*** and so on adapted for our largest (and smallest) stages. I am not a typical dramatic author, I am rather a man 'approaching the theatre'. I think, however, that my suggestions (my mistakes and my achievements) may halt the decline of ambition which characterises our theatre repertory in the forthcoming season. Adaptations of *Little Red Riding Hood* or of the telephone directory and the torturing of our classics will not create a contemporary Polish theatre. Despite the 'enthusiasm' of foreign visitors our theatre lacks its own image. Is it not worth thinking and talking about this?

8 October, 1963

---

*Stanislaw Witkiewicz (1885–1939), painter, dramatist, novelist and philosopher. His plays are now seen as early important manifestations of the theatre of the absurd. He experimented with the effects of drugs. Committed suicide when he felt that civilization was coming to an end in September 1939.

Leon Chwistek (1884–1944), philosopher, mathematician, poet, painter, created the Formist theory in art. (A.C.)

**Respectively the celebrated epic by Adam Mickiewicz, a versified novel by Maria Konopnicka and a vast novel of peasant life by Wladyslaw Reymont. (A.C.)

STAGE DIRECTIONS AND REMARKS

The stage represents a large room. The door on the left leads to the right and the door on the right leads to the left. There is also a door in the third (middle) wall. The room contains furniture and pictures completely devoid of character. Three white hairs, not visible from the auditorium, are lying on a shelf. Two, perhaps three, flies buzz around the room but they will not play any significant role in the development of the action.

A beautiful shapely girl holding a big suitcase walks across the room. She has just said goodbye to her father, a well-known civil engineer, and is leaving for ever to America to the family of her dead mother. Her father is not seeing her off because he is lying in his study on a divan with his leg in plaster. It is his left leg. We cannot, alas, prove on the stage — with the help of 'theatrical' means — that the girl is leaving for ever or even that she is leaving for North America. We are helpless. True, we could employ a narrator, a telephone, the father's voice coming from the next room, but all these are very primitive half-measures. In exactly the same way one can go (with a suitcase) to college, on a holiday or take one's washing to the laundry. True, the father could have cried out 'As soon as you land in America, let me know' but he would have had to add, for example, 'in North America'. Using the telephone the girl might make enquiries about air connections with Hamburg, Lisbon and New York. Alas, all this has already taken place before the curtain rose and the girl is crossing the room in a quite ordinary way although she is on her way to America. The girl's father is enjoying a well-earned convalescence and holiday. A week earlier, under his supervision, the last cofferdam under the last pillar of the last span was filled with concrete. Work on the construction of the longest bridge linking east-central Europe with south-west Europe took ten years. Last week teams of workers met in the middle of the bridge. We provide these considerable details of the worthy Engineer's achievement because we are unable to present on the stage the gigantic enterprise, the failures, the achievements and frustrations which accompanied the Engineer and the crew in building the bridge. Like an (almost) vulgar realist I did indeed ponder the possibility of placing the first scene in the draughtsman's office or in the foreman's cabin in the middle of the works, of, possibly, showing the construction of (at least) a sector, a pillar, a span, of showing the moment when the Engineer slipped and fell into the water.

His cry. Of the clinic in which they set his left leg and put it in plaster. His conversation with the pretty nurse. I could even show the Engineer's youth by making use of the Medical Registrar who was the renowned Hero's (I am not afraid of this word) schoolmate. I came to the conclusion, however, that all these scenes would have taken about 45 minutes, while during that time the actual 'drama' might have completed its course. In his room the Engineer is in fact experiencing a great drama but, alas, this we cannot see. Had I transported the action into the Engineer's study I would not have achieved any stage effect because he is a very reserved man. It may be that at this very moment he is breaking down or even has broken down but we are not able to show this internal struggle because we lack the external means. Various types of facial expressions, gestures or even cries are not 'capable of' representing the suffering. Naturally one could dispose of all this with the aid of dialogue but it is a singularly vulgar and base method. Even a monologue would be better. But in order to explain the whole tangle of tragic events one would have needed 20 minutes and again the action would have suffered terribly. He could have told the audience 'I am suffering' but the fact that a young girl with a suitcase has left home does not justify a man's suffering and some of the audience would (in any event) gain the impression that the Engineer is suffering on account of his leg being in plaster. Alas, we have no time to show in our theatre (through pictures and dialogue) the causes which led to the young person's departure, although in this instance I have yielded to temptation and I will show a little scene in which lies the seed, the cause of the drama (or rather the departure) of the young person. For the time being let's return to the stage. If during her passage across the stage the girl had turned her head and said 'Bye bye daddy. Farewell father, Goodbye, etc' the whole case would immediately have blossomed out and made dramatic sense. Alas, the girl has uttered these and many other words in her father's study. When she passes across the stage she has already done with all 'farewells'. She can, of course, turn back. Let's say she picks up the key to the door. Since this key will not be of any use to her (in America) she takes it back to her father. This shows that the situation in contemporary theatre is difficult and at times has no solution. I have of course in mind the one realistic theatre worthy of the name — poetical theatre. And it's not enough to perform trepanations on *The Forefathers* and *Mazeppa**. It's not enough to have grotesque student

_____

*Two well-known plays by Adam Mickiewicz and Juliusz Slowacki respectively. (A.C.)

jokes. Even our stage designers are helpless. Only a new realistico-poetical theatre may open – (not the door, I don't say that) – but a chink in the door leading to the exit. In this case we do not disdain minute details, small, even microscopic, stage props (which cannot be seen from the auditorium), we do not disdain information contained in the stage directions. On the contrary, I want to use this information as a spring of the whole 'show'. (At the moment I have, alas, no better definition.) Stage directions must be included in the theatre programme. They are as important for my theatre as instruments are for a surgeon during an operation (naturally). They are even more important than my biography, a list of my plays, first nights, prizes, stage productions and other similar elements of a purely decorative nature. My theatre is a living organism. It resembles a man, an invalid, who lost his left leg in battle but continues to feel pain in that leg. For this theatre has lost its dramatic action (that structure which was the goal of the efforts of Greek, Elizabethan and to some extent Warsaw and even Krakow dramatists), but this lost essential member continues to cause me pain. Sometimes, in moments of weakness and despair I make use of this long lost left leg (action) and then I resemble certain foreign and native dramatists. But giving to Witkiewicz what belongs to Witkiewicz and to Gombrowicz what belongs to Gombrowicz I wish to declare that as far as I am concerned they are both authors of classics. Great writers who have taken their place next to Slowacki, Norwid, Krasinski, Wyspianski, Fredro, Zapolska, Chwistek and others. I bow to all these great ones and pass on. I say nothing about 'the young' because one never knows how they will end up. Following this (polemical) interlude which however throws a certain light on my stagecraft and its (hidden) roots I proceed to complete the recording of my stage directions. After the young girl, who is (probably) the daughter of the Engineer lying in the study, has left the room the stage is empty. One of the three flies (which I mentioned at the beginning of these remarks) buzzes across the room and alights on a lump of sugar. I forgot to add that on the table there is a sugar bowl filled with lumps of sugar. After a pause which, depending on the producer and the critic, may last anything from one to five minutes (the five minute pause may only be used in the case of either a very sophisticated or a completely unsophisticated audience); after a pause, then, a woman slowly walks across the stage. She is carrying a pair of well pressed men's trousers. These trousers may be cream, blue or grey, with turn-ups. The width of the leg at the turn-up is 29 to 34 cm. At the moment of her appearance on the stage the woman is sixty. She has smoothly combed black hair, a slightly shrivelled face and an ordinary dress lacking character and shape. The woman stops by the table with the sugar bowl. She chases the fly away. She glances at the trousers. She scratches at a stain which (from the auditorium) is invisible. She hangs the trousers on the back of one of the four chairs which stand round the table. She takes a lump of sugar out of the sugar bowl and puts it in her mouth. She sucks the sugar. This action deforms her cheeks and lips to some extent. The woman is listening to find out whether anyone is moving next door. She stands thus for almost 60 seconds. She then leaves by the middle door which she leaves ajar (not wide open but only ajar). There is a click and the sound of a key in the lock. Apparently someone has entered the hall. Through the door left ajar we can hear him taking off his coat. It is a stiff green waterproof oilskin or tarpaulin. (But this we shall not be able to see on the stage during the course of the play.) The person who has entered splutters like a wet cat. A shower must have caught him in the street but we cannot be certain of this. 45 seconds after the woman has left, a grey-haired man in a dark lounge suit enters the room. He takes a handkerchief out of his pocket and wipes either his whole face or just his mouth. His actions are very free, he feels 'very much at home' (or maybe even better). He sits on one of the chairs. The woman must have told him that the host is still asleep. The guest has decided to wait. He looks around the room. He walks up to the cabinet or sideboard (possibly a bar) and pours himself a glass of brandy. He drinks appreciatively. He sits at the table. He is scrutinizing his left hand, or rather his fingernails. Then his eyes move to his foot shod in a black patent leather shoe. He examines his black sock with a red stripe. Rubs his brow with his hand. This scene may last one to three minutes and in favourable circumstances even seven. This man, who in five days' time will be 42, had only 24 hours ago been released from prison and fully reinstated. He is rather pale, but this pallor could also be the result of the previous day's drinking. Our play still hasn't begun and it is difficult at this moment to foresee when it will. But, after all, I do know it will start the moment the first word is uttered. For in the beginning of the contemporary theatre there was, there is, and there will be, the word. An instrument of communication so imperfect and yet irreplaceable. Primitive and indispensable. Like water, devoid of taste but essential to life. As a realist writer I strive, however, that the word in my theatre should not have a larger meaning than it has in life. The man in the lounge suit stays in the room for a while longer. He drinks the brandy and leaves. Apparently didn't wish to wake the host. Admittedly he had certain urgent business to transact with the host, but he has left it till the following day. He departs and we have not established whether he was the host's younger brother, the young girl's fiancé, a commissioner of police, a pastor or the co-creator of the design of the middle span of the great bridge. He left (and what is stranger[!] in a theatrical show) he never returns. He doesn't appear on the stage during this performance which lasts (according to my intentions) from 30 to 70 minutes. Even the avantgarde theatre did not have such things. And yet they do occur in my realistic theatre, my poetic theatre. I warn any possible simple-minded producers of this play that he is not a symbolical character or a ghost nor a dream vision. For this gentleman had already exchanged a few words with the woman behind the door. Alas, these words reached neither us nor the (perhaps) intrigued audience. As a realist I do not recognize any theatrical, film or novel 'time'. My time is identical with the time mirrored by our watches. The 'dramatic' incidents which I have so far described last, let's say, three minutes. My wish is that the potential producers should extend these events to last ten minutes. But I do appreciate that in our times such dreams are futile. Theatres and producers (not to mention the public) will not stand for such consistent and brutal stage realism. In these circumstances, having sketched the likely course of the development of my theatre I once more disclaim all responsibility, I reach a compromise and proceed to build a spectacle based on elements of a traditional pseudo-avantgarde theatre, but at certain points I shall realize the assumptions of my true theatre about which I have spoken in these stage directions. In principle, a part of the spectacle has already been put into effect in accordance with these assumptions — I will nevertheless repeat once more the first scene in the compromised version.

SCENE ONE

A large room in the apartment of a distinguished CIVIL ENGINEER. It's midnight. The clock on the wall strikes twelve. When the last stroke sounds a very beautiful shapely YOUNG WOMAN enters through the door leading to the left. She is carrying a large leather suitcase. The room also contains a door which leads to the right and a door in the centre. Passing by the table the GIRL trips against a chair. She drops the suitcase on the floor. She sits at the table and holds her head in her hands. A moment later she goes to the door on the left and presses her face against its white varnished surface. She is motionless and speechless. Then she returns to the table with a swift decisive movement. Her hands are stretched along her sides. Her palms slowly clench themselves into fists. There is a silver sugar bowl on the table. The lumps of sugar glisten in the electric light. There is something eerie in this landscape. Something clean and cruel at the same time. A black fly sleeps on one of the lumps of sugar. At a certain moment the fly takes off in a droning heavy flight. If it were possible to make use of a real fly in this scene that would have a considerable significance for the development of the action. Alas, limited resources do not permit such experiments on the large stages of contemporary professional theatres, although I did see elephants in a certain opera and horses in a certain play, another had dogs, cats, etc . . . . Because of these difficulties I decide against introducing a fly on to the stage. I had forgotten to add that the action of our play takes place in one of the neutral rich smallish capitalist countries where the percentage of suicides is higher than in economically under-developed countries. Psychological and mental diseases also have a richer harvest there than in other countries. Of course you can base the action in any country you can think of. In that case however you would have to alter certain props like furniture, doors, chairs, and so on. The GIRL started up from the table. And yet the calmness with which she uttered her first words seems to have immobilized and paralyzed her. Her lips opened with difficulty as if somebody were prising them open with a metal tool from outside. In an animal grimace she bared white almost cruel (in this empty room) teeth. Although I appreciate at this moment the risk (I may simply become the laughing stock of our poor theatre critics) of an unduly detailed description of the GIRL's teeth I will do it, giving way to the dictates of my theatre. The GIRL has two fillings, they are however fixed so discreetly and adroitly that a member of the audience could see them only with the help of glasses (not opera glasses but field glasses employed by the military and by explorers). Please forgive me the little joke on the subject of glasses. This allows me to catch my breath. I put off the decisive moment but of course I know the GIRL must speak. Although at the moment I have an inclination to remove her from the stage, she ought to pass across it without a word. But I lack the courage and the logic. Let's therefore begin the show.

GIRL:

They (*pause*)
they there
(*louder*) they there together

(Silence. She stops her mouth with her hand as though with a gag. She takes her hands away slowly, very slowly. In the light her lips appear swollen. bloodshot, they move like suckers of parasites. She speaks softly but clearly.)

They are doing
they are doing that there

(Silence. She closes her eyes. She speaks with her eyes closed.)

how long
how disgustingly long
how long are they doing it
how revoltingly
how long
they will never finish
they will never stop
twice three times five ten twelve

(She runs to the door, raises both her hands, stands thus for a while, returns, sits at the table, buries her head in her arms.)

after all I am a living being

I hear feel see
through that door
I am not a chair
animals
filthy animals
frogs apes dogs rabbits tortoises
how long can one go on doing this
one hour two three four

(Silence)

they've stopped

(Silence. She is listening.)

they've stopped

(She breathes.)

O God what

they

(She listens.)

they are starting
how can they
they don't take any notice of anyone
like dogs
beneath the statue of Bismarck or Columbus
in a square under the gaze of children
under the gaze

(The GIRL's body grows taut and stiff, she falls on the floor and turns into a trembling bundle of hair and rags.)

stop

(Whispering)

I beg you stop
I
I wished
I beg you

(She crawls towards the door on her knees. Suddenly she begins to strike with her fingers at the silent white door: rhythmically at long intervals. She talks to herself.)

I am mad
how can I
how can I behave like that
they are adults
it's I who am disgusting

(Listens)

they are starting again
my head's splitting
how it creaks
how cruelly it creaks
how it cracks
my poor head
as though in a forest
or a sawmill
what the hell
are they sawing that divan with a fretsaw

(She sits at the table, now under control she talks smilingly to herself, to the potential audience.)

joke after all it's a joke coke smoke broke stroke trough tough torture vulture vault malt fault lout loot love lust life lifeblood strife rife wife wed wedded wedlock

(At this point she speaks seriously, harshly)

random ripple rubbish rubble rupture reddish rhinoceros rescue rest roll rush rich rough rack hack hack saw saw with a knife with a saw

(She falls silent. Listens. Silence. Silence reigns in the room, silence behind the closed door. An absolute and intolerable silence. The GIRL writes something on a pink card and slides it under the sugar bowl.)

how quiet
how quiet it is here
how quiet it is there why is it so quiet there
why don't they speak why aren't they talking
no cries no laughter no moans no groans
why do they

(She gets up from the table and walks on tiptoe.)

breathe
what are they doing there

(She speaks softly)

I beseech you speak
laugh
say something
do you hear say something!
dumb animals
damned reptiles amphibians crustaceans protozoans
slipperworts

(The GIRL runs to the door and begins to batter it with her fists.)

Speak! Speak!!

(She utters wild cries. She picks up her suitcase and runs out of the room through the centre doorway.)

SCENE 2

> *The clock strikes the hour. An elderly but robust and healthy*
> WOMAN *enters through the door on the left. Her complexion*
> *betrays a country origin. In fact the* WOMAN *was born and spent*
> *her childhood in a highland village in an area where even to-*
> *day wolves may be seen. Let me stress once more, she is no*
> *doddery old girl. She is wearing a simple nightdress and her*
> *shoulders are covered with a warm woollen shawl. For twenty*
> *years now the* WOMAN *has been the* ENGINEER's *housekeeper.*
> *After his wife died for a while she breast-fed the poor orphan,*
> *the daughter who a moment ago left for ever for North America.*
> *The 'housekeeper' ought really to 'burst' into the room with a*
> *cry of 'God, what is happening here'. Alas, she is too late. In*
> *any case, she sleeps soundly and did not hear the* GIRL's *cries.*
> *Although it is now an hour since anything happened in this*
> *room, let's allow the* WOMAN *to utter this traditional, well-tried*
> *exclamation. Only in this way will we be able to convey the*
> *terror and turmoil which perturb this simple yet still energetic*
> *person.*

ROBUST WOMAN: (*enters the empty silent room. She looks around and*
as though she had suddenly remembered something she utters
a 'soft cry') God, what's happening here!

(Since however nothing is happening she goes to the table, puts
her hand in the sugar bowl and places a lump of sugar in her
mouth. First one lump, then, after a pause — lasting about
three seconds — a second one, then a third and fourth . . . .
Altogether she might put five to six lumps in her mouth. When
she is about to put in the fifth lump she notices the letter lying
under the sugar bowl. The lumps of sugar deform the WOMAN's
cheeks and lips. Because this simple highlander is not terribly
literate and reads very slowly, the scene with the letter may
even be a very long one. In this way my play begins to stretch
into a full-scale spectacle (not bad, eh?) and may be played

upon even the biggest stages of the established theatres. I must confess I can't (sufficiently) 'marvel' at our contemporary producers and directors who demand plays which are long, that is (as they say) 'full-length'. This demands a huge volume of words. Dialogue. Verbiage. Witticisms. Proverbs. Whereas drama takes place in silence. In an ocean of silence. And words are only tiny (coral) islands scattered in this infinite space. The already dated theatre of Dürrenmatt, Frisch and even Witkiewicz, resembles a text book rewritten in dialogue form. It has very little in common with the realistico-poetical theatre. With the theatre which I now wish to present to our producers and critics. But the trouble is that I too am not without guilt, although . . . the alert member of the audience will here notice that the door is opening . . . .)

ROBUST WOMAN: What's that?

(The WOMAN slowly opens her mouth. One – or at most two lumps of sugar may drop out of it on to the table or the floor.)

What is this?

(She reads the letter attentively once more and sits down on the chair.)

Well, just imagine!

(She wrings her hands.)

The Mistress . . . Holy Michael Archangel!

(Michael the Archangel, the holy prince and leader of the choir of angels withstood Lucifer and the rebellious angels and with the cry 'Mi-ka-el'! = 'Who like God!', led the hosts faithful to God to a victorious battle (Revelation Ch XII). Revered as the protector of the Church, the defender in the fight with Satan, the conductor of souls in their last journey to eternity, in the East also a patron of the sick. The Western Church celebrates two feasts in his honour: the chief one on the 29th September, being the anniversary of the dedication of the Church of St Michael and All Angels at via Salaria in Rome in the sixth century, and the second one on the 8th May in memory of the Archangel's appearance on the Gargano Hill in Italy also in the sixth cen-

tury (according to the Encyclopaedia of Saints *by Bishop K. Rodonski in the 'St Wojciech Library'.)*

Holy Michael Archangel! What does this mean?!

(Puts on her glasses and reads.)

'Daddy, I can't bear this any longer, I am leaving for ever, don't try looking for me. I shall never stop loving you. You must understand. I am no longer a child. I don't condemn you. You do what everybody does. I weep as I write these words. No I am not crying any longer I am smiling at you. Bye, bye. Your little daughter.'

(The WOMAN goes to the half-open door and looks for a while into the dark empty hall.)

It had to end like that!

(She sits on the chair with her arms along her sides. She is holding the letter in her left hand.)

What's to be done now?

(Yes, quite! In an 'avantgarde' play the ENGINEER would have 'burst' upon the stage (through the other door) in his dressing gown and his leg in plaster, his nightshirt unbuttoned on his chest. His chest is covered in black hair. Following him, the trembling NURSE in a diaphanous nylon overall [reaching down only to the middle of her thighs] and in a white cap with a black ribbon. Trembling and yet already feeling herself the mistress of the house. Now the HOUSEKEEPER hands the letter to the ENGINEER who of course makes use of the telephone. He will at once inform the Chief Statistical Office. In five minutes' time the COMMISSIONER would have arrived. There would follow conversations, dialogues, telephone calls and so on. For example:)

ENGINEER: It's your duty, Commissioner, to return my daughter.

COMMISSIONER: We shall do everything in our power.

(Rings)

ENGINEER: Surely, she hasn't already flown to North America?

COMMISSIONER: Please be calm.

(Looks through an international flights timetable. During that time the ENGINEER is pouring out brandies.)

Yes, since November 24th, on Tuesdays, Fridays and Saturdays there is a Boeing 707 flight from Frankfurt to New York via London.

ENGINEER: When does the plane leave Frankfurt?

COMMISSIONER: At 15.45.

ENGINEER: Landing in New York?

COMMISSIONER: At 19.30 local time.

ENGINEER: And what is the difference between our time and theirs?

COMMISSIONER: I'm sorry I don't know.

ENGINEER: So at this moment the plane is already landing in New York?

COMMISSIONER: Yes, but please be calm.

(They are drinking brandy. In the 'surrealist' theatre the Archangel Michael leading a host of angels would have descended from heaven in response to the HOUSEKEEPER's call wearing gilt armour and brandishing a fiery sword. With this sword he strikes the closed white door of the ENGINEER's study. The door opens slowly. A frail GIRL dressed as a NURSE is pushing a chromium-plated trolley. The ENGINEER is sitting on it. His left leg in plaster is stretched out, and even as though on show. This leg measuring about two metres appears rather like some antedeluvian monster. It makes a big impression on everyone. The HOUSEKEEPER [who had earlier been the wet nurse and (perhaps) the ENGINEER's mistress] covers her eyes with her hand. The NURSE pushes the trolley towards the HOUSEKEEPER. The ENGINEER grips the housekeeper by the throat.)

ENGINEER: You dirty nigger.

(The WOMAN speaks in Swahili.)

Where is my child?

(The WOMAN replies in Swahili.)

So here I was not having enough sleep during the last ten years in order to construct the bridge, while you couldn't even look after my girl.

THE WOMAN: (*in a gruff voice*) She has run away to North America.

(*The* ENGINEER *strangles the erstwhile black wet-nurse. Angelic choirs conducted by Michael the Archangel are singing sixteenth century motets.*

My imagination had run amok [the soul straining for Paradise?] But let's return to reality. To our performance. The ROBUST WOMAN *wakes as though from a sleep.*)

ROBUST WOMAN: And what are they doing over there?

(*She glances 'knowingly' in the direction of the* ENGINEER's *study. Shrugs her shoulders [just as in 'life'].*)

What can they be doing there? Nothing. They are sleeping.

(*She talks to herself.*)

You have a hundred kilos of plaster on your left leg!

NOTE: *I have been caught in my own booby-trap. When I sat down to write this play I was in excellent good humour. I must confess that when writing the stage directions I was amusing myself. What was the source of that carefree optimism? Simply that together with the whole of humanity I took a deep breath. The apocalypse veiled its countenance. For some time now the world has seemed to me a more durable and more solid construction. I will not conceal the fact that the change of my mood has been influenced by a political act of significance for humanity as a whole. I am thinking of the nuclear test ban. Despite stupid gossip I am a man who likes to have a laugh; as for the fact that I hadn't done so in a cemetery . . . ! So I started writing this comedy in a cheerful mood. It seems to me that there is an atmosphere favouring the rejuvenation of the theatre, of the theatre as a game. I admit that in my previous plays I had tried to create just such a new theatre. I failed. Breathing apocalypse, I could not entertain others (and entertain myself). Thus, my plays were not quite accurate realizations of my intentions. At a certain moment they would turn into the so-called 'true*

*theatre'. But where does the continuation of the 'true theatre'
lead? To such monstrous works like* The Physicists, Andorra
*and many plays by American, Krakow, French, Warsaw, Aus-
trian (and other) playwrights. Dialogues on the subjects of
politics, sociology, religion and sex, lasting for several hours
and fitted into traditional 'dramatic' peripateia of the 'Heroes'
have simply become a nightmare. The writers try to astonish
the public, shake it, amuse it and at the same time they write in
dialogue form naive stories which have occurred in the family
of some solicitor, industrialist, scientist and so on. B is quite
close to the theatre in the 'spirit' of entertainment . . . yet theatre critics have turned him into a mystic, a nihilist. A tragedian.
Whereas his plays are wonderful entertainment. They ought to
be performed in music halls and student theatres. But to understand this one has to be an optimist. This Shakespeare of
our times (despite the fact that he has written only three or four
plays) is being interpreted so onesidely that he will eventually
cease to be readable and acceptable. This is the fault of producers and critics. Surely* Waiting for Godot *may be interpreted
as an excellent comedy. But to do that one has really to be a
realist, a person of serious intent who 'is not waiting for Godot'.
As it is the metaphysical beagles have smelled carrion for themselves and are indulging in mysticism, they terrify dumb
common people (who believe for example in Michael the Archangel, Lucifer and so on). This reciprocal mystification which
is played at by stage designers, directors, critics and the public
leads to . . . a dark room in which the children frighten themselves with ghosts. Unfortunately, the children are now grown
up and the whole show is changing into a lurid ritual. (NB: I
am aware that I am at this moment stretching B too much in
support of my thesis but at a time when I propose a completely
new interpretation of his plays I can't avoid extremes and over-
emphasis.) This same mystification appears in relation to other
plays by B. Instead of enjoying themselves at his* End Game
*people are searching for lousy nihilism. Surely, a right thinking
person will not accuse one who is grown-up, wise and indeed a
dramatist (almost) of genius that he is treating the 'theatre'
seriously when he places the aged parents in rubbish bins. The
same applies to another play where the 'heros' are buried in*

sand. *The action should of course be set in a large sand-pit among children who are building sandcastles, throwing sand at each other and, when necessary, peeing into the sand. As it is, all this is placed in some metaphysical sand and a macabre (and of course a quite devoid of sense) spectacle is mounted. So one can't be surprised that the 'Frankfurter Allgemeine' reviewer writes nonsense on the subject of the world première of B's latest play which took place in Ulm. 'Classical' plays (from the Greeks right up to Dürrenmatt) have so restricted the horizons of our reviewers that they treat all plays (the contemporary ones too) 'seriously'. A theatre which never had anything in common with the so-called 'real life' became the field of the strangest and most entertaining misunderstanding. Had this 'spiritually' impoverished reviewer of the 'Frankfurter Allgemeine' eventually understood that the theatre is not a dramatized reflection of 'real life', he would not have been ironical (causing amusement among the uninitiated) on the subject of live corpses 'buried up to their necks in something or other'. These same people who easily swallow* A Midsummer Night's Dream, Balladyna *(Slowacki's),* Goldoni, Ibsen . . . *these same people suddenly become impoverished realists and deride the poet-dramatist who dared to place people in rubbish bins, in the ground or in urns. They raised no objections to people being placed in hell or in heaven but they can't come to terms with people who entertain themselves with conversation on a rubbish heap. This is strange indeed! After this brief explanation which will perhaps give you a clearer idea of my theatre I return to the interrupted dramatic action:)*

ROBUST WOMAN: *(talking to herself)* Enough of this game, my doves. That old tomcat! Just look at him. His leg's in plaster weighing a ton I shouldn't be surprised and all he can think of is dalliance. And what can they be doing over there. In such a position.

(Takes a book from the shelf, skims through it, reads not very audibly.)

Carezza or coitus reservatus . . . mmm . . . hmmm . . . mmm . . . well . . . standard position . . . mmmm *(mumbles)* Ah well, yes! Soixante-neuf . . . or as we would say sixty-nine . . . the things people think up ... twenty-one ....

(Replaces the book on the shelf, dries her hands against her blouse in a peasant manner as if she had a moment before been feeding the poultry or blowing the children's noses.)

My young Mistress, my poor child is gone to North America without a coat. She hasn't put on anything warm. That rain! That rain! Won't it ever stop? And just before her finals. She packed and ciao! All the same, the old one could also have arranged things differently! Ah well, if it's got to be 'bye bye' then it's 'bye bye'.

(Goes to the door. Listens. After a moment, knocks gently.)

Nobody answers. They must be asleep. And that little viper has twisted the Master round her finger. A nurse. Well, and couldn't even an old one like me pull it and even set it ... ? There came the little thing in its cap and clutching a bag. Such a little wet hen. Only had one lump of sugar in her tea. And then, just watch that little hen! Just my luck. The old Tom. He snatched the hen on to a spit and crunched her up but she too knows what's what. Oh God, God. In one's old age one can't even remember whether one says 'crunched' with a 'c' or a 'k'. The old head is in a terrible spin.

(The clock on the wall strikes the hour. The WOMAN *sits at the table. From a little bag on her bosom she pulls out a little notebook bound in stiff green covers. She opens the notebook and begins to write. She talks aloud as though she were dictating to herself ....)*

'That night from the 6th to the 7th of September 1963. An hour ago the Mistress left the house for ever and departed to North America. She has left a farewell letter under the sugar bowl. The Master is still locked up with his nurse in his study. For the past 24 hours they have not been partaking of any nourishment. At first I condemned him but I don't think I was right. The late Mistress was a true Viridiana: ice, marble and wood. Often enough the Master would return straight from the bridge and the water cold and shivering and she wouldn't cuddle him. Cold. A wretched frigid soul. Last week they cemented the last pillar in the cofferdam. What's to be done? But one can't be surprised at the young Mistress. I ought to leave domestic service and set up a poultry farm. I have been dreaming of this for the past 20 years, although the state of the market at the moment is not too good. We don't know the outcome of the Brussels negotiations regarding the reduction of tariffs on chickens imported from North America. The raising of tariffs on European products would have been a severe blow for France, Italy, West Germany and other countries of the Common Market. Tariff on cheeses would have risen from 12 per cent of their price to 35 per cent. But what are we to do with our chicken and eggs! Only ten years ago a French or an Italian chicken would lay on average 80 eggs a year, now poultry batteries produce on average 220 to 250 eggs a year.'

(The WOMAN *stops writing and thinks. There is no sound behind the door of the* ENGINEER's *study.)*

I'll go to bed . . . .

(She stretches and yawns.)

I feel hungry . . . . Omne vivum ex ovo.

(She goes to the cupboard, takes out a mug, two eggs, a saucer and a small spoon. She breaks the eggs, at the same time skilfully separating the yolks from the whites. She slips the yolks into the mug which has a little red rose painted on it.)

ROBUST WOMAN: *(beating the eggs into a gogel-mogel sings softly)*

Two eggs	Two
will I beat	will I
for you	two for you
my child	my bonny
my bonny	my child
child	a sweet
a sweet	just for you
gogel-mogel	my child
just for you	for you

my child	will I beat
my bonny	gogel-mogel
child	for you

(The WOMAN is beating the yolks in the mug. How long? As long as it is necessary to beat the eggs. This may last 5 minutes and with intervals even 12. Here again is a place where the [potential] producer may intervene. Depending on the size of the stage and of the managing director one can either shorten or lengthen the egg beating scene, although within the limits set by the author. All exaggeration in either direction would push the spectacle down to the level of a farce — which at present is the standby of all impotents in the theatre.)

SCENE 3

The same room. The door to the right and the door to the left are closed. The middle door leading to the hall is ajar. There is no sugar bowl on the table. Evidently it has been put away by the ROBUST WOMAN. Nor can we see the flies which were to appear in previous scenes. Although at the moment the stage is empty, tension rises continuously. The situation is tense. It seems that something ought to happen. The closed door leading to the ENGINEER's study gradually changes its shape. It seems to acquire larger proportions, it expands to achieve (perhaps) a symbolic role. All this is of course happening exclusively in the spectator's imagination. In reality the door remains as it is.

Before I start writing this scene I wish to share (with those interested) the thoughts which accompanied me while I was planning it. I am here introducing the STRANGER (who is not connected in the 'dramatic sense' with any of the characters appearing in this play). This MAN lives in a very similar street, in a very similar house and in an almost identical apartment to that of the ENGINEER. Both houses have been built by the same firm. The apartments possess identical furniture, carpets, pictures. The people who live in these apartments read the same magazines and books. At the same time they watch the same TV programmes, listen to the same speeches, sermons and concerts of light and serious music. They have very similar fashionable clothes and information because they have been to similar schools and universities. On their walls they have almost identical pictures. Their fridges are stocked with identical food products e.g. frozen chicken, bananas, sausages and so on. With similar interiors they live similar lives. They have similar pleasures, problems, deviations, illnesses and children. They have an identical vocabulary of words, expressions, sayings, jokes, curses and so on. They have a similar pattern of life and death. They differ in their surnames but often their Christian names are identical. Their reminiscences from the past and plans for the future are almost identical. It is the same with their shirts and their cars. The same doctors tell them the same things at the same time and so do politicians and priests. They spend their holidays in the same resorts, look at the same land-scapes, castles and archeological sights. Only their faces (partly) and fingerprints prove that they are not the same people. We shouldn't be surprised that the MAN who entered the ENGINEER's apartment feels quite at home. Almost throughout the whole scene he doesn't realize that he is in somebody else's apartment. So, contrary to ap-pearance, our drama develops consistently and this is my constant concern. As we know, the 'stranger' has played and is still playing a large role in various old and new plays. But in the development of the usually naive (dramatic, Gold help us) action this 'stranger' sud-denly turns out to be the father lost in the war, the prodigal son, the uncle who has come back from Africa (or America), a school friend, a suicide who has been cut off or fished out and is restored to life, an insurance agent, a thief and so on and so on. Worthy classical and avantgarde (!) playwrights make very skilful use of this 'STRANGER' to surprise the audience, tangle the plot . . . and unravel it towards the end. But my 'STRANGER' has nothing at all to do with this drama which I am presenting to you. He has found himself in the ENGI-NEER's apartment for the reasons which I have already exhaustively explained. A similar street, a similar house, a similar door, similarly painted walls, identical furniture, tapestries, carpets, pictures . . . even the brandy in the cabinet bears the same label. Similar glasses. He could have made a mistake. Of course. And he wasn't drunk (that would have been too easy), oh no! Writing, or rather writing the dialogue for the third scene of this play, I was quite aware that this is material for a great, truly contemporary comedy. After all, it could have transpired that 'the wife' is so little different from 'the wife', 'the daughter' from 'the daughter', a 'conversation' from a 'conver-sation', 'love' from 'love', that right to the end our 'hero' would not realise that he has got the apartments mixed up. Perhaps one day I shall make use of this idea and in this connection I request sundry speculators not to try to . . . they know what.

Following this 'intrusion' we return to the room and to the play. A MAN who will be 42 in three days' time enters the room. We cannot, alas, show this to the audience (from the stage). He is wearing a fashionably cut coat (I don't indeed know what cut is fashionable but the producer or the stage designer can look this up in a glossy). It's a black coat, maybe even a jacket of thick fashionable (?) mate-rial. The coat is unbuttoned, apparently the man is in a state of

excitement. He has no hat and his hair is damp (of course this fact
is of no consequence). The man has entered the room warily but
not on tiptoe. It looks as though he was trying to surprise someone
(but not quite). Rather, he is undecided. He sits at the table, lights a
cigarette, looks at a 'fixed point'. He sees 'nothing' around him. His
formal suit (it may be a dinner jacket) demonstrates that the man
has returned from an official reception at an embassy or from a
concert (maybe he is the conductor). It pains me to write about a
certain small detail but unfortunately I am forced to do this by the
poetics of this drama: well, this (almost) elegant gentleman has a
hole in his left sock. This is a remnant of very ancient times when
women darned socks and Ibsen was worshipped. I can't, alas, explain how this sock with a hole found itself on the foot of a well
situated conductor or bank manager. Of course the hole in the sock
is tiny and is (definitely!) invisible: it is hidden away in the patent
leather shoe. 'If this hole is not visible, why do you write so much
about it', a simple-minded member of the audience or a crafty drama
theorist might ask. Quite so. In this play I write not only about the
visible world but also about the invisible (real) world. But our producers of course demand that we should occupy ourselves with
holes in heaven (because a hole in the sock is too small for the large
stage of the national theatre). Hold it, gentlemen! Sometimes a tiny
little hole may be more dramatic than a hole in heaven. I personally
do not ignore even a hole in cheese. True, 'a hole in heaven' opens
possibilities for stage designers, composers, reviewers and so on
and so on. Stage settings for 'a hole in heaven' are quite a spectacle,
a self-sufficient spectacle! But here? It's a flop. Our ways part, gentlemen. You see a huge stage with a huge hole in heaven, while I am
satisfied with a hole in a sock. Again, I am rambling on, while 'nothing is happening on the stage' (a fact which is an underrated asset of
the poetic theatre — apparently nothing, and yet everything . . . .)
The MAN is still smoking a cigarette. He goes to the cabinet, pulls out
a bottle of brandy and a glass. He pours. He looks around.

SCENE 4

The same room in the ENGINEER's apartment. The STRANGER has apparently realized that he has entered someone else's apartment and has gone. He has left behind him an empty brandy bottle and a glass. A MAN in a rubber raincoat and rubber boots reaching above the knees bursts 'like a bomb' [this superb simile is however very difficult to put into effect] into the room. He looks as though he has been fished out of water. He is dripping. To the extent that in the spot where he has stopped a large pool of water is forming on the parquet floor under our very eyes. He is the FIRST DEPUTY of the CHIEF ENGINEER. He is followed by two well-built handsome WORKERS in boiler suits. Their pockets are bulging with spanners, spirit measures, set squares, micrometers and other instruments indispensable in building large-scale edifices.

FIRST DEPUTY: *(looks around confused. The door to the left and the door to the right are both closed.)* Is anybody there?

(Silence)

Hey, is anybody there?

(Silence)

What does this mean? The water has broken through the embankment and has washed away the dyke, the dam, the lock and even the island! It's rising every minute. Any moment now it will flood the boulevards and the whole town! Hey, is there anyone there?

(Sound of a cannon shot. This is the flood alarm. A moment following the shot the ROBUST WOMAN holding a candle in her trembling hand enters the room.)

ROBUST WOMAN: Was it you who knocked?

FIRST DEPUTY: Yes.

ROBUST WOMAN: At last! I have been waiting these three days. Please follow me.

(They all disappear in the open doorway but the ensuing dialogue is clearly audible.)

Everything's blocked up. The shower. The tap, the tank, the window, the waste pipe, the lavatory seat, the water-closet, the bidet, the thermometer, the children's bath, the toothpaste . . . they throw hair everywhere . . . fluff all over the place.

FIRST DEPUTY: Where is the Engineer?

ROBUST WOMAN: What do you want the Engineer for? He is asleep.

FIRST DEPUTY: Don't you understand, woman, that the steel ropes of the suspension bridge which was dedicated last week may snap at any moment? The balustrade is twisted, the tower is leaning over, water is already lapping against the bridgehead.

ROBUST WOMAN: Against the icebreaker.

FIRST DEPUTY: The icebreaker, the icebreaker! Both the pillar and the central span are caving in.

ROBUST WOMAN: What pillar? In a suspension bridge?

FIRST DEPUTY: Where is the Engineer?

ROBUST WOMAN: He is in bed with his leg in plaster.

FIRST DEPUTY: Then wake him up!

ROBUST WOMAN: *(shrugging her shoulders)* Well?

(FIRST DEPUTY taps delicately on the door. ROBUST WOMAN looks at the empty brandy bottle and sniffs the glass. There is silence behind the door.)

FIRST DEPUTY: Hey, hey, Chief!

(Pause)

I am very sorry
but the pillar of the middle span is caving in
Chief, please get up

we must drive at once
to the place
of the imminent disaster.

(Silence)

FIRST WORKER: *(with a face of a smallholder)* I smell a rat.

ROBUST WOMAN: And what are you up to?

FIRST WORKER: If they hadn't fiddled the cement the pillar wouldn't
have given way.

FIRST DEPUTY: Go towards the bridge. For the time being secure the
icebreaker with sandbags. I will try to wake the Engineer.

*(WORKERS leave. FIRST DEPUTY bangs on the closed door with his
fists.)*

Chief, Chief
I implore you
in the name of our old friendship
from our schooldays
will you please come with me at once
don't you remember our old history master
or our biology master
with his tinted beard! Was it green or
ginger — I can't quite remember. . . .
We used to call him alga . . . protozoan . . . .
slipperwort . . . .

(ROBUST WOMAN nods her head indulgently and leaves the room.)

Open up! You lazybones!

*(FIRST DEPUTY strikes the door with his fist. Silence behind the
closed door. DEPUTY runs and hits the door with the whole weight
of his body. Like a battering ram. Once, twice, three times . . . .)*

THE FUNNY OLD MAN

CHARACTERS

AN OLD MAN	An old man in a threadbare but neat suit. A live actor.
THE JUDGE	A beautiful young woman in judge's robes, beautiful hands and hair. A dummy of natural size. After the interval a live actress.
FIRST ASSISTANT	A man with a moustache and grey hair. A dummy.
SECOND ASSISTANT	A bald-headed old man. A dummy.
THE LEARNED COUNSEL	In barrister's robes but without a head. A dummy.
CHILDREN AND DOLLS	

The PRESIDING JUDGE and his two assistants sit behind a table. The SECOND ASSISTANT sits on the JUDGE's left and the FIRST ASSISTANT on his right. All three face the audience. The OLD MAN is standing with his back to the audience. In the course of giving evidence he wipes his nose with a handkerchief two or three times. His face becomes visible when he leaves the courtroom.

The LEARNED COUNSEL sits next to the OLD MAN his back to the audience. On the right of the stage, partly behind the wings, we catch a glimpse of gymnastic equipment.

During the interval well-developed live GIRLS use the equipment for exercise. Something like a ballet. After the interval CHILDREN play on the stage during the performance. They run about, shout, play hide-and-seek and hopscotch. The smallest ones are building sandcastles in a sandpit. These could be life-sized dolls.

One of the GIRLS pushes a doll's pram up and down the stage. Her 'daughter' is inside the pram. What the CHILDREN say and sing is of no consequence. Sometimes their voices grow loud and drown some of the OLD MAN's words. The choice of quiet and noisy moments is significant. The CHILDREN's games are a performance in its own right which has no connection with the OLD MAN's case. The adults too pay no attention to the CHILDREN. The DUMMIES have realistic human faces. All grotesque elements are to be avoided. The OLD MAN speaks clearly. Parts of the OLD MAN's evidence ought to be illustrated with tableaux vivants.

SCENE 1

THE OLD MAN: ... the elder one used to lie in wait for me and always threatened me each time I passed the corridor. She had teeth like a mouse very tiny and sharp. She would bare those tiny teeth at me and stick out her prickly little tongue. I would pretend that I didn't see anything. And then I tried to turn it all into a joke and I even stroked her head. She caught me by the hand and wouldn't let go and I heard somebody coming. I offered to buy her a chocolate and only then did she let me go. At the very last moment. In order to pacify her I bought her a bar of chocolate and gave it to her. But it didn't help. Did I ever give sweets to other children? Never. I couldn't afford it. Anyway I like sweets myself. I've always like them ever since I was a child. That's why my teeth decayed. I'm a bit ashamed of this passion. But we all have our favourite dishes and sweets. I even began to walk with my head bowed as though I were guilty. But it's always been like that: whenever anyone caused me distress I would feel shame and blush. I began to hear giggles behind my back and even rude words which you wouldn't expect from such little girls. It is I who ought to be complaining about these children to the court. I had never accosted them. Right at the beginning when I first moved in, there weren't any small children at all. There was only one little boy, no bigger than my stick. Later these children multiplied terribly. You simply wouldn't believe it.

   For many years there were no children in the whole building. And then suddenly there were plenty of them. What noise! Not far away from here there was some school or other, or perhaps there wasn't. I never accosted women. Nor girls. Nor little girls. Throughout my whole life God had protected me from the female sex. I remember I bought myself a bird. A bird in a cage. I couldn't stand large strange creatures. There were several of these girls. Nobody will believe me but they molested me and persecuted me terribly. All this was so hideous that I didn't know how to defend myself. In the old days things were simple. Either one would oneself wallop them on their bare behind or one would go to the parents or guardians and everything would be settled on the spot. I had intended to go to the house committee, to the school, to the police. In the end I went to see a solicitor. I felt terrified. The solicitor advised me to go to a doctor. I must confess he gave me an impression of being mental. All the time I was there he would rub his hands, wink at me and make faces. One of the little girls once told me I must return her canary together with the cage. I refused. And she gave me such a severe look and left without a word. I was frightened.

I am greedy but I struggle against this weakness. I struggle against it and this ought to be a point in my favour. As far as this vice is concerned I have often fallen. I remember once on pay day I bought myself fifty cream buns which I adored. I ate them during the night. I pulled the curtain across the window and I began to eat. And as I ate I thought of myself as a little boy. But eating these buns became more and more boring. My movements became heavy but I ate with determination. I ate all alone. At first all I felt was the taste in the roof of my mouth. But then I had various thoughts. How empty my life is, I thought, like a bun without cream. I became more and more dejected and I ate the buns automatically. Although I did pause from time to time in order to think. And then I felt like crying. And I did cry. Heavy tears fell down my cheeks and I felt their saltiness on my lips. I ate unwillingly. In the end I got so upset that I closed my mouth and went on eating with my mouth shut. I felt very angry. I was pushing the bun into my mouth but my lips were so tightly closed that even the cream couldn't get through. And yet I continued to squeeze the buns against my face. Then into my ears. I was sobbing. What good is all this cream, I thought. What good is the cream of the whole world. I don't want pastries I don't want pastries I don't want pastries. I rubbed the cream into my hair. One of the buns fell on the floor. I didn't notice it and I slid on the cream. I fell on the floor. My hands were all covered in cream. But then I really got upset and I began to crush all these buns. On the chairs on the table on the wall and even on the ceiling. Even though that was difficult and I had to climb on to a chair. Eventually, tired out, I dropped on the bed and fell asleep in my clothes. In the morning I washed myself. Well, I thought, that was nothing dreadful, all I did was to squash a few cream cakes. Napoleon abandoned a million soldiers on the limitless steppe not counting horses and cannon. He didn't even look back. And no one minded. And I, when I was a little boy, wanted to be Napoleon. It wasn't until I was about 40 that I realized I would never be Napoleon, never in my life. I didn't tell anyone about this. I remember I took sick leave. I shut myself up in the house with dry biscuits. I didn't want to see anyone. It was a dreadful experience. I would sit whole days and even nights staring at my face in the mirror.... But eventually I concluded that, after all, there is only one such face in the world. That there never was and never will be such another. That cheered me up. And yet mirrors are devilish inventions. Yes. The day that I realized that I shall never be Napoleon was probably the most important day in my life. From then onward I was a mere vegetable. That is, I lived like everybody else. I grew humble and began to take notice of how my fellow humans looked at me. Of their opinion of me and so on. From then on I talked very softly almost in a whisper. I would never raise my voice, never gave orders. I kept apologizing to everyone although I knew that they wouldn't be Napoleons either. I would wake up in the night and persuade myself that this was all to the good. But if one isn't Napoleon one has to take into account every petty little thing. This precisely is life. The moment a man realizes that he will never be Napoleon he begins to pay attention to his comforts. He avoids all efforts and discomforts for he no longer sees the point of giving things up. He doesn't wash himself in cold water. Before my very nose someone slammed the door to greatness. But who? Shall I ever find an answer to this question? I even began to turn into a rag ... but not a 'rag' in the vulgar sense of the word. A moral rag and so on. On the contrary I was turning into a rag in the organic physical sense. I notice for example that I hang down from a chair like a pair of trousers. Or that I lie on the bed any old way. Sometimes I would sit with my tongue hanging out and I couldn't pull it back into my mouth. Anyway, there wasn't any need to. I spent a whole month in such a state. Then I returned to normal life and lived for 30 years. When I retired I applied to the Historic Monuments Trust and got a job as a guide. Part-time. But together with my modest pension this was quite enough. Days passed. At that time I found myself longing for the company of some creature. At the same time I read in a newspaper that our planet is inhabited by three billion people. This globe of ours is getting crowded and yet I have no one close to me. So despite the growing population it is not easy to find companionship. I began collecting tin cans. Then ladies' shoes and pigtails. But I had to give this up because there was no room in my tiny flat for such collections. It was then that I bought a canary. The first canary died after a week. He grew sadder every day and eventually died. The flat was empty again. I do have a radio of course and so I listen to the news. Including Radio Free Europe, The Voice of America and whatever else they are called. What they talked about most often was the atomic bomb, the hydrogen bomb, missiles and polaris submarines. And so it went on for several years. I cried only once when I heard a song by a French singer but I don't remember what it was called. So as time went on I stopped listening to those broadcasts about bombs as they were both terrifying and boring. I don't read many books for my eyes have grown weak. So I used to sit at the window in such a way that nobody would see me and I observed the street. In the autumn the streets were empty. Sometimes I would sit like this for an hour, sometimes several hours. I would look at the window-pane covered with rain drops and I would have stray thoughts but I would never think anything through to the end. Sometimes when the rain stopped I would go out for a walk. People would be sitting in their houses. The asphalt was black and glistening. There were clouds above the houses and the windows had curtains drawn across them. This street looked as though it led to the next world. But it only looked like that after the rain on a cloudy November day. This street led to the railway station. And in the winter I would sometimes sit the whole of Sunday from morning to night watching the snow fall. From the sky onto the earth. For the first few hours the street would be white. Sometimes in the morning it would look like a dream. It was utterly quiet. I would see the footsteps of one man that led to the door of my house, but these were my steps. I didn't have much work because few bothered to view the ancient buildings in the autumn and winter. But in the spring and summer it was like a madhouse. You had to watch the walls and ceilings. They would all scrawl their initials everywhere. Some would write their full names and addresses. They also drew various obscene things. One had to go on scrubbing them away. And the things you could see there. We had to cover them up with tar and whitewash. What did these historic walls look like! Some inscriptions were filthy and pornographic, some were political and some were a bit of both, some had rhymes. The work I had to do then. Outside my working hours too. In fact I ought to have been paid overtime. I mentioned this once in the director's office. They didn't take my request seriously and they laughed at me. Yes, they laughed at me. It was terrifying to look at those inscriptions. They were about various politicians and even about the Greatest Man of our time. Even now I couldn't say it. I got so frightened at the time that I had the whole wall whitewashed at my own expense. The following day the scribbles reappeared. Some were against dictators, some against other statesmen. Some criminals even drew swastikas and wrote revisionist and revanchist slogans. So long as all this was confined to the lavatory I slept soundly. But then it spread to other walls of the monument like rising damp or a disease. These inscriptions were the work of ordinary hooligans but often enough one could come across just remarks about our economic situation which you wouldn't see in any of our newspapers. I remember one such inscription which began with something about 'success' and ended with the words 'The Polish eco-

nomic mess', but I don't remember this too well. I had a
nervous breakdown in those dangerous times. But although
I kept scraping and covering up these inscriptions and drawings I never felt quite safe. What's more when I thought
about all this during the night I felt like one of these hooligans. For although I kept clear of politics various things did
enter my head. But I never revealed it to anyone. Anyway
even in bed I was always alone. And the lavatory did not
even belong to me. Once a month an old woman would
come to clean up. But I wasn't blind. Every morning when
I went there to perform I would lift my eyes to the ceiling
and naturally I would be scanning the walls. And then I
would see those figures of naked women and men. Or just
the genitals. They would be drawn with a black pencil, char-
coal or chalk. Some would even use a nail or a piece of
glass. There were also drawings of the various positions of
human bodies and members which an old man like me had
never dreamed of. And beneath these drawings there were
inscriptions. The name or the address and the date of the
rendezvous. And various propositions as well. I must admit
that on one occasion I was tempted to go to one of these
addresses. I was very taken. But somehow it all passed,
thank God, and I was spared this thoughtless step. Perhaps
these problems are too great to be brought up in this way. I
have in mind the political problems. And my point of view
may appear silly and narrow but at that time I was exposed
to such provocations. But perhaps these were the catacombs
of our times. Perhaps this was the voice of the people or
something of that sort. I beg the Court's pardon for raising
a political matter which throws no light on my case but I
wish to present myself to the Court in all respects as a human being so this is not irrelevant. Madame Judge will forgive
an old man for mixing up various subjects but I see no
other way of untying this Gordian knot which these innocent devilish little creatures have contrived to bring about
my ruin. But I shall revert to that subject only once more
and thereafter I shall keep strictly to the events which have
led me to this tragic situation, to the witness box. The times
were difficult and one could stumble over any kind of sh

... I beg your pardon, my tongue must have slipped because of the place I was telling you about. Well Madame Judge, one fine day when I was scraping away at one of those dangerous inscriptions I felt a hand on my shoulder. I was paralyzed. I was frozen stiff. I felt, if I may say so, my soul leaving the body. Oh, yes, I do believe in the soul. And even now when my fellows are pushing me into a quagmire, I shall not cease to believe that one day in years to come .... For allow me to refer to a parable taken straight from life, straight from the street. Well, our urban rubbish disposal unit is now equipped with garbage lorries. These are huge machines and along their sides they have various slogans painted for the edification of the citizens. The lorry which comes to our district has the slogan 'Beauty and Cleanliness a Responsibility of every Citizen' and the other lorries also have interesting thoughts painted on their sides, but this particular one attracted my attention. I pondered this over for, if Madame Judge will allow me, it is very strange the way things are ordered in this world. A container carrying filth and garbage has the inscription 'Beauty and Cleanliness a Responsibility of every Citizen'. Sometimes it's the same with a human being. Inside he is full of refuse and all sorts of muck, but on his front and his back he carries the inscription 'Beauty and Cleanliness a Responsibility of every Citizen'. This is not what I wished to say and I got a bit muddled just now but please forgive me, I am in a high state of excitement and nerves. I am struggling against a libel and an ignominious accusation. And in this case everything is important. Some people imagine that a man who pokes about a rubbish heap or collects garbage is himself a dirty, smelly piece of rubbish. This however is in conflict with reality. I have read in a book by a certain traveller that the beautiful temples and statues in India have a wonderful golden sheen and that this wonderful polish is the result of the statues and temples being rubbed with manure and you can even see the sun's reflection in this manure. And whenever this refuse van with the slogan 'Beauty and Cleanliness a Responsibility of every Citizen' passed me by I would think: here we have a proper inscription in its proper place. And yet surely, often enough it's quite the other way round. But already I have got too far away from that thread which I have lost. When I felt that hand on my shoulder in that lavatory I was paralyzed. From that moment my life turned into a nightmare. I feel slightly embarrassed that my experiences, if you will pardon the expression, of what they call the Stalinist period are on such a small scale and at such a low level. However all things have to fit into some scale. The pattern of my life was such that I never tried to overreach myself. Various people are good at standing things on their head and excusing themselves but I will say quite modestly that I felt paralyzed in that lavatory and I lost my speech. I will describe the scene to you. I didn't turn round, I only heard an unknown young voice in my ear: 'Got you, pal.' That is what he said. He didn't address me either as 'sir' or 'comrade' but just said 'got you, pal.' And the Court ought to know that at that time I had completed my 70th year and my hair was as white as snow. And this voice continues: 'So it's you who decorates the loo, well who would have thought, it's chaps like you who go on at the young ones for being cynical, but you are at it yourselves.' And there I was scraping off the name of the Greatest Man of our time which was placed next to an offending expression. 'So it's you, you old bastard, who's organising an underground job around here' and I feel that the whole of my body is growing numb and I also feel that this man is thinking in an odd sort of way; what sort of underground and subversive work could you be doing in a lavatory? That is what I thought rather than that here I was accused of a serious crime and that I could easily spend several years in prison. 'You two-faced agent, you are planning to upset the framework of the System, like a mole you wish to blow it up from inside.' Who is burrowing like a mole? I thought for no particular reason and my hand holding the scraping knife fell down listlessly. And somehow I turned and faced the young man. Anyway it's difficult to call him a young man, he was just a boy. A miserable snivelling little boy. He might have been fourteen or fifteen. I look at this green specimen and say 'Sonny.' And he says to me: 'For a handful of silver you want to destroy the alliance, Judas, Colorado beetle.' And I say to him, 'Sonny . . . .' 'Listen old boy, if you don't give me a fiver, I'll put you behind bars.' Ah, I think to myself, this is no idealist, just a young crook and blackmailer and something like a shadow of hope enters my heart now dead with fear: 'You see,' I say to him, 'I am an old man, I work here part-time and all I get for this job is a fiver and it is already halfway through the month and I am penniless.' 'Let's go then,' he says and takes me by the hand. And so we stand in front of that wall, two representatives of two generations, one might say. Slowly I regain my composure and I say to him 'So it's you, you little viper, who has smeared all this over these walls. I've got you by the hand now,' I say and although I feel that I am not being quite honest, I push on in order to frighten him, 'I have been waiting here for you for the last month. What school do you go to, eh?' So he thought he'd got me but I'd got him. This is how low our morality has sunk during the Stalinist period. The boy blenched and tears appeared in his eyes. 'Please Sir, forgive me and let me go,' he says. I was moved and I started looking through my pockets. I dug out the last few coppers. 'Here you are,' I said, 'Buy yourself some sweets and never play at being a provocateur again.' He smiled through tears and kissed my hand. He was young and foolish and a moment later he was helping me to rub off the dirty pictures and inscriptions, both the sociological and the political ones. When I got home I was so shaken that I went to bed without a meal. For even the most innocent person has various thoughts, both in relation to women as well as in relation to the political system and his superiors. But these are involuntary thoughts.

I beg the Court's pardon for straining its patience but I did wish to reveal myself so that I would be standing here in the full light, hiding nothing. Apart from this political shock I have had no momentous experiences. But in that lavatory at that time I was afraid. Now all of a sudden we have the astronauts flying around. Soon people will be flying to the moon. I have lived to see it. But it is difficult to get rid of one's old fears. Such is human nature. You get frightened as a child and it stays with you for the rest of your life. I was preoccupied with my professional business. And although I had been repeating the text that I recited as a guide in that ancient monument for the previous ten years, all the same I would sometimes wake up in the morning with certain gaps in my memory which I had to fill. Intellectual work at my age isn't all that easy. And I was doing housekeeping at the same time. It was at that time that I began to collect dolls. Why? For no reason at all. It simply is a pleasure to collect something. Collecting matchboxes isn't interesting, worse, I'm of the opinion that it is an occupation that tends to dull the brain. I used to buy the biggest dolls they had in the shops. All in all I bought five of them. It wasn't a large collection but the dolls were expensive. Each item would cost several pounds and this is by no means a small sum for an old pensioner who makes up his income with a little pittance as a guide to an ancient monument. After work in the evenings, or sometimes even at night, I used to play with my dolls. I can't see anything queer in that and I don't think this throws any shadow over my reputation. Nobody objects when adults shoot partridges which clear our fields of colorado beetle. Or when a man hits his wife on the head with a boot in front of their children. And once there was a drunk who was relieving himself outside my door. I had to clean it up with my own hands after midnight. Or perhaps he wasn't drunk for he rang the doorbell, woke me up at midnight, pulled me out of bed and then the scoundrel ran away. And there are plenty of other worse things that our fellow human beings perpetrate. So I wasn't doing anybody any harm when with my own money I was buying these dolls and playing with them. I would dress and undress these dolls. I also bought one nude doll. A girl. Made of pink plastic. She had beautifully set black hair and a blue ribbon. When you laid her down she would close her eyes. I taught her various exercises and tricks. She had to stand on her head, walk on her hands and sometimes I would punish her. One evening I drilled two little holes in the naked doll. And then I poured water inside.

But one day for some reason I got upset. I pulled out the doll's arms and legs and I threw the body into the stove and burnt it. At that time I often had stomach pains but considering the great epoch in which we are privileged to live I'm ashamed to raise this matter. Anyway there was no one to tell this to. I used to lie under the eiderdown and tremble until I started sleeping with hotwater bottles. These were really lemonade empties not, God forbid, vodka ones. Because I'm a teetotaller and the last time I ever drank vodka was during the lifetime of my late brother when dizzy with alcohol I accompanied him with songs. I nailed the remaining dolls to the table. Surely there is nothing wrong in that. I didn't hurt anybody. But neighbours who some-how got to know of this began whispering behind my back. They smiled and made faces which I didn't like. Well, chil-dren do many worse things. Children, the only heavenly dwellers on earth, ha, ha, ha! Forgive me this laughter, but I can't contain myself. I know these little angels all too well. As a matter of fact, one couldn't tell whether that nude dolly was a boy or a girl. They just make dolls like that. But why? Nobody can answer me that. But I can. They are made like that because adults are stupid and . . . I'm sorry . . . .
What do I do with my time? I work. What do I do with my time? That depends. I go for walks to preserve my health. I study to keep up with my professional duties. During the winter I listen to the wireless and read the historical novels of Henryk Sienkiewicz written to sustain the morale of Poles. I watch the falling snow. It's worse in spring. Then I feel weak and I sleep badly. I prefer the summer. Although I don't swim any longer, I sunbathe in my beach costume. I have a very respectable costume. The legs are perhaps a trifle too long because sometimes I see the young ones look-ing at me critically. Well, I can't help it. Little remains of the good old days. A moustache. I go to the bathing place by the river and I watch. I cover my head with the newspaper I've just read and I say to myself that nobody knows what lies beneath this paper, what face hides beneath this news-paper. What eyes and lips. That is terrible. I am as shy as I was fifty years ago. I was terribly frightened when I read in

the newspaper that they found the body of an eight-year-old girl that was murdered. It's just as well it happened in another town. 100 kilometres from here. I only watch these naked dollies when they paddle or pee in the sand. I don't even carry sweets with me. Just in case. I take visitors round the castle. I have a good grounding in history and I work part-time as a guide in a national monument. I keep expanding my knowledge of the kings of the Piast dynasty.

SCENE 2

Thank you for removing the public from the courtroom. This will save my life story from becoming fodder at casual gatherings of the curious. They foregather in courtrooms like vultures ready to tear the accused's body to shreds. And yet surely it's enough to have a close look at people's faces to read their dreadful hidden thoughts. How is it possible that a man who, for half a century, was a spotless citizen and member of society, should be placed before the law on the basis of evidence given by children, that is little girls? What we really need here is a whip and instead what do things look like? It looks as though the learned Court is going to believe these tiny disgusting schemers. In the old days the proceedings would have been brief. Bend over, pull off the pants and ten smacks on a bare bottom. Whereas now everybody in the whole world has got mixed up. It's all because of those psychologists and pedagogues. In our home we had a deer's hoof with a leather strap hanging on a nail. It used to hang there until we got sensible. It was very rarely used, usually we were just given a 'whiff' of that hoof, but all the same it used to hang there. And what is hanging there now? What is the sign, what, if I may say so, is the symbol of authority? Stupid psychological questions which we have acquired from those mad Americans. And we all know what these psychologists and star performers have brought about over there, don't we? I won't elaborate for you know it all well yourselves. Meanwhile what our national poet has said will remain topical for a good while yet. He said 'The spirit of the Lord advises that little children ought to be birched.' I think he said that. And what have these damned psychologists brought about?

The result is that in Warsaw a boy beheaded his own mother like a chick and then displayed the head on his window-sill. And when they asked him why he did it he replied that he wanted to punish Mummy for not giving him money to go to the pictures and buy a bottle of fruit wine. But ladies with very wise and understanding eyes, some wearing spectacles, some not, proved that the boy was deprived of maternal affection. And whenever there is a discussion about the criminal code various gentlemen argue that punishment has no corrective effect on people. I'm only a simple guide with an incomplete secondary education but I must protest strongly. We have to punish and most severely at that. Let's leave all talks and discussions till we reach heaven! The logic of the facts is simple and society as a whole is single-minded about it. Only false friends of man and false teachers create confusion in the head, whereas the logic of facts is this: a crook murders a respectable person. Or beats him up and maims him for life. Then the crook goes to prison while his family sends him food parcels. Lard, meat, cakes and fruit. Perhaps cigars and brandy as well. Whereas, as we know, decent and educated people are so overworked that all they have time for is to snatch a bite of something and work twelve hours a day. And with ulcers to boot. But a crook and a thief has leisure. Apparently they even have film shows. I am not denying that a crook is a human being. But this is the very reason why he should be given an exemplary punishment. I'm being asked to speak on the matter. What matter?

You mean the doll which I burnt? Then I must also explain that she could make sounds. She had such tiny parted lips and inside that orifice you could see tiny teeth and a little tongue. I don't remember exactly, but you had to push the doll a good way forward and when it straightened itself out she would emit this sound. But instead of saying 'Mama' she would make a bleating noise. She could turn her head and lower her eyelids. Her eyes moved and she could give you a sidelong glance. She was plump, if you could say that of a toy. Those children who swarmed our building, the street and the courtyard used to yell without a moment's pause. They cried, they screamed, they screeched, they yelled. Day and night. The din would be so terrific that I would often wish all these children turned to stone. We all have moments when we curse ourselves, our fellow-men, the whole world, but after all, our curses have no practical significance, and one cannot judge a man on the basis of his involuntary thoughts and curses. And so I wished that those tiny creatures would all perish, that a blight should liquidate them, and so on. For after all, they produce heaps of children and afterwards we solitary men have to bear this burden too. Very often you get some antisocial individual taking as much pleasure as possible with another harmful individual, producing as many children as possible and then the children are dumped on the shoulders of society. It means either a babies' home, if it's an infant, or a remand home if it's a youth, or a prison should certain individuals reach maturity. We have to prohibit anti-social elements from doing what a decent citizen cannot afford to do during the whole of his life. For, Madame Judge, what did I get out of life?

Everything here is topsy-turvey and the Church too is not without blame, for it encourages the production of little angels and little dollies without end. Without any consideration. The burdens are then borne by decent people, and some of them are not believers and this is not right. But it's not my job to mend the world and I must admit I calmly look forward to death, for the earth is in too much of a muddle, there are too many voices and noises which are of no value at all. Now it is bitterness speaking through me but the disgrace which has fallen on my white hairs through human stupidity and female tongues has turned me into a Job. But in fact I watch pigeons and playful children with amusement, although these latter have shattered my nerves. I remember that when I was young I used to show children various tricks. Using my hands and a handkerchief I could throw the shapes of dogs, hares and wolves on to the wall. And those children with plump little arms and dimpled faces, with darling little feet and hands were for me a paradise on earth. Irrespective of whether they were the children of my brothers and sisters or completely unknown. A neighbour who worked a night shift had just such a tiny tot. Of my own accord I would very often amuse it and put it to bed in the evening. I would undress it, tuck it in and even sing it to sleep.

What are little girls made of?
Sugar and spice
And all things nice
That's what little girls are made of.

And if necessary I would put it on the pot. And perhaps
it is a detail unworthy of the Court, but for this purpose I
would lend the widow my own private chamber pot. Well,
years have passed and before one realised it, the baby grew
into a maiden like a doe, for it was, of course, a baby of the
female sex. This is a difference in which an adult does not
see anything extraordinary. And this is why my heart bleeds,
for whenever I greet her, she, like a doe, blushes all over,
gives me a contemptuous look and does not respond to my
greeting.

What was that, Madame Judge? Yes it was a child of the
female sex. Did I previously speak of it as a boy? I must
have made a mistake. Or perhaps it was a boy, I don't remember. Am I giving you a cock and bull story? Oh, no! I
never allow myself such a thing in the Court's presence.
But I've got myself mixed up? Yes, of course, it is true, it was
girl, for I would sometimes tease her, saying where is your
little birdie, the birdie's flown away and I would laugh. These
were just little amusements which even a curate would allow himself. As to the fact that 'bird' is also a symbol of the
male member is no secret for adults. Anyway this member
or penis has so many names that one couldn't possibly count
them. For schoolboys have one name for it, boarding school-
girls have another, ordinary soldiers have their terms,
learned persons have theirs, so that perhaps the word 'birdie'
is not so reprehensible when uttered by a man with one
foot in the grave. Why did I attend sporting events The
Learned Counsel thinks fit to smile. But I don't see anything amusing in that. Why competitions involving female
teams? Some go to horse races, some to bullfights and I
must emphasise that such amusements are detrimental to
society ... or take boxing for example! There have been
cases of people being killed in the ring. But I go to watch
basketball and netball matches. Only once did I go to watch

an athletics competition. But these were school sports in
which both boys and girls took part. I found it terribly ex-
citing. I also used to attend elimination matches at various
gymnastic competitions in elementary schools. The Learned
Counsel wants to know what sort of schools these were.
There were also some girls' schools and girls of various
ages would take part in gymnastic displays. From 8 to 14.
And would it have been better for boys to indulge in gymnastic displays? As far as I'm concerned I see no difference
but it is a fact that these were sporting events in which girls
in groups and singly performed displays. But there's nothing wicked in that. On the contrary I was sometimes moved
to tears when I watched the development of these little
things. They were still so gawky and shapeless. Almost devoid of any shape. A wisp of something under the arm. Still
no hair in the armpit. And yet, something of the female
would shine through these forms. After these displays I
would sometimes feel like giving the participants sweets or
bars of chocolate. But I never did. A false modesty wouldn't
allow it. And yet surely, Madame Judge, this is very natural
when one hasn't got a child of one's own. This I couldn't
afford under the pre-war capitalist regime and after the
liberation it was too late to think about it. What did these
girls do? I don't know what all these figures are called.
They would walk on their hands or form a bridge or a
spiral or something like that. And they would also leapfrog
over each other and when the displays were over they would
curtsy gracefully. A blessed age!

What are little girls made of
Sugar and spice
And all things nice
That's what little girls are made of.

God forbid that I should show contempt of court. All I
want to do is to describe the innocent, mutual relationship.
For, to tell the truth, I too am still a child. There is something terribly moving in children's tiny little feet, irrespective
of sex. Dimples in the hands above the fingers or the lines
beneath the knees. I'm getting lost, I know I'm getting lost

but surely these physical developments have been studied by judges and teachers. And not all of them young either. I would often hum those innocent lines. At home, in the park, on the bench or during a walk, but when I noticed that people were smiling I stopped singing, I just went dumb. I won't deny that during a game of basketball or netball I admired the efficient movements of the fully-developed female bodies of the competitors. But there are officially sponsored beauty competitions and many other attractions which do not scandalize anyone. I beg your pardon? Yes, of course, I will be brief. It's the stupidity and credulity of women, of so-called mothers that has resulted in this misunderstanding. These hags live like parasites, like cows, though this isn't quite right, for cows are not parasites, but there is something in that. They always have been carriers of evil. Uncleanly vessels, and that is why they are not allowed to be priests. Begging Madame Judge's pardon. First, as I have already said, let me repeat once more, I am the victim of little girls' intrigues. Because of these innocent angels I have often wept bitter tears. I used to live on the ground floor and these girls would peer at me through the window. During the evening as well. They would even throw sand at the windows. Glued to the window-pane they tapped and stuck their tongues out at me. I had to get undressed sometime. Yes, of course, I did pull the curtains. I would block it with newspapers. I even used my own jacket, although it didn't do the garment much good. I couldn't wall up that window, could I? And now I regret that I didn't wall up the window and the door. For ever and ever. Amen. I've lately even stopped looking through the window. For they would play their little games outside the window. We had an iron bar there for beating carpets and these girls would use it for their little tricks. When a grown-up happened to pass they would curtsey sweetly and produce picture smiles. But they would always find a moment when they could perform their tricks. Supposed to have been a gymnastic display. They would perform such lightning movements that only an experienced eye could see they had no panties on. They would hang on this bar, heads down, sticking their tongues out at me. So whenever I slammed the window I could hear terrible screams. Or they would squat on the ground with their skirts tucked up above their knees pretending to be drawing something in the sand. And again they would keep glancing at my window. This apparently is the way they bring them up nowadays. They shook their fists at me and poked their tongues out. And all because of that birdie I mentioned previously. This is libellous nonsense cooked up by parents and guardians. True, one could blame me for spanking one of these girls. Like a father. I didn't spare my hand. I do not deny responsibility for that. For that I don't. I can't remember how many times I did slap her, perhaps five, perhaps ten. I didn't count. And where was I to spank her, Your Honour, if not on the bottom. Children have always been smacked on the bottom and the world hasn't come to an end. Except that now we have scores of these educationalists and pedagogues. I have no idea whether she had her panties on or not. I simply felt like a father. What am I to swear on for the Court to believe me? On my honour? Upon my parents' ashes, the Redeemer? This is where the use of foreign terminology and opinion polls have led us. In the past when a child misbehaved, it was spanked and that was the end of it. Madame Judge is younger but I am sure she must remember those days. You misbehaved, you got a wallop on the behind, you kissed the punishing hand, and that was that. And surely they were as good as we are. Now we have these foreign words and opinion polls. Children are bored, the young ones are bored, while I by God's grace have passed my seventieth year and have never been bored. If they are bored and stand around with their hands in their pockets they should be given a broom or a shovel. Let them sweep the street. But no, they have more interesting occupations: they smash street lamps and wastepaper bins. And they all philosophize and use foreign words while the stock of commonsense diminishes all over the world. And our People's Republic too, although it is a socialist country, in this respect reminds one of the most advanced capitalist states. One could go on in this vein but who will listen to an

old man peering into his grave, who has had such a griev-
ous accusation flung at his head? Who will cast a stone at
me? How often do we get a child, even a small one, that
irritates its parents beyond endurance. How often would a
mother or a father tear its darling to pieces. While the
stranger has to endure it all. Yes, I often had ugly feelings
and thoughts in my heart: 'A plague on you'; 'I wish the
earth would swallow you up' — nothing extraordinary. Anybody in a tram, on a bus, in a shop, addresses evil thoughts
to his fellow human beings. If all these curses were granted
our mother earth would look like . . . how shall I say . . . one
can't even express it. Such a ten-year-old creature is not so
defenceless and weak as the Learned Counsel seems to
think. She tore my ear and bit my finger. And when I asked
the doctor to make an official inventory of the bodily injuries, I was treated like a man out of his mind. But I will seek
justice both in this and the next world. All my life I have
been laughed at for blushing. But I won't blush in the grave,
Madame Judge, I won't blush there! But now I blush for
society as a whole and for the administration of justice. I'm
sorry. But I will not take up the offer of the Learned Counsel who wants to show that I am of unsound mind. I'm
neither mentally ill nor a pervert. Surely the explanations I
have given here are sufficient proof. I, an old man will not
go to a lunatic asylum because some snivelling little girl has
dreamed up a common lie. Children lie as often as adults.
No, children lie a hundred times more often than adults
and their lies are so perfidious that only some complicated
machinery would be capable of uncovering them. But unfortunately we have no such machinery in our town. And I
demand that the girl be examined by an impartial lie-de-
tecting apparatus which I heard about on the radio. The
Learned Counsel, out of the goodness of his heart, thought
fit to speak here of senile infantilism and even that my brain
has softened up and as proof he mentioned that fact that I,
an old man, played like a child. But what was it I played at?
At theatre, my dolls acted in it. What did they act? Plays.
Either ones that I made up myself or things taken from
history. Yes, there was also one life-size. This was an old

mannequin. I bought it secondhand. I brought it home in a suitcase. First the arms and legs and then the body. I made two trips. I didn't wish to carry the whole thing in public. I wasn't concealing anything then and I am not concealing anything now. There is no reason for this, there is no need. That doll was partly made of fabric and stuffed, and partly of wax and some other material, but I don't remember. Her form was well-developed, although the figure as such was quite slim. I don't remember the measurements. I had it all written down in my diary. The waist, hips and bust and even thighs as well as the measurements of hands and feet. When shopping I would often forget and this would some-times lead to unpleasantness. But I got quite a lot of pleasure out of this because I could wander around shops with ladies' dresses and underwear. I often went shopping. I wasn't doing anybody any harm. Often enough everybody in the shop would get quite a lot of fun out of this and I too laughed. But I loved buying underwear best of all. Bras for instance. The variety you get nowadays in this item of female under-wear. I can't stop marvelling. The girls would jump for joy when I brought my lady panties, nighties and all those com-binations that I can't keep in my head. They would ask me for various details of my lady's build and I often had to glance in my diary. But I also had to describe her bust and her hips. These shopgirls are very polite and I can't say a word against them. They would often try these things on themselves. They would also ask me to sing my song:

What are little girls made of?
Sugar and spice
And all things nice
That's what little girls are made of.

One asked whether she could stroke my moustache and she did. Well, so what? A moustache. And the others gig-gled terribly, quite mad. But the atmosphere in the shop was very merry. When I would leave they would invite me to visit their shop again. One day just as I was closing the door behind me, one of them said: 'It's killing, what a funny old boy,' or something like that. I never set foot there again.

People in the prime of life and such tomboys imagine that an elderly person can be treated like a child. This is the great mistake that our world makes. Such slobs .... What is it ...? I beg your pardon. A chick like this thinks the whole world is funny and that only she with her girlish problems is serious. Days and nights these chicks twitter ... not chicks but parrots, twittering about some Jimmy or Frankie with a scooter. I blushed. Ashamed of those girls who had no respect for the old. At that time I read a lot and educated myself. At that time I read a work called 'Jagiello's Wives'. For I wished to provide some entertainment for the parties that came to look at the monument. Another work was a critical study called 'Suicide' by Dr Eugene Rehfisch, a German. I studied this work for many years. It was written in 1892 but even today one could go on quoting whole chapters. I know whole chapters by heart and even if someone were to wake me in the middle of the night I could oblige with examples and figures. If we wish to judge men we must take into account the motives of their actions. Had statistics been the source of our actions, I can assure the Court that our actions would have been more sensible. But the average citizen in our country never draws any conclusions of his own accord unless he burns his own fingers. Wretched are the creatures who have to burn themselves in order to draw the conclusion that fire burns. So from the statistics quoted there I attempted to draw the most far-reaching conclusions and consequences. Thus for example I compared the incidence of suicide in the German and the Austrian armies in the year 1887 to 1888. These figures gave me food for thought. Thus fear of punishment led to 507 suicides in the German army and 704 in the Austrian army. Suicides caused by worry, quarrels and provocation were respectively 192 and 279. There were 111 cases of suicide due to mental illness in the German army, while there were as many as 198 in the Austrian army. The situation was even worse as regards passion and other offences, for on the German side there were 84 people and on the Austrian as many as 178, and finally there were no suicides in the German army over debts while the Austrian army had 208, in the German army only 18 soldiers committed suicide because they were weary while there were as many as 162 on the Austrian side. Has anyone ever drawn any conclusions from these statistics compiled by Dr Eugene Rehfisch? No one has. And with what result? We all know from the history of the first world war. Had Emperor Franz Joseph read those statistics ... Madame Judge, my dear, please forgive an old man who could have been your father! I do not wish to obscure anything. On the contrary I wish to make a confession covering my entire life. And if I am not talking about my childhood and my schooldays that is only because I have written it all down in separate diaries which I have deposited in the hands of the Learned Counsel. Perhaps my diaries too will find a willing buyer and will become part of that treasury of human experiences to which everyone of us is obliged to add his widow's mite. In reading the work of Dr Rehfisch's I was struck that cases of suicide are much more frequent in the summer than in the winter. This representative of German thought speaks very beautifully about the influence of the seasons on man: 'Just as nature after a long winter sleep, warmed by sun's kisses, unfolds its buds in the spring and with its creative power calls everything to life again, so man too feels a greater creative urge in the spring than at any other time of the year. Apart from the fact that practically everyone has noticed this in his own case, Lombroso, in his famous work, *Genius and Madness*, has given us tangible proof of greater productivity in the summer than in winter. According to his researches it is an indisputable fact that the thought of discovering America and of inventing the galvanometer, the barometer and the telescope have all occurred in the spring. It was in the spring that Michaelangelo completed the design of his best work, and the same is true of Dante's *Divine Comedy* and Goethe's *Faust*.'

... the Court asks me what happened to that female mannequin? And how does the Learned Judge know that this mannequin was of the female sex? I have never said so. It is surely a fact known to mature people that these mannequins, like angels, have no sex and I must say that I am

rather amused by Counsel's knowing look directed towards
the Learned Judge. I had stopped playing with that mannequin although its lips had a dreamlike smile. The human
mind is active and constantly searches for new directions
and occupations. I laid my lady under the bed. How long
she lay there I do not remember. One night, which was
pitch-black and silent as only the nights of lonely old men
can be, I heard something like a squeal, like a baby's cry.
My bed and my clothes were expanding while I was growing smaller. Everything grew large except me. These are
the inevitable symptoms of ageing. The skin grows thin
and disappears, the amount of fat under the skin diminishes, hair roots disappear, the hair grows white and drops
out, teeth are loosened in the gums and fall out, while man
goes on living even longer. I could hear those squeals several nights running. I got up, it was autumn. I got up shivering
at dawn. An autumn dawn in my room is a bit like something of the next world. Like this and yet like the next. Still
in my underclothes and a jacket which I hurriedly put on I
began to move around the room. I lit the gas. I made some
tea and then I emptied the chamber pot. I recalled a clown
I used to play with as a boy. That clown always lay around
the bed or somewhere in the corner and was all broken.
His feet were somewhere above his head and everything
was always twisted. Then I heard those squeals again. I saw
a pair of lady's legs in gilded party slippers. The old feeling
came over me again. I pulled my friend into the light. She
was wearing a black lace combination which I had bought
her during our honeymoon. Her stomach was eaten away
and something of a dirty, pink colour was moving inside. I
bent down and the pink thing moved and squealed. A nest.
I felt sick. It was a nest. I get nauseated very easily. Practically all living organisms nauseate me to such an extent
that I couldn't eat a dish of kidneys. If I touch something
live, warm, covered in hair, that gives me such a shudder
that I get ill. I would never put my hand or finger inside any
opening, any hole. I've always been like that since childhood. It is the same if in bed during the night I would touch
a live cat or something that moved. That is why I bought

myself a bird. That canary which later became the cause of all this misfortune and misunderstanding of which I have fallen the victim. And a grey, grown-up animal had just scurried out of her. It was a nest of domestic mice. They were pink and only just covered in a film of hair. I then poured the boiling water from the kettle over the lot. Because just then the water for the tea had boiled. I do my own cooking. I was not to have a family nest. Providence did not allow that I should bring a woman under my roof, a life companion, the priestess of my hearth. And surely we all harbour an instinct which compels us to perpetuate our kind in this vale of tears, to put all our efforts into building a nest. When those chicks with wide open beaks squeal hungrily waiting for food, when father and mother bring tasty morsels to their darlings, we see a picture of happiness which has been denied to me. At moments like these I am not an old man in a worn-out coat but that blackbird who brings earth worms, caterpillars and flies into the nest from a nearby garden. And then my heart beats happily. And you, Madame Judge, you too have once been a child, a young girl who played with her little dolly.

What are little girls made of?
Sugar and spice
And all things nice
That's what little girls are made of.

When I look at Your Honour's distinguished figure my imagination paints a picture of a small girl with dimples, podgy little arms and sand covering her knees . . . all right, I will say no more.

September–November 1963

GONE OUT

CHARACTERS

HENRY

EVE

GIZELA

BENJAMIN

OLD MAN

YOUNG MAN

STRANGER

MALE AND FEMALE VOICES

DANCERS

FIRST LADY

SECOND LADY

SERGEANT

TWO AMBULANCE MEN

FAT MAN

ACT I

TABLEAU ONE

*A large room with a variety of clocks, all of which have stopped.
Each one shows a different time. In the corner there is a green
palm and a comfortable armchair. A newspaper is lying on the
floor and next to it a pair of well-worn slippers. A table and
chairs. EVE, her face buried in her hands, kneels in front of the
armchair. We can see the nape of her neck. Light lies still on
the taut white skin. On one of the shelves there is a figurine or
perhaps just a wooden block painted black. One of the clocks
starts and then stops again. EVE talks indistinctly, then sounds
turn into words, but we hear only some of the words and sentences.*

EVE:

lord I am not worthy
I am not
no

(A pause)

I will not touch thy robe
why do you hide
you are afraid lord
you run away
lord only say the word
and my soul shall be healed

(Pause)

I am yours my lord
an idiot
an old woman, my lord

*(EVE's back begins to shake with sobs, then she gets up, we see
her face; she is laughing, but we also notice signs of tears.)*

what am I saying
she wants the lord does she?
I am talking to the lord
to the wall
oh lord lord lord
but you are not there!
pity

(Now EVE *is speaking clearly.)*

I have made a vow that if he comes back
to me I shall never to the end of my life
I shall never to the end of my life
to the end of my life I shall fast
I shall
each Saturday I shall
maintain silence

if he returns
and if he does not return what shall
I eat — sweets?
I my lord, thy vessel
thine
why was Jairus' daughter worthy?

(Reflecting)

Jairus? What Jairus?

A CLEAR VOICE is heard on the radio: Attention please, there is a
special announcement. In the early hours of this morning
. . . he left home . . . and did not return . . . here is a description . . . height, face, eyes, nose . . . he was dressed . . . anyone
who can give any information about the missing person is
requested . . . .

(The announcement is followed by dance music, then silence.
EVE *gets up and walks about the room.)*

EVE: 'Eat something' . . . they say to me . . . .

MALE AND FEMALE VOICES *(heard from various sides)*:   Eat something,
eat something, eat something, eat something eat.

EVE:

> I can't eat
> I can't swallow anything

FEMALE VOICE:

> She really can't swallow
> anything

EVE:

> this house this furniture
> these odds and ends
> made sense
> only in connection with him
> it was he who
> filled this armchair
> these slippers
> me
> with himself

FEMALE VOICE:

> it was he who filled her with himself

EVE:

> it's not only I who wait for him
> my body does too
> I mean
> not only my soul
> but also these hands
> lips

> *(Pause)*

> What use is this hand if he is not touching it
> it is only a limb
> it is a tool for gripping carrying washing up
> what use is my face
> what use is it to you

> *(EVE turns to the audience and in the course of her monologue gradually comes forward.)*

> she is an old crumpled shell
> in the eyes

of this or that student this or that
booking clerk passerby rent collector
only for him
has my face an inner side
is young
to you my face means nothing
it is one of the million faces
in this city

MALE VOICE:

this old face means nothing to us
it is one of a million faces in this city
one of a hundred million
an average face
of an average woman
meaning nothing
or meaning little

EVE:

only he can take my face
see it once again
in a bus in a crowded train
with a drop of light on its cheek
That was in a cellar
during an air-raid
that was in the field beneath the clouds
in the forest
I was twenty
I was sixteen
I was thirty

(EVE shuts her eyes, listens . . . .)

MALE VOICE:

your face beneath the sky
with eyes shut
rain fell on it
and she lay smiling
asleep
a bird sang around her eyes and lips
it nested in the corner of her eye

leaves fell
about the rosy shell of her ear
the sea roared on the sands
and then your face
began to close
then turned away it fell
into the sand
then your head revealed
the other side
covered in hair without a mouth blind
I felt it under my palm
it grew
full of weeds pine scent dampness

in the cellar
buried under white lime-dust
pressed and torn apart
with holes for eyes
with a rat's face
giving birth to man
giving birth to humanity
a huge face
with huge tiny
lips
your evil face
giving birth
and then through all the lines
furrows
light began to flow towards me

(VOICE *fades.* EVE *stares at the white blind clock faces. Talks to herself as though she were remembering something with difficulty.)*

EVE:

today I swallowed time
these clocks tick in me
in my
in my throat
belly
in my underbelly

in my heart
in my stomach
they tick in me harder
louder
heavier
the clock hands enter
into me
pierce me

now these clocks tick
in the joints of my hands
they tremble in my knees
they tick in my thighs
they tick in my hair
they tick in me
in mine
they go deeper
it's not true I am talking about the weather
I am talking about him
it's not true I am talking about dresses
I am talking about him
it's not true I am talking about the weather
I am talking about his lips

FEMALE VOICES: (*variously pitched, repeat*)
it's not true she is talking about dinner
she is talking about him
it's not true she is talking about the weather
she is talking about him
talking about herself she talks about him

(*Pause*)

EVE:

I have nothing to talk about
when I do not talk about him

(*She walks over to the table, touches its surface with her fingers and examines them.*)

how dusty it is
how much dust is gathered here

I must kill this time
I must somehow kill this time

FEMALE VOICE:

she must somehow kill this time

EVE:

I will read

FEMALE VOICE:

she will read

EVE:

I will answer letters

FEMALE VOICE:

she will answer letters

EVE:

I will phone

FEMALE VOICE:

she will phone

EVE:

I will fill this time with something
I will find a way of filling this time

FEMALE VOICE:

she will fill this time with something

EVE:

I will be busy from morning till night
I will be a father to the children
I will sew on a button
I will dust
I will have a manicure

(She turns to the armchair. She sits 'enthroned' in it, quite still, her arms stretched along her body.)

I feel sand
running through my windpipe
the sand grates against my teeth
time seeps from
the upper half

of my body
through some vessel
into the lower half
and lower
still

(She speaks in a tired sleepy voice.)

now I feel like a queen
the queen of hearts
who has two heads four breasts
two upper halves
touching each other
but lacking that other half
the lower half
the part essential for
a mother the world the male
for the hive
I am a paper queen
I have a head here and there
alas
this is fatal for a simple
woman

(Lights slowly fade. They come on and fade again. In the darkness there is only one source of red blood-like light whose intensity fluctuates.)

TABLEAU TWO

A herd of 'suitors' bursts upon the stage. They dance a courting dance. Something like a ballet in which amateurs and understudies jostle alongside excellent dancers. They are both young and old. The young ones are in tights. They represent distinguished-looking civil servants, soldiers, athletes, and clerks, as well as petty provincial officials carrying briefcases and wearing light overcoats. The lights come on and off, on and off. The suitors carry flowers, ostrich feathers, strings of pearls and colourfully woven cloths. Sometimes they laugh, squeak, bellow, neigh like stallions, and grunt.

Two men in dinner jackets stand in the corner of the room. They offer cigarettes to each other and whisper in each other's ear. In the silence the light grows in intensity. The suitors are now gathered over something and are examining it, bending over it, sniffing. They are very quiet now, as though we were seeing them in a dream. Some of the dancers are dressed in skins of dogs and baboons. They wear dog and monkey masks, others wear glasses. The baboons have pink and violet bottoms. One of the suitors is picking lice in his fur. Two others bite each other in silence. One of them is licking another on the face. The light dims. In the darkness the eyes, teeth and the pink, moist, protruding tongues and the baboons' bottoms shine with greater intensity. We hear quickened, gutteral breathing. The light continues to dim. The suitors run off the stage in silence. The lights come on again. The last one to leave is a drooping figure in a light coat and carrying a large yellow leather briefcase. He blinks as though surprised, looks back, lifts his hat and leaves. EVE lies with arms outstretched in the middle of the room. She rises slowly. Sitting on the floor, she stretches herself, yawns and stretches her whole body once more.

TABLEAU THREE

> *Full daylight. Scene as in Tableau One. EVE is lying on the floor, her hair dishevelled. She wakes up, stretches herself, yawns, sits up and looks around.*

EVE: It's very stuffy in here. What's that pungent smell? Stinks like a stable, sperm and phosphorus. Hair everywhere, cigarette ends, socks, matches. I have such a heavy head. Such a weight of dreams. Never before have I carried such a burden.

(She gets up, looks at the white clock faces and goes over to the mirror in which her whole body is reflected.)

Oh God, I am bruised all over.

(Examines her reflection.)

my body

he shouldn't go out
he shouldn't leave me like that
he shouldn't leave my body alone
my corpse
these shackles
dig into my flesh
it struggles
I begged him don't go
he left me
he left my body
I shall wait for him
eternally young
but my body will grow old

(Two elegantly dressed LADIES enter the room. They sit at the table as though it were a table in a café. They look at EVE. EVE hasn't noticed them. They don't exist for her. One of them touches the table with her white-gloved hand and examines her dust-covered palm.)

EVE:

I shall wait for him

LADIES:

(*Together*) she will wait for him
(*Amused*) she will wait for him
(*Seriously*) will she wait for him?

EVE:

But my body
doesn't want to wait for him
it changes hour by hour
it moves away
it doesn't know the past
it doesn't remember itself young
this body stretched over me
worshipped derided
this body doesn't remember
it's only I who am remembering
what am I to do now
what am I to do with myself

FIRST LADY:

>what is she to do now?

SECOND LADY:

>what is she to do with herself?

>*(She lights a cigarette.)*

EVE:

>he would have found a way out
>something to do
>he would have filled my day
>put the books in order write that card
>sew on a button
>stuff a teddy bear
>water the flowers
>polish the silver
>bath the dog wash your hair
>have a look at Satre
>sew on a button? what is a button
>if there is no eternal life
>what do I care about a button
>if there is no salvation
>what good are buttons to me
>does the other world exist?

FIRST LADY:

>she wants to know whether the other world exists

SECOND LADY:

>the other world does not exist

>*(EVE goes to the palm and carefully wipes its leaves with a cloth.)*

EVE:

>no one will believe me
>that I am a mature woman
>that I sometimes think about about immortality
>and in the most unexpected places too
>in the shop for instance
>sitting at the table after lunch
>or in the kitchen

> can one think about the soul
> while one is seasoning the soup

LADIES:
> yes one can

EVE: (*touching the palm leaves*)
> don't laugh at me
> here I am a forty-year-old woman

FIRST LADY: (*to SECOND LADY*)
> she is forty-five

EVE:
> here I am a forty-year-old woman
> I wish to be saved after death
> perhaps I will be an angel
> Lord! will I rise from the dead?

FIRST LADY:
> naturally, like all of us

EVE:
> oh, Lord, my Lord, when the trumpet sounds
> will the gravestone lift
> and my young body
> emerge from the earth
> pure
> like a mountain crystal
> will my thighs rise from the dead
> will my breasts
> arise from the dead
> my lips the skin of my neck
> funny questions
> will my hair rise from the dead
> Lord I ask you
> funny questions funny and stupid questions

FIRST LADY:
> My Lord, she is asking you
> funny and stupid questions

SECOND LADY:
> will her dyed hair

rise from the dead

(The LADIES get up and leave the room.)

EVE: *(covering up the mirror)*
    if he doesn't come back in an hour
    if he doesn't come back at once
    I will tell the police
    perhaps he *(clutching her throat)*
    he had no cause
    surely he has not done himself
    any harm

(A slim seventeen-year-old GIRL enters the room with a light dance-like step.)

    ... he drank his coffee changed his pants
    changed his pants drank his coffee
    said nothing
    behaved normally
    surely a man who changes his socks and shaves
    has no intention of ... leaving this world ...
    unless he is English or a Lutheran
    ... how silly I am

(The GIRL kisses EVE on the cheek.)

GIZELA: Isn't Daddy back yet?

EVE: No.

GIZELA: Maybe something unexpected turned up.

EVE: I don't know. Quite frankly, I'm terrified ....

GIZELA: That something might have happened?

EVE: Father went out and disappeared.

GIZELA: What do you mean, disappeared?

EVE: I don't know ... he's simply not here.

GIZELA: *(embracing her mother)* Daddy always comes back.

EVE: You were the last one to speak to him.

GIZELA: In the morning ... I noticed nothing special. He kissed me and asked what time I would be back .... I saw he took a clean handkerchief .... Mother, surely a man would not think about a clean handkerchief who ... really, you have no reason to worry....

EVE: I don't know. I phoned the ambulance, the radio, the television, the office ....

GIZELA: We just have to wait ....

EVE: We can't wait .... This time I'll phone the police.

(*She phones and says something. Puts the receiver down. At that moment a police* SERGEANT *arrives and salutes.*)

SERGEANT: Is this the address where a citizen has been reported missing?

EVE: Yes, my husband .... Do sit down.

SERGEANT: Please describe the incident.

EVE: My husband ....

SERGEANT: Please relax.

EVE: He has disappeared without a trace.

SERGEANT: Please give a description of the missing person.

EVE: I'm so sorry.... I've simply lost my head ... everything's gone out of my head .... I can't remember ... perhaps my daughter ....

SERGEANT: That's unfortunate. (*Salutes and turns to* GIZELA.) Well, then, maybe you ... ?

GIZELA: Well, really, Daddy was quite nondescript, that is ... similar to ... what I wanted to say ... he wasn't like anything ... he was like everybody....

SERGEANT: Yes.

GIZELA: I don't know. I never looked at Father carefully. Daddy is fair-haired. Wears glasses.

EVE: What on earth are you saying. Father has blue eyes .... You know, Inspector, when people are together all the time they don't notice niceties of features so much.

SERGEANT: And what about special marks.

EVE: I haven't noticed anything special. It all rubs off after so many years.

GIZELA: It all rubs off, Mummy....

EVE: It's the second time in my life that I've had to describe him, you'll understand, Inspector.... (*Aside*) What is he like? The first time I described him in detail was twenty years ago. To my best friend ... now I have to describe him to you....

SERGEANT: (*sitting down*) We'll do all we possibly can.

EVE: Perhaps you'd like a cup of tea. I'll collect my thoughts.

SERGEANT: Sorry, I'm on duty.

GIZELA: Don't go yet. With you being here everything is less terrible.

SERGEANT: (*taking off his cap*) I'm sorry I keep coming back to the same thing, but I forgot to ask about a certain important detail concerning the missing person.

EVE: I won't hide anything from you....

SERGEANT: Something's just come to my head.

EVE: Doubtless you want to know what the relations between us were like lately.... Gizela, leave us alone....

GIZELA: Mummy, you're forgetting that I'm grown up.

SERGEANT: What I want to know is what type of frame did your husband's glasses have?

EVE: Gizela, please leave us.

(*GIZELA leaves, frowning.*)

SERGEANT: You will forgive me, madam, for asking about such a trifle.

EVE: I won't hide from you even the most intimate aspect of a mature woman's experience....

SERGEANT: God forbid.

EVE: I will not hide from you that our relationship . . . .

(Telephone rings. EVE picks up the receiver.)

Yes. No. Yes . . . he hasn't turned up . . . .

(Covers receiver with her hand.)

That's his mother . . . .

(Talking into the receiver again.)

No, I don't know what to do next . . . . Yes, I know you are
his mother . . . . No, you have no right to speak like that . . . .
I'm sorry . . . I wanted to ask about a trifling detail. Do you
remember what kind of frame Henry had? Of what? Of his
glasses . . . yes . . . he didn't wear glasses? I'll phone you . . .
we're waiting . . . .

(Replaces receiver. SERGEANT gets up.)

EVE: What was it I wanted to . . . .

SERGEANT: Please relax.

EVE: You've put a very important question to me.

SERGEANT: Oh, that's nothing, it's merely a formality.

EVE: I know, but I will do everything I can.

(There is a knock.)

GIZELA: May I come in?

SERGEANT: *(finding it difficult to make himself heard)* Because what
we are concerned with is when did the missing person leave
the house?

EVE: He shaved and drank his coffee, changed his socks . . . . *(Grabs
SERGEANT by the hand)* Surely a man who shaves in the morn-
ing with such care can't go out and do himself any harm?
You're experienced in these matters. Please tell me.

SERGEANT: I assure you, madam.

EVE: Well?

SERGEANT: We are concerned to know how many days the missing
person has been away from home.

EVE: What did you say?

SERGEANT: How many days is it since your husband left home?

EVE: Today.

SERGEANT: Please relax. We want to know when he left the house for the last time.

EVE: Today at 7.30. He changed his socks, drank his coffee.

SERGEANT: (*wiping forehead with handkerchief*) At what hour and on which day did your husband leave the house?

GIZELA: He took a clean handkerchief . . . .

EVE: Today in the morning.

SERGEANT: What do you mean 'today'?

EVE: Just like any day, excepting holidays and weekends.

SERGEANT: At what time does he normally come home from work?

EVE: At five.

SERGEANT: Never later?

EVE: On one or two occasions he got back at seven.

SERGEANT: (*looking at his watch*) It's now eight.

EVE: Eight.

SERGEANT: In other words, your husband is an hour late.

EVE: An hour?

SERGEANT: One hour.

EVE: I don't know; I've stopped counting the hours.

> (SERGEANT *puts on his cap, salutes, stands to attention, shrugs his shoulders, and leaves.*)

One hour.

GIZELA: There, you see, Mummy. (*Kisses her*) I'll take Cleopatra out for a walk. She must want to go.

> (*The bitch* CLEOPATRA *is heard squealing.* GIZELA *takes the lead and leaves. After she is gone all the clocks begin to go; then, one by one, they stop.*)

AN INTERLUDE

An open space on the outskirts of the town. Perhaps a cemetery, perhaps a refuse dump. Grave-diggers or maybe municipal garbage collectors. One old, one young. One fair, one dark. They are eating pineapples and bananas and drinking water from a bottle. Spades, pickaxes, boards, ropes, bones, tins and stuffed rats are lying around on the frozen earth.

OLD MAN: The earth is frozen two feet down.

YOUNG MAN: Maybe even three.

OLD MAN: You won't bite it without a wedge.

YOUNG MAN: If you can't bite it, you'll have to lick it. (*Laughs*)

(A middle-class MAN approaches along a little avenue, rubs his spectacles with a velvet cloth and looks at the little heap of earth and at the tiny burrow which the grave-diggers have dug up.)

STRANGER: What are you doing here, good people?

OLD MAN: Blowing into our hands.

STRANGER: This isn't much of a hole.

OLD MAN: Oh, if you push it in well . . . .

YOUNG MAN: (*with a broad laugh*) Then you can push in even the biggest one . . . .

STRANGER: It's no larger than a mouse hole.

OLD MAN: That's only a beginning . . . . This tiny hole will change into a big hole, into a pit . . . .

STRANGER: Has someone important died in your town?

OLD MAN: No, he hasn't died, only . . . .

YOUNG MAN: (*with a broad laugh*) . . . only he's been born again.

OLD MAN: He's had a resurrection. Almost come back from the dead . . . .

STRANGER: If he's just been born again, why are you digging him a grave?

OLD MAN: To keep warm, sir.

STRANGER: I know something about this business. You go on. (*Turning to* YOUNG MAN) You look the more stupid, there's honesty shining in your eyes.

YOUNG MAN: Chaff.

STRANGER: What's that about chaff? The old man's hiding something in the chaff?

YOUNG MAN: Gaff.

STRANGER: Eating bananas, eh? You are doing quite well.

OLD MAN: Here in the south, sir, bananas are as common as beans and cabbage.

STRANGER: Who is departing from this world? Is it a secret?

YOUNG MAN: And what's that to do with you?

OLD MAN: Where have you come from? Who are you?

STRANGER: From far away, from Paris. Have you heard of the place?

YOUNG MAN: Paris, kiss my ass. (*Silly laugh*)

STRANGER:
Who am I?
I who am
the something which I am not
and I am not that which I am

OLD MAN: See here, mate, nobody's departing, only arriving.

STRANGER: Arriving?

OLD MAN: Like the rosy-fingered dawn.

YOUNG MAN: You wouldn't like a bun, madam? (*With a silly laugh, he peels a banana.*)

OLD MAN: We're making trial drills ... looking for oil, sir.

STRANGER: Are you hoping to get oil out of this man's remains?

YOUNG MAN: (*sharply*) A toady lies here.

OLD MAN: (*nudging* YOUNG MAN *in the ribs and speaking quickly*) Yes, a daddy lies here. Shut up, you bastard. Did you speak, sir? Are you a daddy too, perhaps?

STRANGER: Did you say a toady lies here?

OLD MAN: A daddy.

STRANGER: A toady who was a daddy?

OLD MAN: You are wrong there, sir.

STRANGER: So here lies daddy who was a toady ... hell! If he is lying there, what are you looking for in that frozen earth? Let him rest in the Lord.

YOUNG MAN: ... and light eternal. But what lord? He was an atheist.

OLD MAN: An order's come from Caesar; we've got to dig, sir. We've got to help him. Otherwise he won't rise from the dead.

YOUNG MAN: We've got to search.

OLD MAN: There'll be a ceremony in memory of the deceased. There'll be an artistic performance, then a funeral. There's been a provocation in this ancient town. But this is an old tale ... grass grows on it now.

YOUNG MAN: Gaff.

STRANGER: What did you say, young man?

YOUNG MAN: Chaff.

OLD MAN: He was a noble gentleman, loved people, flowers, even loved human beings.

STRANGER: So you have an order to dig out daddy who was a toady.

OLD MAN:
What's in a name? That which we call a rose
By any other name would smell as sweet.

YOUNG MAN:
He was a good man, but bad men invented a false tale, forged the
dot over the 'i', rubbed out a comma,
and went on quoting
it in this form

> they dug a statement out of him
> from his chest
> breaking standing orders and bones
> he sang like a canary
> hanged himself with his own rope

STRANGER: So it was he who sang?

OLD MAN: When they played a tune on his teeth he not only sang, he danced as well.

YOUNG MAN: Now truth will out.

OLD MAN: And he, the poor stump of truth, will out of the earth.

YOUNG MAN: Truth will shine in the world.

STRANGER: Go on digging and look lively. You must get him out of this hole quickly. Let the rays of the sun light up the error.

OLD MAN: (*indulgently*) My dear friend . . . .

YOUNG MAN: You've got fiery blood, sir. Every inch a Frenchman. A real dandy.

OLD MAN: (*to YOUNG MAN*) Light a fire, the earth will warm up. My tongue will loosen up in the warm. The world will melt like frozen shit. The gentleman here doesn't know our customs.

STRANGER: The dark one is telling tall stories.

OLD MAN: Sit down and listen. Listen and sit down. (*He lights a pipe*) We're digging slowly because experience tells us not to hurry. Since morning we've had the messenger here twice running and giving us contradictory orders. We started work on this bed at midnight . . . . The hole was very tiny, a finger's depth, and then the messenger rushes up . . . . Go on, Antek, you tell him the rest, I'll take a nap.

YOUNG MAN: The envoy, sir, had steam billowing out of his mouth. 'Bury it, bury it quickly,' he says, 'so that the eyes won't see any trace.' But why, I ask. He gave me a terrible look. He whispered. He spit in my ear: 'Let this degenerate specimen get lost and rot. That dog, that crook, murderer, swine, and provocateur. The prosecutor has presented fresh evidence. They found forged documents today and a new truth flows out of them for us .... Bury it and stomp it down: there is nothing lying here.' So right away Bamba and I, we covered up the hole. That old dark one, his name is Bamba, even though he's been washed in baptismal waters. So we covered up the hole and stomped it down well. Uncle stuffed his pipe ... he's no uncle of mine, but I call him uncle because I'm an orphan, sir, and an orphan without an uncle in the world is like a tiny finger. So I call Bamba 'uncle'. 'Let's go,' says uncle, but again there's someone rushing towards us from over the gate, his tongue hanging out. 'Brothers,' he says, 'listen brothers, everything's changed, there is a mistake which we shall put right. We have to dig up the martyr's body, we have to commemorate this murderer.' And so he babbles, sometimes he says 'martyr' and sometimes he says 'murderer'. You could see he was so frightened his tongue got twisted, poor thing.

OLD MAN: He who dies of fright gets a farting funeral.

STRANGER: The only fear I know is the existential fear, when the essence is too weak and existence has no taste.

YOUNG MAN: 'There's been a mistake,' he says to me. 'We'll put up a statue. He was no nigger. Never touched a woman. Someone else raped grandma. He was a white man and so were his ancestors. But they talked him into it, so he turned dark all over. And black he lies in the earth, although he was wholly white. Now we'll give justice to the ashes and tomorrow a funeral for the bones. The family which had cut him off from its trunk like a rotten member is now adopting him as husband, son, brother and daddy.' But that's an old tale. He is rising from the dead.

OLD MAN:

I stood over the grave, my mouth open wide,
there was something and there was nothing inside;
but I see, sir, this wearies you and you balk
at the truth of ordinary, dim, simple folk.

I say to the messenger: 'Orders is orders, sir.' He went away, quickening his pace, while we got back to work digging up the bed. And you, where are you from?

YOUNG MAN: That's enough from you, Ancient. The gentleman from Paris has told you already that in his shadowy existence he's lost the taste of the essence. Now he walks about the world, begging for bread and, like every French atheist, he's winking at God.

OLD MAN: Godspeed, good sir! I'm going to dig other pits; the little angels are waiting their turn. You've got to shove the white little angels into the ground before they begin to stink. Such is the fate of flesh . . . .

(The OLD MAN walks away.)

YOUNG MAN: Uncle has hidden . . . .

STRANGER: Yes, tell me . . . . Here, here you are . . . . (*Takes some beads out of his pocket.*) Go on . . . .

YOUNG MAN: Uncle hasn't told you there is nothing in this grave.

STRANGER: What?

YOUNG MAN: We've dug right through the night and no go.

STRANGER: Nothing?

YOUNG MAN: Nothing. Seems nothing was buried here.

STRANGER: But they want to dig something out.

YOUNG MAN: That's the orders. When in Rome, do as the Romans do.

STRANGER: I don't understand what's going on here. It's like some cadaverous pantomime.

YOUNG MAN: You travel a lot but you don't see nothing. Yes, when it comes to it, sir, you are very stupid.

He spits into his hands and takes hold of a spade.

ACT II

TABLEAU FOUR

A ten-year-old boy with a satchel on his back enters the room.
He is pale and dishevelled but good-looking. Takes off his satchel
like a sack and throws it on the floor.

BENJAMIN: (*walking about the room and talking to himself*)
... childhood
the childhood years! he! he! he!
they talk so much about this happy childhood
about children, the only heavenly inhabitants of earth
who after death swell the host of little angels
well I am a child
and so what

adults waste my time
first they played with me as if I were a little monkey
threw me up in the air
till once I fell and got bruised

father used to tell me fairy tales
about dwarfs they kept beating me
on the paws
well take mum as an instance: what was talking to her like?

year in year out
from morning till night:
    wash your hands
    have you washed your hands
    your hands are grubby
    don't eat with your hands
    don't wave your hands like that
    take your hands out
sometimes I say to myself
well cut those hands off and that will be that
they never talk seriously to one

when I was little
they treated me like a little dog
they invented strange words and lisped
even now one has to wait months and months
for a sensible answer

all of them are always dissatisfied with one
one would like to know something
about politics metaphysics astronomy
all one hears is 'stop picking your nose'
you ask them about demographic policies
about population explosion
and instead of an answer they give you
chit chat about spinach
but these are things that concern me to the quick
go — they say — go and play
don't sit around with adults

there is no peace even in the toilet
the moment I get in there
rightaway somebody is calling what are you doing in there
so long
what were you doing in there
get out at once
wash your hands
remember you mustn't play with your ding dong
that's what the penis
is called in our family —
don't play with it you will become an imbecile
sometimes whole days pass
and you won't hear anything sensible
from the adults

(*Enter* EVE)

EVE: Ben, what are you doing under the table?

BENJAMIN: I'm not doing anything.

EVE: Don't be rude.

(BENJAMIN *comes out and stands politely by the table.*)

Look at your hands.

BENJAMIN: It's ink. I've been working.

EVE: Go and wash your hands.

BENJAMIN: Yes, mummy.

(He goes out with a grim expression.)

EVE: Poor children. Deprived of a father . . . .

*(A knock on the door. Louder. The door opens. Two AMBU-
LANCE MEN lead in HENRY with a bandaged head. The bandage
covers the whole face, giving the head the appearance of an
egg. EVE stretches out her hands as if she were at the same time
pushing the patient away and pulling him towards her. The
AMBULANCE MEN place him gently in the armchair. One of them
hands EVE a wire spectacle frame.)*

EVE: This . . . .

FIRST AMBULANCE MAN: It's the spectacle frame. Found where the
accident occurred.

EVE: This . . . .

SECOND AMBULANCE MAN: The husband. The documents all tally.
Please check.

EVE: Him?

FIRST AMBULANCE MAN: Please relax, the danger is over. During his
walk your husband stumbled or rather slipped on a banana
skin and fell. As he fell he hit the base of his skull against
the head of a statue. He has also suffered scratches on the
face. Apart from the injuries, the fall has resulted in a
shock . . . . The doctor . . . .

SECOND AMBULANCE MAN: The speech cells in the brain have not
been destroyed, merely blocked. The doctor on duty has
diagnosed that the shock will pass and that the patient will
recover his speech within forty-eight hours.

FIRST AMBULANCE MAN: The patient's memory is at the moment func-
tioning in response to stimuli. On his own he can't recollect
anything. Please leave the patient in peace. Don't tire him

and don't ask him any questions.

EVE: What I don't understand is where the bananas come from.

SECOND AMBULANCE MAN: Please relax.

EVE: I've never seen a banana skin lying about anywhere in the streets.

SECOND AMBULANCE MAN: Well, madam, you get some fool who eats a banana and throws the skin on the pavement.

EVE: Thank you, gentlemen, thank you from the bottom of my heart.

FIRST AMBULANCE MAN: Oh, it's nothing, madam. Will you please be kind enough to certify the delivery .... Yes, please sign just here.

EVE: Does he take any food?

SECOND AMBULANCE MAN: Only liquid. The patient will not be able to eat any meat, bread, or fruit for the next two or three days. At the moment he is not able to think logically.

FIRST AMBULANCE MAN: It will all pass after a good sleep.

(EVE kneels in front of the armchair and touches the sleeper's hand with the tips of her fingers. The AMBULANCE MEN look at each other, smile with understanding and sympathy. They leave.)

TABLEAU FIVE

HENRY is sitting in the armchair which has been placed next to the palm. He has his slippers on his feet. The bandage has been partly removed so that one can see his eyes and lips. EVE comes into the room with a small red watering can and waters the palm. She turns to her husband. A serious tone is maintained throughout the scene.

EVE: Are you going to the meeting tomorrow?

(She is watering the palm. She takes no notice of the patient's silence and continues to question him in a lively tone.)

The doctor said you could go back to work tomorrow. Why don't you say something?

(She comes close to the patient and looks into his face.)

Do you hear me, Henry?

HENRY: I do.

EVE: So why don't you answer my questions?

HENRY: *(as though he were trying to recollect something and this is causing him difficulty. At last he says with relief)* Why are you calling me Henry?

EVE: What should I call you?

HENRY: I beg your pardon?

(EVE puts away the watering can, sits opposite HENRY and takes him by the hand.)

EVE: Henry, tell me what's your name? *(HENRY does not reply.)* How old are you? *(HENRY does not reply.)* What's your profession? *(HENRY does not reply.)* What's your religion? *(HENRY does not reply.)* How much do you weigh? *(HENRY does not reply.)* Are you married?

HENRY: What does 'married' mean?

EVE: Oh God!

HENRY: I beg your pardon?

EVE: *(terrified)* God .... 'I beg your pardon'? I didn't really mean ....

HENRY: What does 'God, God' mean?

EVE: I'll explain that later, Henry. But now try to remember in what country you are living in, and in what town.

(HENRY moves his head in a negating gesture.)

Do you know what you're doing here under this palm?

HENRY: I'm conversing with you.

EVE: Have you got any children?

HENRY: Children?

EVE: Yes children. Have you got a son, a daughter? (*HENRY does not reply.*) Gizela!

(*GIZELA runs into the room. She jumps on her father's knee and embraces him.*)

GIZELA: Daddy, Daddy!

HENRY: (*embarrassed*) What does 'Daddy' mean?

GIZELA: Mummy, what is he saying?

HENRY: What does 'Mummy' mean?

EVE: (*controlling herself, speaks in a matter-of-fact voice*) I am Mummy, you are Daddy, and this is our child, our daughter.

HENRY: I am delighted to meet you.

GIZELA: How funny you two talk.

(*She gets off her father's knees.*)

EVE: Daddy has forgotten that we all form a family.

(*HENRY gets up and moves to the door.*)

EVE: And where are you going?

HENRY: I? I am leaving.

EVE: You can't go now, you have to sit and listen to what your wife tells you.

HENRY: (*politely*) Yes, madam.

(*He sits in the armchair.*)

EVE: So you don't remember my name?

HENRY: No.

EVE: Why then, simply call me 'darling'.

HENRY: 'Darling'.

EVE: So there you are, darling!

HENRY: So there you are, darling!

GIZELA: (*almost in tears*) What does it all mean? Why are you tormenting me in this way?

HENRY: I am hungry.

EVE: Hungry? What would you like?

HENRY: A carrot . . . no, wait a minute . . . ham, I think . . . .

EVE: Gizela, go to the garden and bring father a carrot or two.

(GIZELA leaves.)

And what do you intend to do now?

HENRY: *(looks at her, smiling)* What am I to do? I don't know.

EVE: Have a little sleep, that will do you good.

(HENRY looks at her with a smile.)

You poor thing! *(She pats him on the head.)* You miserable little thing.

(She goes out.)

HENRY: *(writes something on the floor with his finger and talks to himself.)*
happy
unhappy
happy unhappy

(He thinks for a moment.)
I am happy
happy *(crying out)* happy!

EVE: *(rushing into the room)* Did you call me?

HENRY: I am *(in a singing tone)* happy, happy, happy!

EVE: *(with determination)*
You're wrong!
you must have forgotten
what I told you yesterday night
surely I have explained
why you are so very unhappy

HENRY: *(stubbornly)* I am happy.

EVE: Have you forgotten who you are?

HENRY: No.

EVE: Then listen, my poor wretch.

(HENRY regards his wife with a smile; EVE takes him by the hand.)

You were an unwanted child. Your father already had six sons and pined for a daughter. Long before you were born he chose Elizabeth as your name. When your mother found out in her seventh month that it was going to be another son, she was so frightened that she lost her speech. You were born prematurely. It was only thanks to the doctors that your life was saved. During the first few years your mother dressed you like a girl and called you Lizzie. Your father worked so hard he didn't even notice. Anyway, your father's case wasn't very clear either. As a matter of fact, he was found during stock-taking in a supermarket. Someone left him behind in a shopping basket. Unfortunately, his origins were never settled. Blood tests revealed gypsy blood mixed with pure alcohol of unknown provenance. At that time they started building hotels and restaurants designed solely for Mohammedans and vegetarians. Your father lived hapily with that psychological hump on his back. One day, however, he entered a bar where he was attacked by a certain white man with a bottle of dark ale. Struck on the head, he ran out of the bar and never regained his senses.

(HENRY smiles and nods.)

I won't describe to you how unhappy you were at school. You will hear all that from your school friend whom I have just cabled to come. I wish to tell you about some very intimate things . . . .

(Enter GIZELA who places a basket with carrots next to the armchair and gazes affectionately at her father.)

You were a very timid, shy, and clean boy. You passed your childhood amid old calendars and newspapers. One day, when you were a five-year-old little monkey, you were playing with matches. You knew that children who play with matches wet their beds at night — you lived under a constant threat of that catastrophe — but you played on until one night it happened. You woke up and you felt cold and

190 Reading the Apocalypse in Bed

damp below. Then quite independently of Kierkegaard whom you did not then know, you became acquainted with fear and trembling. You stood naked in the face of IT and several years before the contemporary French philosopher you distinguished essence from existence. That was a moment of illumination which recurred in your life only once . . . .

(HENRY reaches into the basket for a carrot and begins to nibble it, not like a human being, but like a rabbit, a hare, or a mouse.)

That moment of the deepest experience recurred fifty years later in Debrecen, where you found yourself on an 'Orbis' holiday tour. Again you felt clearly and terrifyingly, as you had when you were a little boy, the separation of essence from existence. Years later you had the opportunity to talk about this privately with the French philosopher, whose wife was so impressed . . . . Do you remember?

HENRY: *(nibbling the carrot, mumbles)* I don't remember.

EVE: All right, then. Let's reach deeper.

GIZELA: Mummy, stop. Look, he really is happy.

EVE: You are too young to understand.

GIZELA: But he is . . . .

EVE: He is not happy. And if he is, we must immediately make him aware of the tragic situation in which he finds himself. Don't you see that he can't be happy? He is an adult, not an oaf or a poet. After all, he has to prepare a lecture for tomorrow, and his career depends on it. Everything depends on that lecture, our whole future . . . . Don't you understand that? We must make him arrive at a point where he's capable of knowing the correct chain of events . . . .

(HENRY has stopped nibbling the carrot and listens, his head tilted slightly. There is a mischievous flicker in his eyes and something like understanding.)

. . . and to achieve this he must move from sensible to abstract general knowledge. What's the use if he acknowledges

me as his wife, if he doesn't appreciate what the consequences are? We must clarify for him the laws and
obligations which arise out of the relationship of husband
towards wife. The obligations of a father. . . . (*She takes away*
HENRY's *carrot and throws it into the basket.*) So you see, my
poor wretch . . . .

GIZELA: He isn't a poor wretch at all. It's a long time since he's had
such a happy expression . . . . At last he is free, really smiling. He's no wretch, mummy.

EVE: But he will be. Can't you see that he must become what he
was in order to be what he is? Don't you understand that if
he won't be what he was then he will be what he was not?
He will simply be nothing. And this I will not allow!

can't you see Gizela
that he wants to leave home before lunch
he comes and goes
but he doesn't know why
I will bring him down to earth
I will take him by the hand like a child
like a little doggie
I shall bring him to the place where he used to be where he
raised his family
where he lived where he's done his dirty work
where he did beautiful and ugly things
— in the last resort it's all the same —
I will bring him to this little nook
and he will have to sniff it
and when he sniffs it he will remember
and understand . . . .

But all of you must help him. We have only forty-eight
hours, Gizela. Where personal, intimate matters are concerned — the whole work of the body, love, and the kitchen
— I will reconstruct him from his foundations. But I have no
head for politics. You are younger, Gizela, you do politics at
school; you must take care of that side. I must go and prepare lunch. Yes, child, everything must be as usual. No
changes. At home nothing has changed . . . do you under-

stand? Now go and remind him about all those sociologico-
political problems. About political systems, about the road
to socialism, to capitalism, to feudalism. In other words, make
him conscious of the world he lives in. Remember that for
the time being father's memory functions in response to
stimuli. And don't forget either that you are his daughter.
You may of course now and again throw in a few words on
the relationship between daughter and father, what a father means to his daughter, what a daughter means to her
mother.

*(EVE intends to leave the room, but stops in the door, thinking,
then returns.)*

Gizela . . . .

GIZELA: Yes, Mummy?

EVE: I'll strike the iron while it's hot. Lunch can wait.

HENRY: *(nibbling his carrot)* I am very, very content.

EVE: Gizela, leave us now.

GIZELA: *(looking beseechingly at her mother)* Please don't do him
any harm!

(She strokes her father on the head and leaves.)

EVE: *(walking slowly about the room. HENRY has now finished his carrot and follows her with his eyes.)* Well, whatever you may
say, you've no right to forget that you suffered, that you
were very unhappy at school, in the army, during your holidays. Even your name was awful. Hoopoe, or something
like that. Stinks like a hoopoe. Those birds apparently smell
pretty badly. You've changed your name. You call yourself
Lavender. But people always smell out everything. Let's
stop all this nonsense, Mr Hoopoe.

(She stops in front of her husband.)

Look at me carefully. Does anything strike you?

HENRY: No.

*(EVE leans over him and whispers in his ear. She breaks off,
examines his face, and again leans over to whisper something.)*

EVE: And now?

(HENRY shrugs his shoulders.)

I was young, gay . . . . When you met me in the dentist's waiting room I was a vain happy young thing in love with life, and now I am almost old and almost an unhappy woman. That's what's left of me after twenty years. No, this is madness! *(Aside)* No, I can't tell him what my body was like twenty years ago.

(She goes over to a built-in cupboard and opens it. Old and new suits hang on hangers. She pulls out a black worn-out dress suit.)

Do you remember this?

(HENRY examines the old suit. EVE takes the trousers in her hands.)

Look at these pants. They are like a topographical map. How many years have you passed in them with me by your side? How many good and bad moments, how many disappointments and exultations? How many government crises in France! Don't you remember a terrible scene of jealousy in these trousers on Lake Balaton? Take them in your hand. Sometimes an inaminate object says more than a host of choirs. There are tears in the heart of things . . . .

(HENRY takes the trousers in his hands.)

You gaze at these pants as if they were an exotic plant or the flag of a toy kingdom. And yet you've passed your manhood in them. You've left a particle of your soul in them. They were with you step by step at receptions, weddings, funerals. One mustn't despise one's clothes . . . . They are a part of our organism and our personality. We are born naked. They are our wrappings and we are the stuffings. Birds, cats, and rabbits don't wear clothes. They grow out of their organisms, out of their chemical substances. We too grow hairs, but how many hairs do we have? One can't call them a covering.

(During this passionate speech the husband carefully examines the old trousers. He looks at them against the light which shines through the worn-out seat.)

Remember those concerts, conferences, banquets, break-downs, crises, jubilees, anniversaries, blunders, excesses of power, fiascoes, inflations, dinners . . . . Give me those pants. (*She takes the trousers from him.*) I remember when you came from a funeral reception . . . . What am I saying, you came from a party at the embassy. It was just before midnight. 'What a pity about that sauce,' you said to me in bed after midnight. I got up. Your trousers were stained at the knee with something greasy and you were quite drunk . . . .

(HENRY takes the trousers from her and holds them like a seer who has been given an object belonging to a missing person. He remembers something with effort. The broken sentences and words which he utters seem to flow from a very far distance, from a deep well of memory.)

HENRY:
Colbert sauce
Genoese fish sauce
Calves' brain sauce . . . .

(EVE is watching his face intently and prompts him.)

EVE: 'Soubise' sauce, very thick, goes with lamb cutlets or arti-chokes . . . . Bechamel sauce? This sauce must be quite thick so that it doesn't pour but has to be laid on with a spoon. Goes with fish or cauliflower during Lent. You dilute it not with chicken broth but with milk or fresh cream . . . .

(HENRY makes a despairing gesture.)

Sauce Madeira? Sauce hollandaise? Say it, say it . . . . A sauce to go with tongue?

HENRY: A grey sauce?

EVE: Yes, of course, grey . . . . You do remember?

HENRY: *(repeats)* A sauce to go with tongue . . . grey . . . no.

EVE: White truffle sauce . . . .

HENRY: To go with boiled beef?

EVE: Oh God!

HENRY: What did you say?

EVE: Later, later I will explain everything. Also this bit about the Creator. For the moment let's stick to the sauce. We mustn't let go of this sauce.... We'll use the sauce as a stimulus.... You were at the embassy then.

HENRY: Knockwurst in mustard sauce *à la* Sierzputowski?

EVE: White caper sauce.

HENRY: Caper sauce?

EVE: But of course!

HENRY: What?

EVE: Melt butter and stir in flour, taking care not to burn. Blend well with stock. Chop and add capers, lemon juice, and rind, and season to taste. Let simmer for ten minutes ... make sure the sauce is thick enough....

(HENRY presses the trousers against his chest. A VOICE comes from over the loudspeaker.)

VOICE:
Der Ausserordentliche und Bevollmächtigte
Botschafter.... A l'occasion de l'Anniversaire
de Sa Majeste le Roi ... de ... de ... de ....
Le Ministre de la Republique Bim Bom et
Madame ... Zefirina prient Monsieur
Henry
Henry!
Henry!! Hoopoe ....
de leur fair l'honneur de venir a la reception ....

BALLET SCENE

Lights fade, come on, and fade again. In the half-light, as in a waking dream, the stage begins to fill with guests in formal dress. Dinner jackets, uniforms, ribbons, stars, gowns, tiaras, smiles, and bows .... Light grows and with it the clamour of voices. There are both white and coloured guests. Diplomatic moves, cutting ripostes, puns, succinct analyses of the international situation, aphorisms, earrings, busts, backs, bald heads . . . . We hear snatches of sentences.

. . . pas semblable . . . votre metier est infernal . . . poetry is the feast of the intellect, man is a thinking reed, Fourierism, she sells sea shells, will you have a banana, madam, e sempre bene, e pur si muove, entre nous soit dit . . . eat thou honey, because it is good . . . I went by the fields of the slothful and by the vineyard of the man void of understanding . . . use your life while you can, my pussy-cat, are you keeping it for the children . . . ?

The stream of words flows and glistens amid the lights, the bodies of men and women move with unusual grace, their movements are light and well-timed.

These insubstantial, exquisite conversations are accompanied by music on the harp and cor anglais with its soft melancholy sound (being a fifth lower than that of an ordinary oboe) . . . words, lights, and music fade . . . .

When the lights come on again, there are now sumptuously decked tables set against the walls; the buffet shines and glitters with silver, it is opalescent with wines, vodkas and liqueurs . . . snow-white table-cloths . . . in a word, the author's (limited) language is not only incapable of describing, but doesn't even dare to sample, this culinary orgy . . . . Let the producer unleash his imagination.

The great door is closed. Sound of horns in the silence. ('Horn' comes from 'Waldhorn', i.e., a forest horn. A brass instrument developed out of a bison's horn, first employed as a sacred instrument — cf. the 'shofar' used in synagogues — and to play the 'hallali' closing a successful hunt. Brass horns were also used by stage coachmen.)

A force like an unseen battering ram strikes the closed doors: once, twice, three times. The doors creak and eventually burst open under the pressure of this elemental power and the stage fills with guests in formal dress. This scene takes place in glaring light. Not a word is spoken. The same people who a moment ago moved with exquisite grace, who respected the autonomy of their own and others' bodies, who weighed every gesture and every word, now mob the buffet. The horns sound. The first line of guests falls and is followed by succeeding waves treading over the sprawling bodies. The scene is like a whirlwind — or panic in a burning theatre. If I were to say that this scene is reminiscent of Michelangelo's 'Last Judgment' in the Sistine Chapel, that would be a gross exaggeration. In the first place, Michelangelo did not include a buffet and did not dress his people in official uniforms (even the most perceptive spectator will not spot there a sauce dish or crystal champagne glasses among the twisted bodies). But, above all, in such a crowd one cannot distinguish the sinners from the saints, the damned from the saved. Such folk beliefs are here almost completely obliterated. As not everyone has had the chance to see Michelangelo's work, I will compare the storming of the buffet to Matejko's painting of 'The Battle of Grunwald'. In the general melee there is an occasional flash of a knife, a hand or a fork . . . . And yet the participants aren't starving. The psychology of crowds. (My picture is not a condemnation either of the capitalist system or of petit bourgeois morality!) But let's return to the stage and to factual details. What role (in all this) is played by the sauces? In what sauce is everything happening? The stage reveals the imagination of the author who comes from (an exceptionally insignificant) white-collar family! Caviar, salmon, tongue in Malaga . . . 'peacocks and bananas upon the king's table . . . .'

Meanwhile, they are swarming over the buffet like ants. In the silence one hears lips smacking, hissing, scraping and the crunching of bones. They are fighting — an eye for an eye and a tooth for a tooth . . . . A distinguished looking elderly gentleman loses his false teeth in a sauce dish (this isn't funny). The scene changes into a ballet. The huddled crowd covering the buffet now moves like the rump of a piebald butterfly larva. Synchronized movements of rump and feet. And the ladies' gowns, their hairdos, breasts . . . in what sauces and caviars are they dipped? From this crowd, this jumbled pulsating pile, our 'hero' HENRY (nee Hoopoe) crawls away to the side in a crumpled dinner jacket. He stands against the wall and wipes the sweat off his brow with his hand and clears his ear of (red) caviar. His trousers are stained with a thick white sauce. It is white caper sauce.

Lights fade and the gentle, melancholy, soft music of cor anglais and harp is heard again. From the infernal swarm (amid complete

silence) comes a thunderous voice. 'Man is a thinking reed' (etc, etc.)
The producer may throw in a handful of aphorisms, witticisms and
diplomatic (?) expressions — the author hasn't got anything at hand
at the moment.

TABLEAU SIX

> EVE *is walking about the room. It is mid-day.*

EVE:

> stimuli
> our only hope is stimuli
> we have to stimulate him
> with these stimuli
> unceasingly
> like a bull with its horn
> stimulate Henry
> until struck
> he will come to his senses
> to me
> to the family
> which despite the crisis
> is the basic cell in society
> I will not allow the disintegration of this cell
> is the family today exposed to greater dangers
>   than in the days of our parents and grandparents
> yes there are more pussies gnawing at the roots of
>   this cell
> now it is pussies in the past it used to be grisettes
>   cocottes trash
> no my kitten
> this isn't wedding-time
> your wedding's behind you
> now you have responsibilities
> in this cell
> which you have yourself called to life
> so far they haven't invented a better form
> Henry! Henry!

(Echo repeats 'Henry! Henry!' . . . HENRY comes in and stares at his wife with surprise.)

EVE: My dear! A certain fund of general information will allow you to return to active life. Just like a few days ago, you are again a full member of society. These momentary and regrettable disturbances are passing, and in accordance with the diagnosis you will be able to return tomorrow to your lecture and go on that business trip with your delegation. I am sure no one will notice any changes or relapses. But man is not only homo sapiens . . . homo faber, homo eruditus, homo politicus, esteticus or ludens . . . . My dear Henry, stop picking your nose, the nose is not meant to be played with. Adults should pick with the corner of a handkerchief or a piece of absorbent cotton. Man is a being of spirit and body. He is, one might say, homo sexualis . . . no, that sounds clumsy, let's say homo . . . homo . . . well, you see, Henry, the human body is something like a temple of divinity and is not indifferent to what is done with it or in it. Hymen places certain mutual responsibilities on the husband and the wife . . . . Do please stop playing with your ear. However, let's move on to generalizations, to knowledge derived from the senses. Let's begin with parts of the body. If you will not recollect what you are made of, you will not know what use to make of these parts. We must learn, my dearest, to find our way through the formation of the human body and its specific parts using observation and touch, remembering at the same time that these are, apart from measuring it, the two chief methods of examining the anatomy of a live human being.

HENRY: *(suddenly in revolt)* I do object to this! Please don't remind me of anything. I want to have a free flight! Why do you torture me with what Mrs X said about me in 1938? Or that stupid story about razor-blades. I have shed the old skin, I am white and pure. I want to fly high and far . . . .

EVE: Relax, darling . . . .

HENRY: But darling, here is an opportunity for me to forget and start again from the beginning.

EVE: The beginning is an illusion — there is only an end.

HENRY: What I have heard from all of you about myself is neither interesting nor attractive. This isn't even a biography. This is some hoary old joke brought to life again. When I talk about the beginning I mean that I can now relive my life once more from the beginning.

EVE: You can, but with us. With me, with the children, with Mummy . . . .

HENRY: (*roused*) Me?!

EVE: You won't be able to go to the office if you are in such a state.

HENRY: All superstitions come from the bowels. The thing is to be sedentary for as little time as possible and not to believe in any thought which wasn't born in the fresh air or during spontaneous movement . . . .

EVE: And what are these theories, may I ask?

HENRY: The patience of the hams — I have already said it once — is the true sin against the Holy Ghost.

EVE: Sitzfleisch was always your Achilles' heel, but that is no reason to despair. Please sit down. All these theories may be all right for geniuses but we must look after our petty affairs. So let's start with parts of the body. Please stand facing me and repeat every word after me.

(*HENRY obediently stands facing his wife. GIZELA enters smiling.*)

GIZELA: May I come in?

HENRY: Good morning, pretty miss.

GIZELA: (*laughs*) Have you made any progress, Daddy?

EVE: He has realized that his place is in the cell, that is, in the family which is the cell; that he can fly high but must take his whole family with him.

GIZELA: You are over tired.

EVE: (*claps her hands*) Henry! Let's begin.

(*HENRY claps his hands.*)

EVE: I will mention the names of the various parts of the body and you will repeat. Each time I mention a part, I will touch with my hand the appropriate part of my body or your body and you will do the same. Of course, we can do it the other way round. That makes no difference. The head — caput.

HENRY: The head — caput.

(EVE takes HENRY's head in her hands.)

EVE:

This is a head.

(She rubs her forehead as if she were remembering something, then recites a fragment of the poem 'Glimpses' from Rozewicz's Forms.*)*

This is the head of the family the head of the world
so long has this head been the right hand the left leg
this poor head was
this head was a stool a shell a seat
a box a pulpit an amoeba a tribune a catalogue
a wardrobe a waiting room a magazine
this head has been filled stuffed loaded choked
with the categorical imperative imitation imperialism
import rapport
impotence inscription insurrection intention
idiom . . . .

GIZELA: *(shaken)* Mummy! You are delirious.

EVE:

My head my husband's head
seen for the first time
in a dentist's waiting room
or maybe it stood in a line
for whipped cream in the ice-cream shop
let's return to the stimuli!

(She touches in turn the various parts of her body.)

Neck — collum.

HENRY: Neck — collum.

EVE: Trunk.

HENRY: Trunk.

EVE: Limbs — membra.

HENRY: Limbs — membra.

EVE: Gizela, please leave us alone for a moment.

(GIZELA *goes out.*)

Belly.

HENRY: Belly.

EVE: Navel.

HENRY: Navel.

EVE: Loins.

HENRY: Loins.

GIZELA'S VOICE: May I come back now?

EVE: Not yet. Pelvis.

HENRY: Pelvis.

EVE: Mons veneris.

HENRY: Mons veneris.

EVE: Flanks.

HENRY: Flanks.

GIZELA'S VOICE: May I come in now?

EVE: Yes, but don't interrupt us .... The upper extremities.

HENRY: Upper extremities.

EVE: Arm elbow forearm thumb digitus minimus.

HENRY: Arm flanks mons veneris hand thumb digitus maximus.

EVE: Once again. Arm elbow forearm hand thumb digitus minimus.

HENRY: Arm elbow forearm hand thumb digitus minimus.

EVE: Gizela, leave us for a minute.

(GIZELA *goes out.*)

Chest. Bosom pectus.

HENRY: Chest. Bosom pectus.

(He touches his wife's breasts.)

EVE: *(her voice changed)* Breast — mamma.

HENRY: Breast — mamma.

EVE: Nipple — papilla mammae.

HENRY: Nipple — papilla mammae.

GIZELA'S VOICE: May I come in?

EVE: Come in. *(Her voice now under control.)* The lower extremities.

HENRY: The lower extremities.

EVE: Thigh — femur.

HENRY: Thigh — femur.

EVE: Knee.

HENRY: Knee.

GIZELA: Will I have to go out now?

EVE: *(thinking it over)* No, stay. The back of the knee.

HENRY: The back of the knee.

EVE: Shin calf ankle.

HENRY: *(quickly)* Shin calf ankle.

EVE: *(quicker)* Face eye nose tip of the nose.

HENRY: *(quickly)* Face eye nose tip of the nose.

EVE: *(quickly)* Mouth upper lip corner of the mouth tongue.

(She sticks her tongue out.)

HENRY: Mouth upper lip corner of the mouth tongue.

(He sticks his tongue out.)

EVE: Teeth — dentes.

HENRY: You have forgotten the lower lip.

EVE: So, after all . . . ! Henry . . . ! Gizela, we've won! Unaided, Daddy has remembered his own lower lip! In time he will remember everything. The lot! Gizela, leave us for a minute.

(GIZELA *kisses her mother and father and goes out.*)

EVE: And now, darling, let's pass on to the parts of speech . . . .

HENRY: Is that strictly necessary for an adult?

EVE: Most certainly, darling. He who lives must talk, he who talks must know what use he is to make of the various parts of speech. First, we shall talk about the grammatical peculiarities of the feminine gender.

TABLEAU SEVEN

HENRY is walking about the room. He is wearing a black jacket, pyjama trousers and a pair of shabby old slippers. He is holding some notes in his hand. He stops in front of the mirror, adjusts his tie, smooths his hair, and begins to talk to the mirror. . . . He is talking fluently, quickly and clearly, now and again consulting his notes. Here and there his face is covered with plasters.

HENRY: Our Single-Family Homes Building Society is next year planning to build houses out of straw bricks and coffee dregs with a living area of three square feet. Experience of past years has shown that the development from monogamous families to polygamy is not only a general occurrence, but that it is also socially harmful. And in this connection our technicians and moralists have reached the conclusion that smaller dwellings will serve better the cause of tightening the knots between the several members of the family. Under such conditions there will also be no place for jealousy which arose in feudal times. The shape of the cross-section of the joint will prevent the hardened mortar from falling outside. Our Society has called upon experts to examine the durability of the straw bricks which might be employed to construct the cell called 'family' . . . the hand press of engineer Boboli has fairly wide application in the moulding of family bricks . . . in order that the family should preserve the shape it has received during the pressing, the members of the family should be tied together with paper, string or wire. We shall also find instructions in the Book of Genesis. The well-known idealist philosopher Bertrand Russell has declared that the nuclear arms stored throughout the world (HENRY *laughs*) have already achieved an explosive power equal to hundreds of millions of tons of TNT. In order to use up this arsenal, it would be necessary during the next 146 years to cause daily explosions of nuclear power equal in explosive power to all the bombs and missiles used during the Second World War . . . .

Due to this potential danger, although I can assure you that there will never again be a war, nevertheless, in connection with this possibility of explosion of stored-up material, our Society is employing straw bricks in the construction of ceilings. Such a new ceiling used by us, that is a 'naked' ceiling, will successfully withstand tremendous atmospheric pressures. A specialist abroad has said that the source of jealousy lies in the urge to monopolize feelings, to desire to have exclusive possession of the beloved person. This feeling originated during the formation of class-society and the transitions from polygamy to monogamy which is seen as an archetypal cell of private property . . . but as soon as this feeling arose it became subordinated to that logic of the evolution of feelings which was born under the system of private property. In other words, man treated woman as if she were his chattel, not allowing anyone other than himself to possess her . . . .

The abolition of private ownership of the means of production has lifted marriage out of its sordid condition. Practice proves that families with many children are — in the majority of cases — happy families cementing the love of husband and wife, a love which grows from year to year . . . .

(He stops and tears a plaster off his face. GIZELA and BENJAMIN enter on tiptoe and sit quietly near the armchair. GIZELA is holding a book and BENJAMIN a cage with white mice.)

Cement is bluish-green in colour or dark grey with a bluish tint or white with a greenish tint. In principle the colour of the cement has no influence on quality, only the binding power of the cement influences the durability of the concrete. In its dry condition cement behaves neutrally. However, after a time cement loses some of its binding force although, as I have already remarked it is the basic material in the production of roof slates and ridge tiles with which we cover the individual family nests in the single-family homes. It will not be out of place here to point out the theologians' views on matters of the cell, that is, the family. The fundamental instructions for the family and the frames within which it realizes the aims of humankind we shall find in the Book of Genesis. They are: (1) 'It is not good that man should be alone'; (2) 'Therefore shall a man leave his father and his mother and shall cleave unto his wife: and they shall be one flesh'; and (3) 'Be ye fruitful and multiply.'

Naturally one should not use stale cement in binding. That is why, on receiving a consignment of cement, one ought to note the date when it was poured into the sacks. Stale cement is no longer a material of full value because it loses about 20% of its binding power.

It is against these conditions that we must on each occasion measure the family structure. The social significance of marriage and of the family nest is the subject of our inquiry which has shown that we may use straw bricks to insulate the walls of family nests. If, however, we wish to insulate a building affected by damp, then naturally we must remove the damp. It follows, therefore, that marriage may be a successful struggle against loneliness. A man and a woman may operate a hand-press for the production of straw bricks but they achieve mutual knowledge only through love . . . . For it is only in the flesh that people arrive at the full realization of their personalities.

(*HENRY sticks a plaster on his forehead and continues.*)

The press employed in the manufacture of straw bricks

consists in principle of a base, a fixed frame, a movable frame, two pulleys, chains and other elements, including a wooden hammer, a sieve for the cement, a box for the cement mixture, a moulding press, a frame, and a measuring cone for checking the thickness of the clay suspension.

During the production of flat tiles normal apparel — that is a white linen overcoat buttoned up at the back — is obligatory. The sleeves of the shirt and the coat ought to be rolled up above the elbows. White caps. Women should wear head scarves. Rubber gloves are not generally used.

When laying ordinary roof slates we fill in the ridge grooves with mortar and animal hair. When laying tiles on the roof, start at the bottom and work your way up. Slop dishes make for cleanliness both on the table and on the floor. As far as laying out a body is concerned, it should in principle be laid out on a special table or tray with a protruding edge all round . . . the body laid out flat is supported on two wooden blocks, one underneath the shoulder-blades and one underneath the pelvis. Flat tiles are laid out in the same way but without mortar. In order to insure the insulation of the covering, we tuck in flax fibre dipped in tar. The skin, fat, etc, which have been extracted in the process are at once placed in dishes. The flax fibre . . . flax dipped in the slop basin . . . .

(HENRY *is rubbing his forehead. He has forgotten . . . tears a plaster off his forehead and speaks slowly.*)

The flax . . . flax . . . (*trying to collect his thoughts*) Toadflax — linaria vulgaris, round-leaved toadflax — linaria spuria . . . sharp-pointed toadflax — linaria elatine . . . pale-blue toadflax — linaria repens . . . perennial, smooth . . . corolla violet with dark lines and yellow palate . . . flowers July to September . . . ivy-leaved toadflax — linaria cymbalaria . . . with egg-shaped leaves . . . hairy . . . sandy cornfields . . . July . . . .

(*He stops, sits down in the armchair and repeats, mumbling.*)

. . . bastard toadflax . . . thesium humifusum . . . bastard toadflax — humifusum . . . toadflax . . . bastard . . . bastard . . . .

(HENRY covers his face with his hands and sits in silence for a while. He puts his hand on BENJAMIN's head and talks quietly but clearly.)

I feel I am departing
I don't want to leave you without a blessing
but I don't know how it's done

BENJAMIN: You've still got a temperature .... Mummy was saying that you are coming to your senses.

GIZELA: Slowly coming to your senses.

HENRY:

I would have wished to bless you
but I honestly don't know how our father did it
it's disgraceful that there is no manual of some sort ....

(BENJAMIN shifts about because he is uncomfortable under his father's heavy palm which rests on his head.)

I wish ....

BENJAMIN: Don't force yourself, Daddy, we know you have nothing to say. That's only natural.

HENRY: *(stubbornly)* I wish to leave you with certain directives .... True enough, no one has sufficient experience in these matters .... Your grandpa fell into a well when he was drunk and had no time to compose his last will and testament. He had no time to transmit to me anything of his great experience. I find myself in a more fortunate situation and I wish to transmit to you that which your grandpa had no time to transmit to me.

GIZELA: Then transmit it to us, Daddy ....

(She shifts about on her chair and looks intently at her father.)

HENRY: Gizela, be patient. And now, Benjy, be a man to the end of your life because this is your duty and your right as well. Brush your teeth, wash your hands; even when you are a grown-up defend your convictions, brush your teeth, wash your ears, protect the values which are the most precious deposit transmitted from generation to generation. What if your father should go, if he leaves you everything and even more . . . .

BENJAMIN: (*trying to remove his father's palm from the top of his head*) But Mummy . . . .

HENRY: And you, Gizela, be a woman. Do not depart from this under any circumstances. Had your grandpa had the time to leave me any directives regarding bringing you up . . . but after all, I know what he could have thought in his last hour . . . . He was a very good man but a little irresponsible. Yes, Gizela, be a woman always, train your character. One day you will be a mother. I know you wanted to be a boy . . . Benjy, don't fidget so much — after all, my words are for you too. It makes no sense if someone talks very wisely but his breath is foul. Such, unfortunately, is our contemporary world. Anyway, at all times one must think not only of oneself . . . . One must struggle with oneself. My children, one must place greater demands on oneself than on others . . . . You are the people of the future . . . .

BENJAMIN: Easy to say that . . . .

HENRY: Don't be so glib, child. You will not even notice when you are a new man. Can't you sit still for a minute? Wash your ears, Benjy, brush your hair, fold up your pants. And you, Gizela, don't allow yourself to be outdistanced, you are a girl but everything lies open to you . . . .

BENJAMIN: Mummy . . . .

HENRY: The poor thing . . . in her there is a struggle between the new and the old. Do not seek personal gain in anything. I can leave you nothing apart from my name. Remember, Benjy, that no Hoopoe ever stained himself . . . .

BENJAMIN: (*laughs*) Hoopoe, what Hoopoe didn't stain himself?

HENRY: (*realizing suddenly that he has blundered and said something idiotic*) My head is splitting . . . I am afraid I'm going to be sick . . . I shall throw up everything. Gizela, hand me that bucket . . . .

(*GIZELA hands it to him and supports his head. HENRY attempts to be sick but without success. He struggles for a long time, his head hidden in the vessel. He talks with his head inside the bucket. His voice comes out muffled but clear.)*

HENRY: I'm going. I shall leave you nothing but my name. On your father's side, Benjy, you are the inheritor of those values which your grandpa had developed in himself. That grandpa who was unable to finish what he wished to say because a tragic configuration of causes had, like one of the Fates, cut the thread of his life. Whose works were the fruit of above-average spiritual values. Remember, Benjy, no Lavender stained his hands and your grandpa marched with his head held high . . . . (*He is sick and then resumes.*) Be a man, Benjy. When you are on a bus give up your seat to the elderly. What is a man in our times? Neither a protector nor a provider . . . . Defend your convictions with your head held high . . . . Always be an optimist . . . . Fly towards the sun . . . . And you, Gizela, always be a woman . . . . (*He is sick again.*) Wash your hands, Benjy, guard your post, never change your name. Your name includes everything that your fore-bears have collected and with your name you will transmit these values to your successors. What an odd custom we have nowadays in this country. Was there ever a time when a louse wanted to call itself an eagle? A rat call itself a lark, a mouse a cat, a cat a dog . . . ? (*He laughs bitterly, his head still inside the bucket.*) Changes of name are fashionable, but this involves a lot of cowardice, vanity, and stupidity . . . . What is a man without a name? With a name changed he is like a man without a face, without a past and without ancestors . . . . Sometimes when an ancestor stains himself with a terrible crime one can justify such a change, though even Borman's son has not repudiated his father's name nor has Goering's daughter nor had Hitler's sister nor Mus-solini's son. Who then should repudiate his name since even the child of a man responsible for genocide bears his fa-ther's name? Oh, my children, why does Foot want to be called Head, why does Fishman call himself Eaglestone and why does Rat become Pratt? In a free country where love and sympathy rule let Cock remain Cock, let Rat remain

Rat and let Hoopoe remain Hoopoe. And although your grandpa was a mere foundling whom a gypsy picked up on a railway station platform . . . .

(HENRY is sick and then resumes. EVE enters with a bowl of soup. She places the bowl on the table and leaves the room without taking any notice of her husband and children. BENJAMIN, who has meanwhile extricated himself from his father's grip, approaches the table, having left the cage with the white mice on a side table.)

BENJAMIN: Daddy! Soup . . . .

HENRY: *(his face still hidden in the bucket)* . . . one has to know, Benjy, how not to lose face.

BENJAMIN: Don't worry, Daddy, everything will turn out all right . . . .

(EVE returns to lay the table and then goes out. GIZELA supports her father's head and moves the bucket away. She takes a handkerchief out of her pocket and carefully wipes his face.)

GIZELA: The poor thing! How do such thoughts get into his empty head? Probably he overfed himself on his pitiful past. I told Mummy, 'Don't push so much into him, it's already coming out of his ears.' But you know Mummy! 'I must push everything I can into his gut — I'll stuff in to him all of life's gruel and fuel' and so on and so on. You know Mummy, Benjy, don't you? She has had her way.

BENJAMIN: Daddy's throwing up.

EVE: Soup's on the table.

(She pours out the soup. They all sit down and eat the soup in silence.)

Today, Henry, we have your favourite soup.

HENRY: Cucumber?

EVE: Tomato.

GIZELA: Mummy, you forgot that Daddy loves cucumber soup most of all.

EVE: You're wrong, child. I've known father for some little while now. He always delighted in tomato soup. I remember when he was courting me my mother always used to say, 'Henry, today we have your favourite soup,' and she would joke that 'the gentleman will get caught by this soup.' And he did.

GIZELA: (*laughs heartily*) Oh, Mummy, what primitive times those were. Who today would think of catching a man or a boy with soup — and tomato soup at that.

BENJAMIN: Don't count your chickens before they're hatched.

GIZELA: Mummy, tell that child not to talk gibberish.

(HENRY is eating the soup in silence. He is using a fork but no one has noticed.)

EVE: Have you told father about the changes which we have all experienced since the last war? About the political system in which we live?

GIZELA: Yes.

HENRY: Never underestimate the cooking. Don't underestimate sauces! English cooking is like the cooking of cannibals because food weighs down their spirit — and what about German cooking? Those sauces, those meats, those pastries! Piedmontese cooking is best.

EVE: But you could have told Daddy a few things about communism, capitalism, socialism, stalinism, dogmatism, and revisionism.

GIZELA: Recently I read quite interesting things about that. 'Eve's Madness' is probably the last word in these matters.

EVE: And who wrote that?

GIZELA: A Frenchman, a poet. In his view, evolution of love leads to the Age of the Tandem Couple . . . .

BENJAMIN: The age of the tandem? He must have got it wrong . . . the age of the tandem is past.

GIZELA: Mummy, tell him to stop his smart talk. We're not talking about bicycles but about the couple which is formed by man and woman.

EVE: Benjy, leave us for a minute. This topic is not for your ears.

>   (BENJAMIN *leaves.*)

GIZELA: He says that our age is the age of Eve.

EVE: And who is this Eve?

GIZELA: That's his wife . . . . He says that the time of the couple is at hand.

HENRY: Just as before there was competition between blood and iron.

GIZELA: The age of labour in which man and woman create and preserve love.

EVE: It's so very nice of this man. The French are really so charming. Even ideologically.

GIZELA: Yes, he's a charming elderly man. Really charming. Listen to what he says about communism. (*She takes a notebook out of her pocket, looks through it and reads*) 'Let's take the problem of communism . . . .'

EVE: Henry, listen, this is something for you.

GIZELA: 'Not so long ago people talked of communism as though it were something very distant and today there are people who talk about communism as of a thing very close and even give dates: the year 1980. The year 1980 is very close. Each one of us tries to imagine how and what things will look like then. Perhaps falsely and subjectively. But as far as I am concerned — says the poet — subjectivism rests on the fact that I imagine communism . . . .

BENJAMIN: (*knocks*) May I come in to finish my soup?

EVE: Yes, but don't interrupt us.

>   (BENJAMIN *sits down at the table and dutifully drinks his soup.*)

GIZELA: 'I imagine communism as a society whose basic cell will be a couple of close, happy people loving each other.'

EVE: That's charming. Well, really, I never expected . . . .

>   (BENJAMIN, *who was listening with attention to* GIZELA's *last*

words, cannot control himself any more and bursts out laughing. However, his mouth is full of tomato soup with rice. He spatters the soup not only on himself but also on GIZELA *and his* FATHER. *He is choking and cannot catch his breath. Only after a considerable pause he calms down and wipes his tears with his thumbs.)*

BENJAMIN: The idiot. Oh Mummy, Mummy, o mamma mia, what is this idiotic girl talking about . . . .

*(*HENRY *has put aside his fork and is now picking a tooth with his finger.)*

EVE: And you're really not interested in anything. Neither in your children's future nor in me. All you care about is eating your soup and having a night's sleep.

HENRY: *(interrupting his tooth-picking)* Darling, you're unjust to the boy.

EVE: What did you say?

HENRY: Benjy, leave us for a minute.

*(*BENJAMIN *leaves.)*

HENRY: Indeed the boy made a mistake in not swallowing the soup. He had his mouth full and that is what caused the incident. On the other hand, it seems to me that he was right in his evaluative judgment regarding what Gizela, following that charming Frenchman, just told us. Darling, let's for example take the case of the cell which is supposed to be the basic cell of society. I'm not surprised that the child was amused by the babbling of the old intellectual. You see, children have something like a sharpened instinct in their evaluation of phenomena. Children are the only realists on earth. The true cell which will in future form the basis of society will be the family and not this gentleman's tandem couple. That is to say: the husband, the wife, the children, the mother-in-law, grandfather, and even uncle. It's all very well to sing about the couple, of course it's more comfortable when there is a couple, but the couple is not the soul, the couple is only an egotistic association and it's not good idealizing the thing . . . the age of the couple! Benjy was right laughing at Gizela, although he should have done it after swallowing his cucumber soup. I too found it difficult to restrain myself. Gizela is a young miss, she is seventeen, so she can, without any ill effects upon her mind and organism transcribe into her diary these lyrical raptures. Benjy, come here and finish your soup.

(BENJAMIN *enters, sits down dutifully at the table and solemnly consumes his soup.*)

HENRY: You see, my boy, never laugh at adults when your mouth is full of soup. Retain your laughter until you've swallowed it.

BENJAMIN: (*swallows and says solemnly*) Yes, Daddy.

HENRY: And if this gentleman had eleven, or at least four, children, he would sing the age of the couple in a different manner. Well, really, what a load of rubbish.

EVE: Don't cry, Gizela, you can see Father is joking. Wipe the soup out of your eyes.

BENJAMIN: Don't cry, Gizela, I didn't mean to hurt you. Stop whimpering, I'll give you a white mouse, shall I?

GIZELA: You always make fun out of everything. What's wrong with this man imagining communism like this?

BENJAMIN: Don't you know, my goose, that the age of the couple already existed in paradise? Monsieur had forgotten about such details like artificial manure, heavy industry, electrification, social security, cuts in working hours and chemistry. The French are very charming and want to settle everything either in bed or around the bed. That's their national virtue: with them politics, art, and all their literature either happens in bed or under the bed . . . .

EVE: Benjy, will you leave the table at once.

HENRY: Let him finish the soup.

EVE: How can a child at his age . . . the things he hears in the street and on the bus . . . so many drunkards everywhere . . . . He watches television programmes in secret.

BENJAMIN: So what do you want me to do? Feed myself on silly little rhymes in books with coloured pictures? Where imbeciles write about dwarfs and dwarfs write about imbeciles? My God, things have come to a pretty pass in the world of adults. I tell you, Gizela, at school you hear a lot of double talk. The priest tells you about angels and the biology teacher tells you about protein. One's head reels . . . . And now this one comes along with his age of the couple . . . while under the bed there's probably 'that third one' like in all the plays and films.

(GIZELA bursts into tears. She spatters her soup not only on BENJAMIN but also on her FATHER. Hurt, she runs out of the room.)

EVE: Gizela, please bring in the roast.

(A FAT MAN appears in the doorway, bows, goes over to EVE, bows once more and kisses her hand.)

Oh, it's you. I've completely forgotten . . . . The school friend?

FAT MAN: *(bowing)* Yes, a school friend. I received your telegram yesterday . . . .

EVE: Well, as a matter of fact, my husband has come to his senses . . . but do . . . please sit down . . . here, next to me . . . . Benjy, say 'How do you do.'

(BENJAMIN stops eating, bows politely to the FAT MAN. The FAT MAN holds him under the chin and scrutinizes his face. HENRY is feverishly looking for something in his pockets. He draws out a roll of bandage. He is concentrating and his expression is serious.)

FAT MAN: The image of his father.

EVE: Would you like some soup? Here everything's as usual. Henry is slowly recovering his senses.

FAT MAN: *(holding BENJAMIN under the chin)* Yes, please, thank you very much. You like tomato soup, sonny, I can see it in your eyes. And how is school, my dear sir? The very image of father.

(GIZELA enters smiling: there are signs of tears on her face.)

EVE: Gizela, wash the soup out of your eyes. I'm awfully sorry; just a moment ago we had a little incident at table. As you know, with children . . . . My daughter. Say, 'How do you do.' This is Father's friend, a school colleague.

(*HENRY looks carefully at the* FAT MAN *and then slowly begins to wrap the bandage round his head.*)

FAT MAN: The image of his father. (*He lays down his spoon and holds* GIZELA *by the chin*) And how is school? Have you got a boy-friend?

BENJAMIN: May I get back to the soup?

EVE: Yes, please do.

(*BENJAMIN sits down dutifully and finishes his soup.*)

We're waiting for Henry's mother. Perhaps memories of schooldays will prove stronger. One has to get at the roots. I don't really know myself. Mother sees him with a ribbon in his hair. She says he had curls. What do you think about that?

HENRY has finished bandaging his head. Now he again looks as he did in Tableau Four of Act II, but this time his ears stick out from behind the bandage. This apparent detail will make possible the final development of dramatic action. The FAT MAN *stops eating his soup, smiles and winks knowingly towards* HENRY *and then leans over and whispers something in* HENRY's *ear.* HENRY *sits motionless. The* FAT MAN *bursts out laughing, pulls* HENRY *by the ear like a small boy, then returns to his soup. After a while* HENRY *puts down his napkin, gets up, and without saying a word leaves the room.* EVE *follows him with her eyes, opens her mouth . . . .*

THE OLD WOMAN BROODS

CHARACTERS

THE OLD WOMAN SPEAKS

THE OLD WOMAN

A YOUNG WAITER

CYRIL, A WAITER

A BEAUTIFUL GIRL

A DOCTOR

A VIOLINIST

FIRST GIRL — CLOTO

SECOND GIRL — LACHESIS

THIRD GIRL — ATROPOS

A BLIND MAN

A DISTINGUISHED GENTLEMAN

A YOUNG MAN

A POLICEMAN — GUARDIAN OF ORDER

ROAD SWEEPERS AND INCIDENTAL PERSONS

CHILDREN, PUPPETS ENTANGLED IN THE SO-CALLED ACTION

SCENE 1

A floodlit stage with no shadows. The light reaches everywhere. The interior of a huge, modern station café. Plenty of red, black and white tables and chairs. The OLD WOMAN *is sitting at one of the tables. She is covered in a heap of spring, summer, autumn and winter clothes. With brooches, bracelets, watches, chains, earrings and flowers dangling all over her. Her head is covered with three hats and a variety of multi-coloured hair. Her face is still, it is covered with a network of wrinkles but the features are quite clear. A splendid set of white dentures. Tables and chairs made of metal, glass and coloured fibres. They gleam, glisten and sparkle.*

The WOMAN *screeches inarticulately.*

Enter a young, tall, suave and clean-looking WAITER, *wearing a dinner jacket or something equally smart and patent-leather shoes. He is carrying a tray with a jug, a glass and a sugar bowl, he looks around and goes out. Returning a moment later he moves among the tables using a brush to sweep china, vases of flowers, newspapers, menus, bottles and ashtrays on to the floor. From his pocket he pulls out a long cloth resembling a bandage with which he wipes the tables, his face, nose and hands. He picks up a vase of artificial flowers, rearranges the flowers and replaces the vase on the table. He stops in front of a big window which has curtains tightly drawn across it. He has his back to the audience and to the* OLD WOMAN.

THE OLD WOMAN: Sonny .... Sonny ....

(The WAITER *does not turn round.)*

THE OLD WOMAN: Pretends he doesn't hear.

WAITER: *(without turning round)* Yes, Madam ....

(He moves towards her table pushing aside with his feet, various empty cans, boxes and papers. He bows and gives her the menu.)

THE OLD WOMAN: The usual, Sonny, the usual.

(WAITER goes out and returns with a glass, a jug and a sugarbowl which he places in front of the WOMAN.

The WOMAN gazes at the glass. She picks it up and examines it carefully against the light. She replaces the glass on the tray. She picks up the spoon and then puts it back again. She picks up the glass once more. She has rings on all her fingers.)

THE OLD WOMAN: Waiter!

(The WAITER bows in front of the WOMAN.)

THE OLD WOMAN: *(from her smart, patent-leather handbag she picks out a lace handkerchief to wipe the edge of the glass which she again examines against the light and then replaces on the tray)* Waiter . . . .

(The WAITER pretends he does not hear.)

WAITER: *(aside)* Look at that repulsive louse! What use is she to anybody?

THE OLD WOMAN: Come closer. Closer still.

WAITER: Yes, madam.

THE OLD WOMAN: This glass is dirty.

WAITER: It's impossible, madam. This little glass!

(The WAITER picks up the glass and examines it against the light.)

THE OLD WOMAN: Some whore has smudged the edge with her lipstick.

WAITER: *(pulls out his cloth and wipes the glass. He examines it against the light, spits on the glass and wipes it with his sleeve)* I deeply regret this oversight. *(He replaces the glass on the table)* It's as clean as a button. Wonderful weather we're having today. Not a cloud in the sky.

THE OLD WOMAN: You've left your fingerprints on it, just like an identity card or a criminal file. Supposed to be an establishment of the highest class, but the glass is dirty. Bring me another. Are you short of water or something?

WAITER: Just so, madam. The water reserves on earth have diminished terribly. At this very moment people in this town are
allowed a glass of clean water per head. What's more, some
young thugs have destroyed the water system. For two weeks
now we have been practically without water. Rivers, lakes,
seas and oceans have also become polluted. We bring in
water from the mountains but the shortage continues.

*(He picks up the glass once more and wipes it with the dirty
cloth. He pours the coffee into the glass and goes towards the
window. His back is again towards the audience.)*

THE OLD WOMAN: *(poking in the glass with her index finger)* Just a lot
of dregs. It's thick with dregs . . . . *(She picks the dregs out of
the glass and pours them on the table)* And it's all bitter! *(The
WOMAN screeches.)*

(The WAITER moves towards the table after a pause.)

THE OLD WOMAN: *(coos like a dove)* Sugar-r-r, Sugar-r-gr-r-gr-r-gr-r,
Sugar-r-r . . . .

*(The WAITER takes a spoonful of sugar and pours it into the
glass.)*

THE OLD WOMAN: More.

(The WAITER adds more sugar.)

THE OLD WOMAN: More!

*(The WAITER pours out so much sugar that it spills on to the
table and the floor. The OLD WOMAN coos. The WAITER is still
pouring. Wipes his face with a napkin. He is tired.)*

THE OLD WOMAN: I like it sweet — very, very sweet, the older I get
the sweeter I like it. Pour some more.

WAITER: Would you like some butter? Butter with tea is good for
you, that's the way the Mongols do it.

THE OLD WOMAN: It's bitterly cold today . . . . *(The WOMAN tries to get
up. The heap of clothing shakes about violently and then is
still)* I am all in a sweat and he just stands there. Wipe my
face. The sweat is pouring into my eyes.

(The WAITER pulls out his dirty cloth and carefully wipes the WOMAN's face.)

THE OLD WOMAN: *(moans, trying to get up, eventually moves forward toppling chairs and tables as she goes. She is dropping her hats, hair and jewellery. She returns to the table and sits down)* I feel as though I had dropped something . . . . I heard it drop. It must have dropped when I was walking around here. Only I don't know where, in which place . . . . Hey, Waiter, come over here! Hey, you over there, I'm talking to you!

WAITER: Yes, madam.

THE OLD WOMAN: Didn't you notice where I dropped . . . ? The bag must have come undone or something. I don't really know myself.

WAITER: I'm sorry I didn't notice anything . . . . Could you please tell me what it is you've lost?

THE OLD WOMAN: I don't know I'm sure. Look at the floor, or maybe under the table, or, maybe I'm sitting on it. Anyway don't bother. I can do without. I've still got so many different things inside. When I was a young girl it never occurred to me a woman has so many different things. One has to be an expert to grasp it all. But you, Sonny, you probably think a woman is like a doll?

WAITER: I've never given it much thought, madam, I've just come out of the army.

THE OLD WOMAN: What a fine soldier you must be . . . but I like it when it's warm, very warm, very, very warm and warmer still.

WAITER: In the last few days the temperature has varied a great deal. In places it has dropped to minus 15° while the approach of a depression from the west is likely to bring increased cloud and snowfalls. The sun rose at 7.45 and will set at 3.38. Today's saints are Edmund and Telesfor.

THE OLD WOMAN: *(she is spreading the dregs on the table. Burying her fingers in them and then sweeping them into the glass)* I ought to eat a lot of spinach and lead a healthy life. (*After a moment's silence she says with conviction*) I want a child.

WAITER: Yes, madam, a woman ought to have a child....

THE OLD WOMAN: I'm a bit late. I had a forty-year break. I couldn't, I didn't have the time. Now I have the time, the proper conditions — health — and I want to bear a child. Unfortunately I used to be barren but now everything's changed. Arrange for that Romanian to come over. What's his name, Pitulescu, I think. The one that invented the hormone yoghurt. In Translyvania, or wherever it is, centenarians are beginning to give birth. I read in those newspapers of yours that one gave birth to fifteen all at once. Well then, go and fetch me that Romanian or Gypsy or whoever he is. I want to give birth. Well, don't just stand there — go and fetch him.

WAITER: It wasn't a Romanian, that was an Italian.... The Romanian is actually someone in the theatre. As for the septuplets they were born in one of the Brussels clinics. Five were stillborn and the remaining two died soon after. It's worth stressing that all seven were premature births. They hadn't been in the womb for even six months. The mother of the septuplets whose name has not been revealed used to be barren and became pregnant after taking a Swedish fertility drug.... Oh, here we are, I've got the newspaper cutting. I have a scrapbook of all such curiosities about life on Mars, flying saucers and organ transplants.... As for that Italian, he is engaged on the production of artificial children in Bologna.

THE OLD WOMAN: Do you read the papers?

WAITER: Passionately, madam.

THE OLD WOMAN: Well, and what do these papers of yours say? What's going on in that wretched world of yours?

WAITER: The situation is again very tense.

THE OLD WOMAN: One ought to give birth, whoever can ought to give birth.

WAITER: In view of the present state of affairs I admire your courage.

THE OLD WOMAN: The situation was always the same . . . . Phone up that chap in Bologna and tell him to bring that artificial womb of his without any delay.

(The WAITER is not listening to the WOMAN's chatter. He picks up a pile of old, torn-up newspapers and rubbish, sits down at an adjoining table and is engrossed in reading.)

THE OLD WOMAN: *(chews the coffee dregs, then spits them on to the floor and talks without looking at anyone)* And what do they say in those papers of yours?

WAITER: U-Thant has thrown out a dramatic challenge to the world.

THE OLD WOMAN: What sort of warning does that U-Thant of yours throw out?

WAITER: *(from behind the newspaper)* 'Today we are witnessing the initial stage of World War III.'

(The OLD WOMAN laughs, shaking all over.)

WAITER: *(surprised)* All the same, the situation isn't at all pleasant.

THE OLD WOMAN: Sugar-r-r, sugar-r-r. Pour some more sugar-r-r. Can't you hear?

(The WAITER approaches the table carrying rubbish folded up in his paper. Some of the rubbish drops on the floor.)

THE OLD WOMAN: Wait a minute, I've forgotten . . . . You were saying this U-Thant of yours, or whatever his name is, was talking about the Third World War — that it is supposed to be in progress.

WAITER: Yes, madam, it is 'in progress.'

THE OLD WOMAN: Well, let it progress then, as for you, you can go and buy me a sack of flour. A full sack. And you will bring it here.

WAITER: *(bending over confidentially)* You will get maggots breeding in it, you will merely suffer a loss, madam, the situation is not all that critical. I would think that for the moment two or three pounds ought to be quite enough.

THE OLD WOMAN: You will go and buy me flour. I'll eat dough. I'll
fatten myself up. They're making war and I'll make dough.
I will paste the war over with dough. As for maggots, you
don't have to tell me, they breed in everything ... they
even breed in lush flowers as my fiancé, who was killed in
the war, used to complain . . . . Will you please, bring me
immediately a layer cake and a dish of whipped cream.
Maggots. War. Go and frighten miserable fools like yourself. Nowadays they're afraid of everything. Fools. Sugar-r-r,
sugar-r-r! They all ought to bear children. Greta Garbo and
Sartre — and Bertrand Russell — and Cardinal Ottaviani
and Salvador Dali — and Picasso — and General de Gaulle
— and Mao — and Rusk . . . . All . . . . All of them without
exceptions for age, rank, sex or politics.

WAITER: Am I to wrap the cream up or will you eat it here?

THE OLD WOMAN: Wrap it up and I'll eat it here ... sugar-r-r ...
sugar-r-r . . . . You see, my boy, we must perform our tasks.
We have to eat and give birth . . . . And where is that professor of yours? That bearded chap from Bologna. All these
Italians ever think about is 'amore' and 'bambino'. A wise
nation. We have to sweeten and sweat in labour. Cook, labour and sweeten. Without pause. Let them prepare war . . . .
Let it be in progress. Don't care a damn. You have to see to
it that the glass is clean. This is your job.

WAITER: Ah, madam, sugar, flour, lard ... that was fine in past
ages. Now nothing will save us, the radioactive flour will
give birth to monsters, we will all get leukaemia.

THE OLD WOMAN: Une enorme perroquet.

WAITER: I will not worship the stomach.

THE OLD WOMAN: You're talking nonsense, Sonny, because you don't
understand foreign languages. Stomach! Womb! The belly
is a splendid thing but does not get proper recognition. It is
a splendid, colossal thing.

a whole country
it is a defenceless and innocent country

it is vast
vulnerable to strikes
soft, yielding, enclosed
open, embracing
our life
eternal
and yet containing so much shrapnel and shells
so many knives, bayonets, spears, bullets
it is your male bellies that are filled with iron junk
while ours are even more wretched
even more accommodating
they contain foreign bodies
additional instruments
members
children
our bellies
you stupid mule
are true mills
are great white poems
are huge soft warm
loaves
babes born of whipped cream
man ought to wear a plate of armour
on his belly
the belly ought to be subject
to international protection
it ought to be protected
against big blows
from below from above
from the right from the left
the whole of humanity is a belly
warm pulsating
wrinkled like a pig
stretched tight like a war drum
I am curious to know
what generals think of bellies
of bellies they never speak
only of old men women
and children

take note
of generals' speeches
they talk of shields umbrellas swords
they talk of revenge
of the crushing blow
of nuclear arms
meanwhile all these
rockets shells inventions
are aimed at the gentle
white uncovered expansive
defenceless blind
belly of a woman
of a mother
of earth

WAITER: Perruche.

(Enter a young, beautiful, shapely GIRL. She is fully grown. She is dressed in the latest fashion imaginable. She sits at one of the tables and crosses her legs. Or rather she draws one leg over the other very high, very, very high. And why does she do this? In order to enliven the action and the spectators, to give a young actress a chance to shine on the stage. To fall in with the sexual obsessions of the theatre critics. But apart from this second and third-rate reason I do have a true goal in mind. As in that famous saying of the great Chekhov, repeated by critics and others, about the shotgun which hangs on the wall in Act I and must be triggered off in the last act, or something to that effect. So this GIRL whose presence now does not seem to be justified may perhaps play a role in the second or third act, although this is by no means certain for one never knows with girls and this one here is of easy virtue. The GIRL is dressed up in metal and yellow, green and pink materials . . . . The GIRL is sitting in the far corner of the café. Throughout her presence on the stage she is searching for something in her colossal, extremely fashionable handbag. Sometimes she is looking through it slowly and systematically, sometimes nervously, in a great hurry, taking out and replacing a thousand and one items.)

THE OLD WOMAN: I am melting, it is now terribly hot in here. What are they using as fuel? Don't you keep looking over there, listen to me. That table over there belongs to your colleague.

WAITER: Yes, madam.

THE OLD WOMAN: What hot dishes do you have?

WAITER: Tripe, meat balls and stew.

THE OLD WOMAN: Haven't you got any soup?

WAITER: Soup will be ready in an hour.

THE OLD WOMAN: I shan't need your soup in an hour's time.

WAITER: You always make jokes about soup, madam.

THE OLD WOMAN: You will never understand what a spoonful of hot soup does to a human being. (*The* WOMAN *unbuttons her collar and various bits and pieces fall out on to the table, the floor*) I'm terribly hot. Haven't you got a fan?

(*The* WAITER *switches on an electric fan standing on one of the tables. The fan blows up dust, rubbish and papers. The* WAITER *moves the fan on to the floor, raising a cloud of dust.*)

THE OLD WOMAN: Switch it off at once and open the window.

WAITER: (*switches off the fan. Stops in front of the curtained window with his back to the woman. His hands folded. The dust and rubbish float down on the tables and floor*) I am sorry, but the window has a curtain across it.

THE OLD WOMAN: And why has it got a curtain across it?

WAITER: The guests can't bear the view.

THE OLD WOMAN: What guests? What view? But this is the most beautiful view in the whole of Europe: valleys, streams, peaks, cedars, pines, waterfalls.

WAITER: (*mumbling*) Certain changes have taken place.

THE OLD WOMAN: You're lying and hiding something from me. Pull back that curtain, otherwise I'll do it myself!

WAITER: (*in a matter-of-fact, dry voice*) I cannot grant your wish, madam, without the Manager's permission.

THE OLD WOMAN: Silly fool. Call the manager then . . . or rather, no, wait, bring that tripe dish you have, but mind you, it's got to be cold . . . . Sweat's running down my back . . . . Would you rub my back, please.

(The WAITER pulls out the cloth from his pocket. Pulls back the WOMAN's shawls and dresses and wipes her back.)

THE OLD WOMAN: Thank you. That's enough. Add it to the bill. And where is that tripe dish? Silly billy! Wait, where are you going? I asked you to pull back the curtain and open the window. Where is that blessed Romanian or Italian? I don't mind if it's an Italian. Have you found him? I'm melting like butter. What have you done with those trees outside the window? They have blinded the window.

WAITER: We wish to spare our guests a painful sight and anyway a criminal might get through the window. There are gangs of teenagers around. They rape, they steal cats and motor-cars, they riot.

THE OLD WOMAN: You're making it all up.

WAITER: *(shrugs his shoulders)* I have no desire to make anything up because I wouldn't get anything out of it. It's all the same to me and the customer's wish is my command.

(He pulls the curtain away from the window and slowly opens the window. Soot, bones, and general refuse begin to seep in through the opening. The WAITER quickly slams the window shut.)

THE OLD WOMAN: You're making it all up, my pet.

WAITER: There are so many flies about at this time. We have to wait until the night.

THE OLD WOMAN: Open it at once. I have no time to waste.

(The WAITER pretends not to hear. The GIRL has now stopped rummaging in her bag. She turns it upside down and shakes its whole contents on the table or the floor. She sits motionless for a while.)

GIRL: What on earth did I do with those earrings? Well, I could have sworn . . . .

WAITER: (*moves over to the girl, kneels and picks up a few odds and ends from the floor and together with a pile of rubbish stuffs it all into her handbag*) Here is the key!

GIRL: (*moving her tongue over her lips*) Thank you . . . . (*Leaves*)

THE OLD WOMAN: Is that the whore who smeared my glass with her lipstick?

WAITER: (*still kneeling*) The doctor you have called for has arrived, madam.

DOCTOR: Where is our little mother?

THE OLD WOMAN: (*to the WAITER*) Tell this clever showoff that I have been barren for the last fifty years, and it's all my confessor's fault, Nitwit!

DOCTOR: (*to the WAITER*) Let's start with you. Take your trousers off. (*The DOCTOR sits at a table and pulls a tattered book out of his pocket*) An expresso coffee, please . . . you can't work in a distinguished, first-class establishment if you have piles and an itch. Keep your pants on. No need to hurry. This is not an army prick-parade in a barrack-room, oh no. I will give you a prescription and the wisdom of the people. We are turning back to traditional medicine. (*The DOCTOR pulls out a piece of paper and writes out the prescription, talking loudly*) For the dropsy of the male organ and also of female nipples . . . .

WAITER: (*bends over the DOCTOR and draws his attention to the patient. But the DOCTOR continues to read*) If I remember correctly you treated me for the irregularities of my large intestine during the Cuban crisis.

DOCTOR: For external and internal ulcers of the male member there is a simpler prescription for the poor which is salt with unfermented honey with powdered calamint which having stirred together you are to apply to the wounds and pimples of the secret member . . . . As for the itching of the womb . . . .

THE OLD WOMAN: (*loudly*) The secret member, idiot, bore!

DOCTOR: (*to WAITER*) Bring me a coffee and a paper and keep the larger intestine in place with your index finger . . . .

THE OLD WOMAN: (*loudly*) How vulgar! Those draughts again. Who opened those beastly doors?

WAITER: The dishes have been cooking too long, madam, the meat's gone off. In previous ages personal hygiene and communal eating places were of a lower standard. Archbishop Thomas Becket was murdered in Canterbury in the evening of either the 24th or the 29th December, I do not recollect the exact date, and the body lay in the cathedral throughout the night and the funeral was to be the following morning. The Archbishop was wearing an extraordinary collection of clothes. He had a huge brown coat, then a white surplice, underneath that a woollen jerkin and then two more jerkins . . . .

THE OLD WOMAN: Ha, ha, I've got even more on.

WAITER: Then a black Benedictine habit and finally a shirt and underneath that a hair shirt. When the body cooled down the vermin which lurked in these countless layers of clothing . . . .

THE OLD WOMAN: And where is my tripe dish?

WAITER: (*his hands in his pockets*) . . . the vermin which lurked in the innumerable layers of clothes crept to the top . . . .

THE OLD WOMAN: What disgusting things people say to each other nowadays . . . . The irregularities of the large intestine . . . . Where are those sunrises and sunsets? The rosy-fingered dawn with its finger in the chamberpot!

WAITER: (*scratching himself, his hands in his pockets*) It slipped out, madam, and as the chronicler says — it bubbled like water in a pan and of those present seeing it, some burst into tears, some burst out laughing.

THE OLD WOMAN: Some in tears and some in laughter.

DOCTOR: (*pulling a piece of paper out of his pocket, writes talking loudly*) Against vermin which have a habit of multiplying in the private parts . . . . Against childhood fevers which occur with the ringworm . . . .

THE OLD WOMAN: Some in tears and some in laughter?

WAITER: Just so, madam. In order to understand it one has to be a whole human being . . . . We'll return to the subject. For the time being we have to give it an airing and a beating, an airing and a beating.

DOCTOR: You've forgotten the newspaper, my friend.

WAITER: Not at all, here it is (*he hands the* DOCTOR *a torn wet newspaper*).

(The DOCTOR *looks through the paper, tearing apart the glued pages, making holes in the paper. His face is covered with torn newspaper, fragments of his face are visible. The nose. Silence. A burst of laughter. Silence.)*

THE OLD WOMAN: (*she goes to the window and attempts to open it. As she does so she loses some of her hair and her clothing. After a pause she says out loud*) Is there a real man in the house?

(The DOCTOR *is reading. The* WAITER *is doing the same on the other side, crouching uncomfortably on his feet.)*

THE OLD WOMAN: We don't have real men any more. If you were real men . . . but instead you hide your heads in newspapers to avoid responsibility.

DOCTOR: (*putting aside the torn paper which is picked up by the* WAITER) What can I do for you?

THE OLD WOMAN: Please open the window.

DOCTOR: But of course.

(The DOCTOR *goes to the window and opens it wide with a decisive gesture. A mountain of refuse and rubbish pours in through the open window. There is a mountain of rubbish outside the window. From time to time this heap moves and a fresh pile of rubbish pours into the café. We hear the sharp bang of rubbish bins being tipped out and the roar of an engine. These noises accompany the ensuing dialogue.)*

THE OLD WOMAN: (*smiling*) Thank you, a breath of fresh air at last. (*She sits at a table*) My tripe's gone cold . . . . Whatever have they done with those old larches out there through the window!

WAITER: *(calling)* Cyril, Cyril!

> *(A second WAITER enters the café, dressed in a spotlessly white shirt, smoking jacket and gloves. He is carrying a tiny pink plastic dustpan and brush. His movements are stylish and purposeful. He gently sweeps some of the rubbish on to the dustpan, looks around the café as though he was looking to see whether there was any dust left anywhere and slowly goes out, carrying the dustpan in front of him.)*

WAITER: *(brushing his hair)* The larches have been cut down, disposed of, removed because of the increased motor traffic.

THE OLD WOMAN: Fools. I had rather you had cut me down, you buffoons, than those beautiful trees. I feel a positive physical pain at the idea of such an outrage. I remember when I once came here during May. The larches outside the window were covered with delicate, thin, light-green needles . . . . It's a beautiful tree. The larch is probably the most beautiful of all our conifers. It is tall and upright and its branches are not too thick. The sparsely distributed tufts of its needles make the crown of the larch almost completely transparent, strangely bright and sunny unlike any other coniferous trees. So that when looking at it as it stands there, pale-green in the light of the May sun, we often wonder with regret why we have so few of these gay and pretty trees. We ought to plant them with greater zeal so that larch forests will not be a matter of the past . . . .

> *(In the course of this monologue CYRIL returns to the café and pushes away the rubbish under the tables but this is of no avail since fresh loads are pouring in through the window. CYRIL then goes to the window and begins to push the rubbish out with his hands, feet, head and shoulders.)*

THE OLD WOMAN: Even before the larch has time to scatter the previous year's seeds it is already in bloom, preparing to bring forth fresh seeds in the autumn. At the tips of the small branches we notice tiny purple cones . . . .

> *(The OLD WOMAN grabs the WAITER by the hand while he is reading a torn newspaper.)*

THE OLD WOMAN: Cuddle me!

WAITER: Just one moment, madam.

THE OLD WOMAN: Cuddle me!

WAITER: In a moment, madam, but I must first dry my hands.

THE OLD WOMAN: Not in a minute but at this very instant. In a minute it will be too late. I have been waiting 48 years but you're now spending your time clearing rubbish and drying your hands. I have been waiting, I have always been waiting. They were all either as shy as butterflies or as stupid as bulls. One didn't know what to do with his hands, another what to do with his feet, because they were sweating from fear, and a third became a monk. The last one died heroically on the field of battle . . . . Dry those hands and come here at once.

(The WAITER wipes his hands and nose and goes over to the WOMAN.)

THE OLD WOMAN: Why are you standing in that awkward and gawky way? In an hour's time I shall be seventy and I haven't got a moment to lose. Get a move on, you miserable wretch.

WAITER: You are so dressed up, madam, that really . . . .

THE OLD WOMAN: Dressed up! You too are dressed up. Can't you see I'm trembling all over. Dressed up! Then undress me. Why do you keep staring, haven't you ever undressed a woman? Of course, nowadays you don't have to do it. They are all undressed. Like that whore who smeared my glass with her lipstick. You can peer anywhere you like. Life is oozing out of me. Where is that tripe dish, where are the pastries, where is the whipped cream? Wait, I feel like having a pickled cucumber.

(The WAITER tries to get away.)

Wait, Cyril can bring the tripe. Come over here, give me your hand. (*After a pause*) I feel something moving over my leg. It's probably a mouse or a cockroach, why don't you leave poison about? You should be ashamed of yourselves. This is supposed to be a first-class establishment. I can feel something crawling over me quite distinctly. Have a look, I can't see anything. It's probably a rat.

WAITER: That's impossible, madam. Here even a fly wouldn't dare settle on a guest.

THE OLD WOMAN: What do you mean, it's impossible? Surely this can't be a squirrel.

(The WAITER kneels and tries to lift the WOMAN's skirts.)

THE OLD WOMAN: Leave it. There is no need .... It's gone inside now.

(The WAITER looks surprised.)

Why do you keep staring? It's gone inside me and there is nothing more to talk about.

WAITER: I must respectfully point out that you are mistaken. Our establishment has eradicated cockroaches, bats, rodents, sparrows and flies. Here we liquidate flies with all available physical and psychological means. By persuasion and re-education. Cyril has a fly-whip. He is a real terror as far as they are concerned. He's got his own methods, he's been specially trained.

THE OLD WOMAN: Stop this small talk, you're supposed to be cuddling me.

WAITER: What, just like that? Without any cause?

THE OLD WOMAN: Stop babbling and start cuddling.

WAITER: Where, how?

THE OLD WOMAN: All over. You can start either with the feet or the hands. Haven't you learned anything from the cinema and television?

WAITER: *(rubs his hands, appears to be embarrassed)* I've simply lost my head, I don't know where to begin.

THE OLD WOMAN: Everything is open to love, you simpleton, you can love hair, skin, bones, there is love of fingernails and love of tongues, love of hands and feet, love of moles, freckles and birthmarks. The love of a stallion, of a bull, of a chameleon, a ram, an ass and a lamb. You can love in a dog-like, cat-like or bird-like way, you ass! There is love of dreams, of blood, of teeth and this has to be learnt. And as for you, you coprophagist.

WAITER: You're insulting me, madam.

(The OLD WOMAN makes inarticulate noises.)

At least in a public place you ought to restrain yourself. This is in bad taste.

(The OLD WOMAN barks.)

I beg your pardon.

THE OLD WOMAN: Nothing, forget it. Bring me some raw eggs, an onion, truffles and a boiled coal-fish. Do you understand? It's got plenty of phosphates. Wait, don't run away. Bring also some birds' tongues and fish liver. Have you got a pair of scissors? You may cut that hair in my left earhole.

(Engine roar and clatter of rubbish bins. Another pile of rubbish pours in through the window but nobody pays any attention to it. A stuffed rat with pink tail and feet is one of the items.)

WAITER: *(brushing off a speck on his dinner jacket)* I heartily recommend Dr Fagiano's cocktail.

THE OLD WOMAN: And what sort of cocktail may that be?

WAITER: We have here Professor Fagiano who prepares cocktails for us. Its chief constituent is sulphadiazine. This cocktail has rejuvenating powers. He has tried his method on numerous dogs and maintains that he has restored their agility and sexual powers. He has also tried this rejuvenating experiment on rats, on very old rats of course, which following this treatment had recovered all the attributes of young rats.

THE OLD WOMAN: And what attributes are those?

WAITER: Leprosy, excessive sweating of hands and feet, spite and self-abuse.

THE OLD WOMAN: The close of an old year and the beginning of the new always makes us realize in a rather brutal way how quickly time flies. Let us beat our breasts. How often do we give our daughters extra helpings so that the girls shall look well? But they lose their buxomness once their period of bloom is over.

WAITER: Ah! Quel malheur d'etre une fille! You have tremendous experience, madam, you appreciate the capability and wisdom of old women, you ought to become a secretary-general, a president, a governor.

THE OLD WOMAN: I have been everything, my sweet. Both governor and Sartre, and a sacred cow, and an ordinary fourteen-stone pedlar whom a devil tried to possess. But now I have no time for all this nonsense. Now I am brooding on the eggs, metaphorically speaking of course, you silly fool. I have no time to waste, I must give birth continually. Now, here, at once. Get the water ready, plenty of water, a whole cauldron of water, prepare the sheets, plenty of sheets . . . .

The curtain, a huge, white, blood-stained sheet, falls.

SCENE 2

A rubbish dump like the sea from shore to shore. A rubbish dump right up to the horizon. Only one of the café walls (perhaps the one with the window?) is left. There are now fewer tables and chairs and their place has been taken by two or three basket chairs. The illumination increases. A space open on all three sides. Perhaps a battlefield. A colossal rubbish dump. A polygon. A necropolis. And yet a beach. A beach by the sea. A green painted bench. The floor is covered with a layer of rubbish, soot and sand. Several sandpits. (But the sea of course is not to be seen.) Mounds. Perhaps graves. The OLD WOMAN *is sitting at a corner table. She is wearing several colourful dresses.* THREE YOUNG GIRLS *are lying on a white towel. The sun is shining down on them. Either their feet or their heads touch so that their bodies form a star. They are sunbathing. The surface of the rubbish dump cracks in a few places. A* MAN *crawls slowly through it. At the same time he is digging either a ditch or a trench through the rubbish. Finally he stops near the* GIRLS. *He is covered with rubbish, with something resembling a helmet on his head. He has a knife and fork in his teeth.* ANOTHER MAN *is also digging, starting from the opposite direction. Inch by inch. When they finally meet it is difficult to say whether they fight each other, whether they fall in each other's arms, whether they murder or embrace. Two tumbling bodies form a mound. They grow still, move and then grow still again. The* GIRLS *turn over from side to side langourously and sensuously. They rub themselves thickly with suntan cream. They sunbathe, they stretch themselves, they eat fruit and icecream, they read illustrated magazines, they talk.*

FIRST GIRL: *(with a leaf covering her nose)* Lucia . . . .

(The SECOND GIRL, *with dark glasses, listens mechanically pouring sand and rubbish through her fingers. The* THIRD GIRL *plays with a pair of nail scissors.)*

FIRST GIRL: She was married in a basilica.

THIRD GIRL: Of the Prince of the Apostles.

FIRST GIRL: The Archbishop officiated.

THIRD GIRL: The dress was buttoned up to the neck, all white lace . . . .

FIRST GIRL: Every petal of the lace rose had a meticulous finish.

THIRD GIRL: The train was pale blue, twelve feet long and carried by twelve pages.

FIRST GIRL: The bride was accompanied by her father.

THIRD GIRL: She was weeping.

FIRST GIRL: The journalist who described the wedding dress

THIRD GIRL: Was punished by not being allowed inside the church.

FIRST GIRL: He had no right to reveal the secret prematurely.

THIRD GIRL: The bride placed her wedding bouquet at the feet of Saint Agatha.

FIRST GIRL: The patron saint of nurses.

THIRD GIRL: She was trained as a nurse.

FIRST GIRL: Then there was a reception in the grand mansion.

THIRD GIRL: The wedding cake weighed 140 lbs and was 30 feet high.

FIRST GIRL: It had seventeen layers.

THIRD GIRL: In accordance with tradition the bride attempted to cut the cake but had not enough strength

FIRST GIRL: And called the bridegroom to help

THIRD GIRL: And then her father.

FIRST GIRL: But the cake was dry and began to chip.

THIRD GIRL: So the bridal pair took a piece each in their hands.

SECOND GIRL: And then?

THIRD GIRL: They had salmon, champagne, caviare, roast duck and sirloin of beef.

SECOND GIRL: So what?

THIRD GIRL: Nothing.

SECOND GIRL: Well, the Smiths also had champagne, duck and beef.

THIRD GIRL: And so what?

SECOND GIRL: Nothing.

THIRD GIRL: I think so too.

THE OLD WOMAN: (*sitting at her table*) Wash my hair, comb it, take the coffee away, it's got a fly in it.

VOICES FROM THE RUBBISH DUMP: Forward! Forward! (*Voices, trumpets and wild inarticulate roars*)

THE OLD WOMAN: Hurry up, please. Girls, who's making all that noise?

FIRST GIRL: It's the boys playing at war.

THE OLD WOMAN: Idiots. Instead of playing at love. I said, take the hairs out of that coffee. Buffoon. Where is that sugar? Where is that cursed waiter disappeared to again. Hey!

(*A BLIND MAN comes on the beach. He is wearing a coat and holding a white stick. With it he pokes the rubbish bins, cans, the girls and the soldiers buried in the sandpit. The stick has a sharply pointed end. The BLIND MAN sits on the bench and smiles. He pokes around with the stock. He pokes the stick through old newspapers, then removes them, folds them up and stuffs them into his pocket.*

The light grows dim as though the sun were hidden behind a cloud. Rubbish and flakes of soot float down from the sky. The BLIND MAN stretches a hand in front of him. He takes off his hat. He lifts his face towards the sky. He smiles.)

THE BLIND MAN: Snow! The first snow. (*He rubs the soot all over his face*)

(*The sound of a military trumpet. The surface of the rubbish dump splits up in several places. Hands appear. Spasmodic movements of the hands which a moment later disappear in the rubbish.*)

THE BLIND MAN: Boys, don't play at war. Why don't you build yourselves a snowman?

(A drumbeat)

THE BLIND MAN: Stop shooting, boys. There's so much snow around
here. Wait, I will show you how to make a snowman.

*(The BLIND MAN gets up, takes a few steps and kneels in the
rubbish dump. Tries to make a snowman out of the sand and
the rubbish. The rubbish will not hold together but the BLIND
MAN works on. The GIRLS are highly amused watching the BLIND
MAN at work, and then begin to help him.)*

THE BLIND MAN: And on his head we'll put an old blue pot.

SECOND GIRL: *(kneels next to the BLIND MAN and looks at the heap of
rubbish)* And why does the pot have to be blue?

THE BLIND MAN: *(stops working. Smiles at the girl. He is holding a pile
of paper and soot)* You see, my child, this is a long story but
we have no time for stories, we have to make a snowman.

SECOND GIRL: In the old days people used to tell each other fairy
tales, tales which would never come to an end, and now
everybody is in a hurry but we girls love listening so much.
Why were you talking of a blue pot, why blue? Perhaps I
am very childish but somehow it suddenly intrigued me
why you chose just that colour.

THE BLIND MAN: I love this small neutral country. I settled here after
the war. I love this lake mirroring the snow-capped mountain peaks. I brought a seed with me. The last seed. And I
planted it by the stream. And now we can already rest in its
shade. It's a larch. I love larches.

*(Two ROADSWEEPERS are pushing a rubbish trolley. Using either
hands or shovels they push off a heap of old newspapers,
books, encyclopaedias, illustrated magazines, rags, machines,
bottles, animals and people: old ones, children, women. Some
are real human beings, some are puppets. The CHILDREN dig
themselves out of the rubbish and run off the stage. A DISTIN-
GUISHED LOOKING GENTLEMAN tidies a handkerchief in his breast
pocket. He sits down at one of the tables. A moment later a*

waiter, CYRIL, carrying a cloth, comes over to him. He ties the cloth round the GENTLEMAN's neck. He goes over to the rubbish pile and pulls out an old comb full of fluff. Meanwhile the ROADSWEEPERS also sit down at one of the tables. They are smoking cigarettes. They show each other various odds and ends; buttons, old photographs, bottles, all obviously dug out of the rubbish heap.)

GENTLEMAN: Well, Cyril, humanity's on the brink again.

CYRIL: Indeed, your honour, it is on the brink. Shampoo?

GENTLEMAN: No thank you. A few years have passed and it's on the brink again.

CYRIL: And how is your lordship's wife? If I may be so . . . .

GENTLEMAN: Thank you, she is on the brink but full of energy.

CYRIL: A little oil and a parting on the left as usual?

GENTLEMAN: I have no idea, could be on the left I suppose.

CYRIL: There is a buzzing noise here somewhere!

(They are both listening.)

GENTLEMAN: Are you still continuing your campaign against the flies?

CYRIL: Ever since I was a child, your honour, but there are still a few of them left. And I am getting old.

GENTLEMAN: Leave them in peace, let them multiply. You'd do better to concentrate on dandruff.

CYRIL: Oh, no, your honour, I couldn't do that. It's a matter of principle. I couldn't even bear the thought that in an establishment such as ours these insects should defy hygiene.

(CYRIL takes off his belt. Again he goes over to the rubbish heap and pulls out a razor. He sharpens the razor on the belt. Suddenly he throws everything down and pulls out a fly whisk. Now he performs a fly-catching pantomime. He stalks his prey, he runs around, dances and jumps up and down. In the course of his dance he approaches the OLD WOMAN, who is having her hair set. She is sitting at her table, her head in a hair-dryer.

Next to her on a low stool a BEAUTIFUL GIRL is doing the OLD WOMAN's pedicure.)

THE OLD WOMAN: Look up my nose, that's where you'll find your fly.

CYRIL: I've been after it for the last few years . . . .

THE OLD WOMAN: The flies drown in the coffee. Wash my hair but be quick about it. Take the coffee away. Don't forget the pepper!

CYRIL: That is out of the question, madam.

THE OLD WOMAN: You're wasting your life, you don't understand a thing. You're just like a worm in a child's anus.

CYRIL: I'm a great saver, I have a post-office account.

THE OLD WOMAN: I'll buy you a horse. Have you been to Rome? Lead me to the altar this very minute!

CYRIL: I've got to think it over, I've just received news that we are on the brink again.

THE OLD WOMAN: Silly ass. Will you take me or won't you? Yes or no. Get on with it. One, two, three!

(The GIRL on the old woman's feet bursts out laughing. A FIDDLER enters the 'café'. He has a moustache. He is fat with an enormous stomach. A fiery, sweaty, dark-haired character. He is cuddling some instrument in his arms but we can't tell what it is because it is inside a black box. The FIDDLER sweats terribly. There is sweat on his face, on his back, on his hands and legs. He wipes his face.)

CYRIL: *(to the OLD WOMAN)* If you are having the tripe with music there will be a 20% surcharge. Are you still waiting? On the brink everything cools down more quickly and there is music.

(The GENTLEMAN clears his throat meaningfully and even menacingly.)

THE OLD WOMAN: Why is that pig grunting?

CYRIL: *(bends over her in a confidential manner)* He is our regular guest, a European, a man of taste, a conversationalist and wit . . . .

THE OLD WOMAN: Why then does he grunt instead of speaking? If he is a conversationalist, let him converse! What is he waiting for? You have said yourself we are living on the brink.

CYRIL: The Baron can't converse with himself.

THE OLD WOMAN: Why not?

CYRIL: The Baron must have a suitable audience.

THE OLD WOMAN: Damned bores. And where is that coffee? How much longer am I supposed to wait?

CYRIL: I have no idea, madam.

THE OLD WOMAN: What do you mean you have no idea?

CYRIL: Well, to tell the truth, I just couldn't care less about your coffee.

THE OLD WOMAN: You are two-faced.

CYRIL: Anyway this isn't my table. My colleague . . . .

THE OLD WOMAN: And where is that colleague of yours?

CYRIL: He's joined the army. He's gone! Call him if you like, madam, he might come back. But do it loudly, there's shooting going on there. (*CYRIL moves away from the OLD WOMAN*)

THE OLD WOMAN: Sugar-r-r, sugar-r-r! He's pretending not to hear. Wr-r-retch!

(A MAN on all-fours, carrying a knife, emerges from the ditch. He wipes the knife against his sleeve and puts it away in his pocket. It is our young WAITER. He approaches the table. He is all tangled up in dirty bandages which he trails all over the place like intestines. As he goes he smoothes his hair. He stands facing the OLD WOMAN.)

THE OLD WOMAN: The lazy lout, I've been calling him for the last six months. Don't you hear what is being said to you? Take that coffee away! There is a fly in the coffee, a hair in the cream, the cream is in the newspaper, the newspaper has been in the lavatory. Take all this lot away. They move like flies in honey. There's no life in them. So this is modern youth! There he stands, his hands in his pockets, philosophizing. Where is that tripe dish? Where is that fiddler?

(The WAITER feverishly stuffs the bandages in his pockets. He rubs his hands.)

THE OLD WOMAN: I have seen you somewhere. Where was it I met you? Why are you staring at me like this? Just look at his fancy dress! He must have done well for himself. Is it you or isn't it? Where have you been all this time?

WAITER: I was fighting in a war, madam.

THE OLD WOMAN: War?

WAITER: Yes, the third war.

THE OLD WOMAN: The third, the fourth, the tenth . . . . You're in a terrible hurry. Was it you who sugared my coffee? Clumsy fool. Hands like flails. I do remember.

WAITER: The coffee must be stone cold by now. But you look extremely well, madam.

THE OLD WOMAN: What a fancy get-up with all these feathers, twigs, medals, ribbons, buttons. A soldier, eh? Well, angel, meanwhile I gave birth to one boy and three girls. The boy is splendid, I won't give him up. I'm sitting on him. Have a look. Go on, don't be afraid.

(The WAITER kneels and peers. He whistles in astonishment.

The ROADSWEEPERS push on another trolley full of garbage, wastepaper and scrap-iron. This time there is an even larger number of people entangled in the rubbish. The SWEEPERS push it all off on to a heap. Now the beach, the café, the field of battle all turn into one huge rubbish dump. However, life continues as normal. All the institutions, including the Church and the health service, operate with comparative efficiency. There are meetings, conferences, banquets and visits. People enjoy themselves, tell jokes and gossip. At times we hear lively voices and even song. The liveliness and the general mess continue for a few minutes. Everyone says the first thing that comes into his head. This may include the singing of old hit songs, the reading of newspaper advertisements, reports and outdated philosophy and history handbooks. These voices emerge from beneath the rubbish. For example: (A) Few words can match 'unity' in their importance for humanity today. Everything seems to tend towards unity. The great nations of the world consist mostly of politically smaller units .... Unity, unification, union — words which play a role not only in politics, they embrace all areas of cultural and intellectual life. The number of international associations runs into hundreds, consisting of scientists, artists, sportsmen, scouts, stamp collectors, actors, union officials, journalists. In addition we have innumerable trade agreements. (B) The file marked B for 'bust' breaks open. It contains letters of enquiry or complaint about busts being too large, being too small, about shrinking and dried up busts. Letters of this nature are to be found in the mail reaching every newspaper. What size should the ideal bust be? The size is of course determined by the person's height and her general appearance. It is worth mentioning here that women with ideal-sized breasts are non-existent.

To make all this more lively we might introduce short dialogues, questions and answers, good and bad advice. For example: 'What advice should people be given?' 'What commonsense dictates. Live life to the full but avoid adventure, eat a good diet but at the same time discreetly observe your weight. Be attentive and relaxed and at the same time discreetly observe the weight of your body. And when man grows older he should get rid of certain false views. For instance, some people are afraid to eat meat because they've heard that it raises the blood pressure but in fact they ought to eat 100 grammes of meat a day. They've heard somewhere that salt strains the heart, whereas in small amounts salt is indispensable to an organism.' 'And what would you advise regarding daily routine?' 'Every day one must find time for relaxation, quiet and sleep.'

CYRIL goes up to the GENTLEMAN. He carefully wipes the GENTLEMAN's face and ears with a dirty rag. He examines the GENTLEMAN from several sides and looks at him with satisfaction.

CYRIL: (bending over with respect) I think there is a hair in your ear, Sir .... (Looks into his ear) I will remove it quite painlessly if your Honour allows. There! It's all over. Such a small detail and yet it spoils the whole effect. (CYRIL takes out a *mirror and looks into it shaking his head)* A fly has messed up the mirror again. Well, really! How can one look at one's face in such a mirror or ask the clients to use it. (*CYRIL walks around the* GENTLEMAN *with the mirror, while the* GENTLEMAN *looks to see whether his hair has been well cut.)*

(Meanwhile the ROADSWEEPERS *in a sudden burst of energy are beginning to clear up. They sweep the beach, the floor, the whole space. They gather the rubbish together and then scatter it again. They move the garbage and the rags from place to place. The air is full of dust and soot. The* SWEEPS *tuck the rubbish under chairs and tables. They sweep round chairs and tables occupied by customers. They fill their cheeks with water and spit it on the floor. They are working feverishly.)*

CYRIL: Thank you, your Honour. Oh, just one moment, Sir, there is a hair in your nose. Oh, I beg your pardon, that was a mistake. Eyes failing with age.

(CYRIL removes the dirty cloth from the gentleman's neck. The GENTLEMAN *rises. He is a fine, distinguished, imposing specimen and he rises with great dignity. The* WAITER *is brushing him all over, picking off invisible hairs.)*

CYRIL: Oh, there is a louse on your collar. (*Removes the louse with two fingers*)

THE GENTLEMAN: Thank you, Cyril.

CYRIL: Forgive me for being so bold, but your Honour has forgotten and I'm still waiting . . . I am waiting for the funny story. It's the first time in living memory that your Worship has forgotten to tell a funny story.

THE GENTLEMAN: But you haven't told me anything either. No gossip, no titbit of news, but you are right of course, my dear fellow, although in principle it is the barber who tells stories while the customer listens, this way round it is handier and easier. Still, once in a while you can turn things round. And which funny story is it you would like to hear? A political one or . . . .

CYRIL: God forbid, your Worship, that I should meddle in politics. James is the one for that. If your Honour is agreeable, I would like that story about the woman who took her daughter Jackie to buy clothes.

THE GENTLEMAN: Yes, a harmless little story and excellent at that. I always double up with laughter when I tell it but we've had it so many times, perhaps you would like something else about dwarfs?

CYRIL: But that one about Jackie and her mother is excellent. (*Offers the* GENTLEMAN *a chair*) Do sit down, it's a real stunner.

THE GENTLEMAN: No, I won't sit down, my dear friend, I will tell it 'per pedes apostolorum'.

CYRIL: Just as your Honour wishes, but I must take the liberty to observe that a sitting story teller is more impressive. 'Inter pedes puellarum est voluptas puerorum'.

(The GENTLEMAN *takes the chair. Sits down and crosses his legs. Tells the story. Any story will do.*

CYRIL *shakes his head.* EVERYONE *listens in deathly silence. Someone has even taken his hat off.*

The ROADSWEEPERS *who had abandoned their brooms and were listening to the story now turn to another job. They paint white lines through the rubbish dump, the café, the tables, the beach and even the people themselves.*

THE OLD WOMAN: (*knitting either a white baby's outfit or a sock. She sings in a senile voice*)
You've issued from me
in a flow of blood
through a dark stretch
of pain

leaves drown
in a pool of light
and a bird
sings

in a green shade
you dream your dream
white butterflies
flutter and sway

(After a pause she repeats the last verse.)

in a green shade
you dream your dream
white butterflies
flutter and sway

(The distinguished GENTLEMAN *sits at the* OLD WOMAN's *table. Without interrupting her knitting and without looking at the* GENTLEMAN, *the* OLD WOMAN *speaks. The pauses between words become longer and longer . . . .)*

THE OLD WOMAN: How old you are, ugly mug *(pause)* revolting. Quite bald. *(Pause)* You've got dandruff on your collar. *(Pause)* You are moulting and growing lousy under my very eyes. *(Long pause)* . . . Disgusting.

THE GENTLEMAN: I've tried various ointments. I've even tried the skins of young maidens and the warm little bodies of infants. I've tried laurels, foreign coins, dogs' intestines.

THE OLD WOMAN: Your heart has withered. *(Pause)* Your heart, ugly mug, is as bald as a bishop's knee. Cyril was telling me that in your old age you have become a conversationalist . . . . An excellent wit . . . . Is that true? There is wax in my ears and cotton wool over my eyes. Wit. Another one. Aren't you ashamed to be yourself?

WAITER: Am I to serve the pork, my lord? Here are the papers, the situation is again tense to the limits of endurance . . . .

THE GENTLEMAN: And a glass of Tokay 1968, please, my son. And what do the cultural supplements say?

WAITER: That's where the dog lies buried, my lord.

THE OLD WOMAN: *(not paying any attention to them)* Well, let ugly mug talk. Don't restrain him . . . . Let him say how he drank English tea at the stepson's of Wagner's second wife in the presence of King Emmanuel of Italy . . . . Conversationalist my foot! Today's after-dinner belch.

WAITER: Allow me to observe, madam, that nowadays the public takes a tremendous interest in reminiscences, memoirs, diaries, documents and chamberpots of great statesmen, great artists, small whores, great murderers, thinkers and sexual deviants. Everyone throws up to the best of his ability . . . .

THE OLD WOMAN: You're as stupid as that . . . . Well, whatever his name is . . . that critic . . . no not that one, you fool. Can't you see that all this is psychopathology? People find things seeping away, oozing out, falling apart . . . . Caught up in a Niagara of time they flow down with the lavatory water and they want to clutch on to something . . . . They grab hold of the fin-de-siècle, Granny's oil lamp, the baroque, poetry, beauty, nature, other people's lives under a spreading chestnut tree, evenings of yore . . . . They clutch on to old rubbish because they want to take a breath under the arc of an old lamp, you wretched fool . . . . I myself write and paint, so I know what it's like. An autopsy, an autoplagiarism. You're a mess like that . . . what's his name . . . ? That reviewer . . . .

THE GENTLEMAN: Everything is the other way round. Completely and utterly the other way round. Saint Methodius is a mystic . . . naked. And before I grant your request, O my soul, and tell you how I took tea at a certain lady's, I must say a few words in Methodius' defence in connection with the cult of the ephebe. After all, this cult of infantile nakedness is the prime innocence, the revelatory discovery of nakedness in its purity, in the purity of sex without sex and therefore in a certain ecstasy close to saintliness . . . .

THE OLD WOMAN: (to WAITER) Would you pull the cotton-wool out of his Honour's ear, he doesn't hear what or who he is talking about.

(The WAITER respectfully pulls the cotton-wool out of the GENTLEMAN's ear.)

THE GENTLEMAN: Everything is contrariwise, utterly and completely contrariwise, he is a mystic but a mystic possessed by a mysticism of youth and a hatred of literature . . . .

WAITER: But it seems to me, Sir, that he making fun of God and is somehow obscene with that cult of nakedness . . . .

THE GENTLEMAN: It is quite otherwise, my dear boy, he was in love with God and in all his works of genius I sense the presence of God. I would assert that our genius shows great sympathy towards God and knowing the egotism of this genius one has to admit that in his attitude to our Lord God he has shown himself to be civilized, sympathetic and even nice, for all that great philosophy of his is so great that even our professor, doctor and miracle worker was drowned in the critical depths of his existentialist shallowness . . . . (*He breaks off abruptly. The* WAITER *kneels at the* GENTLEMAN's *table.*)

(CYRIL's *voice is heard from the rubbish dump. He has now returned to his old position and is lying in his trench covered with a safety net and a pile of rubbish.*)

CYRIL: Forward! Forward! Over to me!

THE OLD WOMAN: Sugar-r-r-r, sugar-r-r-r, sugar-r-r-r, for Christ's sake.

THE BLIND MAN: Water, water, a drop of cool, clear water. Wasn't there a little lake somewhere? (*He gets up from the bench and pokes around with his white stick*) Where is that mountain stream? Where are the streams, the trees, the lakes?

THE OLD WOMAN: The streams have dried up and the sewage waters have linked up with the wells. Please calm yourself, the boy will bring you a gadget for producing soda-water, together with a funnel and a filter to filter the sewage water. Didn't you know that the great metropolitan cities drink sewage? We consume discharge.

THE BLIND MAN: Accursed witch! She has got me here with her coffee dregs.

THE OLD WOMAN: Buffoon. (*The* OLD WOMAN *talks quickly in a calm and sympathetic voice and without interrupting her knitting*)

WAITER: (*still on his knees, addressing the* GENTLEMAN) Father, I have sinned in thought, word and deed.

THE OLD WOMAN: He has sinned, what a thing to say!

WAITER: I've broken my oath, I have abandoned the colours, I have run away from the battlefield. They painted me black all over and threw me down into a hole at night . . . . I do not believe, Father, I have lost my faith . . . . We are given absolution by priests who do not believe in the life eternal . . . .

THE OLD WOMAN: He is making most of this up . . . .

WAITER: There is only meat, iron and mud . . . . I don't believe in God . . . .

(The OLD WOMAN *shakes her head, smiling. The* GENTLEMAN *shifts on his seat. He has covered the side of his face on the* WAITER's *side with the menu card. There may be holes torn out in the menu for the eyes.)*

THE GENTLEMAN: Don't think about there being no God and don't worry if you do. It's of no importance. Concentrate on everyday problems and Lord God will reveal himself to you suddenly in life itself, in nature which surrounds you, in the trees and birds. In the light, in the rain, in music, in human bodies. You see, my son, God has changed his place. He has come to dwell in human society, in the family of men and he neither needs our prayers nor does he listen to them. For he lives in flowers and streams, in bread, in fish, in mushrooms, in chocolates and sweets, he dwells even in onion soup and meatballs . . . .

THE OLD WOMAN: You're clever, ugly mug, you're always good at making something up. So it now seems that God is in you too, eh?

THE GENTLEMAN: I have disposed of Nietzsche.

THE OLD WOMAN: Show-off!

THE GENTLEMAN: Boy! I would like some spinach croquettes.

CYRIL'S VOICE: Come back, come back to your station.

(The WAITER *crawls towards the ditch in which* CYRIL *lies, dragging behind him a dirty bandage.)*

THE GENTLEMAN: *(continuing his speech from behind the menu card)* When you have shredded the spinach you will add one roll soaked in milk, one egg, as well as salt, pepper, sugar and nutmeg to taste.

(The WAITER has now crawled inside the ditch and has joined CYRIL.)

CYRIL: Why are you getting out? What was it you were looking for there? Lean on me. What were you looking for there? Times have changed. I've told you that . . . . What is it?

WAITER'S VOICE:
I do not want to die
I would still like to see
do not bury me
so quickly
Our Father who art in Heaven
Thy Kingdom . . . tell me are those flowers . . . .

CYRIL: There aren't any flowers here.

WAITER'S VOICE: And what about the horses, and the hares and the drops of rain?

CYRIL: There aren't any horses.

WAITER'S VOICE:
Shut my eyes, bury my eyes
bury me in our mother earth.

THE GENTLEMAN: *(replacing the menu card on the table)* Ah well, we'll make it up somehow. *(Picks up a newspaper and reads)* The development of the embryo outside the mother's womb is possible. Similar experiments carried out on animals are already well advanced.

(The OLD WOMAN stops her knitting and listens with interest.)

The achievements in this area are colossal and have great potential. As early as 1964 an artificial womb constructed in Canada by John Callaghan gave birth to a lamb. Dr Hafer has stimulated the ovaries of select, pure-bred cows to secrete a large amount of ova. He then inseminates them artifically with the sperm of a thoroughbred bull kept specially for this purpose.

THE OLD WOMAN: Just as well the sperm doesn't come from such a genius as you. Old gasbag.

THE GENTLEMAN: (*continues reading*) Herman Muller, one of the most distinguished geneticists, has suggested that the ovaries and the sperm of the best, the most intelligent and the most able people ought to be placed in cold storage in deep shelters. This would be humanity's reserve in case of a nuclear war and the self-destruction of civilization.

THE OLD WOMAN: Claptrap. You and that Italian friend of yours can go on experimenting. A test-tube baby. The baby comes from me. It is me. You are too clever to understand the feelings of an ordinary simple cow.... I won't part with him.

> He has issued from me
> he has gone away into the world
> but I have not bitten through
> the umbilical cord
> I have not allowed
> him to be cut off
> I hold him with my teeth
> let him wander around the world
> he has issued out of me
> into the cosmos
> into the vacuum
> he flies, dreams, sings
> as from a cabin
> but I am holding on to him with my claws
> I won't give him up

(*She pulls out a pair of wire-rimmed spectacles, puts them on her nose and calmly continues with her knitting.*)

> I will pull him inside myself
> I will push him inside
> I will lock him up
> when the need comes
> now I'm loosening the thread
> the hair
> the vein
> he has complete freedom.

(A small LIGHT ORCHESTRA consisting of three or five members, wearing white blazers with golden buttons and blue caps emerges out of the rubbish dump. They are cleaning their instruments. They are preparing for the show. A YOUTH carrying a traveller's bag appears from behind the café wall. The YOUTH is dressed carefully, neatly and colourfully. A beautiful matching of colours. His hair is long, light and radiant. On his face an expression of curiosity and pensiveness, an innocent, coquettish and half-shy smile. The details of his dress are not important, he might be dressed in the late 19th-century fashion. What is important is the expression on his face and the hair style. And the flower in his buttonhole. Black patent-leather shoes with silver clasps. On his breast a dazzlingly white lace frill. The THREE GIRLS who have earlier been sunbathing and chattering are now occupied in weaving wreaths and making bouquets out of the rubbish and dead flowers. Every few minutes they throw the lot on the ground, start again, laugh. They weave garlands of rags and garbage and try to hang these up. The YOUTH looks on while they work. They smile at him charmingly. They whisper to one another. Again they laugh. They pronounce their names as though they were introducing themselves.)

FIRST GIRL: Cloto.

SECOND GIRL: Lachesis. *(She throws a wreath of rubbish and paper flowers round the YOUTH's neck)*

THIRD GIRL: Atropos.

(She is holding a pair of silver scissors and makes a gesture as though she were trying to cut the invisible thread linking the YOUTH with life, but her friends do not allow her to. After a while the GIRLS return to their chaotic occupations. The YOUTH approaches the BLIND MAN and asks him something. Maybe he asks him for the way to a street, a house or a bus stop. The BLIND MAN explains, gesticulating. Soot, down, bits of paper and confetti occasionally float down from above. But at considerable intervals, say every few minutes. Colourful balloons float around and have dirty rags, torn bags, old socks and even threadbare pants and earmuffs, etc, attached to them.)

THE BLIND MAN: What a pity, young wanderer, that you will not be spending the next few days and nights with us. We shall be entertaining the Viceroy and his young bride. They're coming on an official visit, hence all this tidying up. By nightfall the whole city will be like a garden and the sky will be like a bouquet of coloured flares. Well, you're in a hurry and I'm taking up your time. Nowadays you young ones fly, fly anywhere so long as it's quicker, farther and into the unknown. But I know that one comes back even from the longest journey, so I'm saving my legs. (*Points a direction with his stick*) So you will take this lime avenue right up to the white building with a tower. There you will turn right, past the botanic gardens, past three fountains, the sports stadium, the clinic. And beyond the clinic there is a lawn with a statue on it and if from there you walk straight as the crow flies you will reach the beach. And anyway you will then hear the roar of the sea and it will draw you unto itself. Go boldly, young man, and good luck!

(The YOUTH *bows and moves away. The* BLIND MAN *raises his hat and smilingly watches the* YOUTH *go away. He then sits down on the bench and unfolds a torn newspaper. He may be reading aloud theatre reviews.*

The YOUTH *has stopped near a basket chair and has dropped his bag on the ground. He looks around like a man waiting at a bus stop.*

A POLICEMAN *in black uniform with white belt and white gloves and a long white truncheon attached to his belt. He walks with a measured step along a white line. He is utterly unconcerned, as though simultaneously he saw nothing and saw everything.*

The YOUTH *pays no attention to the* POLICEMAN *either. He pulls out a sweet in a green paper. Unwraps it and slips the sweet into his mouth. He looks around as though he were searching for a rubbish bin, then he rolls up the paper and throws it on the ground. The* POLICEMAN *stops in front of the* YOUTH *and looks at him carefully. The* YOUTH *smiles at the* POLICEMAN *but the* POLICEMAN *looks grave. The* POLICEMAN *walks away and continues his beat. The* YOUTH *pulls a mirror out of his pocket and carefully examines his reflection. He smiles to himself and then grows serious.)*

YOUTH: *(recites a poem called 'They')*
The ordinary day is beautiful
it opens with a band of white
lips that are opposite and bitter
consume the dregs of night and sleep
faces strange and blind like puppies
open their eyes open their eyes
from each other's lips they pick
smiles and wonder
they feed each other
upon tongues of birds . . . .

. . . when they perceive the obvious
they stifle a cry
ah! the sun the flower the breast
and the grey ordinary day
turns for them into wonder
like a pink elephant.

(The POLICEMAN stops. Light grows dim, and cold as during an eclipse. Now the YOUTH is not paying any attention to the GUARDIAN OF THE LAW. He pulls out a silver comb and slowly and meticulously combs his long, fine, light hair. The face of the GUARDIAN OF ORDER grows solemn and stony. He utters his words clearly but as though with a certain difficulty.)

GUARDIAN OF ORDER: What are you doing here?

(The YOUTH, combing his hair, smiles sadly but in a friendly way.)

Why don't you answer my question?

YOUTH: What am I doing? I stand, I wait, I comb my hair. *(Continues to comb his hair)*

GUARDIAN OF ORDER: What were you doing a moment ago?

YOUTH: *(finishing his combing)* Just now? I was reciting a poem.

GUARDIAN OF ORDER: And what were you doing before you broadcast that text?

YOUTH: (*smiling*) Nothing.

GUARDIAN OF ORDER: Nothing! Can't you remember? There is still time.

(The YOUTH pulls the flower out of his buttonhole, smells it, touches it with his lips, then maybe kisses it. The GUARDIAN OF ORDER beckons the GENTLEMAN with his finger. The GENTLEMAN looks surprised as though he were asking 'Do you mean me?' The GENTLEMAN nervously adjust his clothes, buttons himself up and almost runs to the GUARDIAN OF ORDER.)

GUARDIAN OF ORDER: (*not looking at the GENTLEMAN*) We have a witness who may be able to remind you of everything.

(The YOUTH, replacing the flower in his buttonhole, gives the GENTLEMAN a friendly smile.)

GUARDIAN OF ORDER: And now do you remember what you were doing before you broadcast the text?

YOUTH: (*laughs heartily. The GUARDIAN OF ORDER moves towards him*) I ate a sweet, but of course, gentlemen, I ate a sweet. (*Laughs*)

GUARDIAN OF ORDER: And what sort of sweet was it?

YOUTH: A sweet with a soft centre. (*Smiles*)

GUARDIAN OF ORDER: And was it wrapped in something?

YOUTH: Yes, in a paper.

GUARDIAN OF ORDER: And what happened to that paper?

YOUTH: I unwrapped it.

GUARDIAN OF ORDER: We're not asking you whether you unwrapped it, but what you did with the paper after you unwrapped the sweet.

YOUTH: I don't remember, (*shrugs his shoulders*) I don't know.

GUARDIAN OF ORDER: We have proof that you first looked carefully all around you and when you ascertained that there was nobody in the vicinity you deliberately threw the sweet paper on to a route which had previously been swept and prepared for the passage of the royal pair.

YOUTH: All right then, I did throw it, but why are you saying all this in such a grave voice? You're terribly sad. Honestly, I didn't want to distress anyone. I do remember now that I looked round for a rubbish bin but I couldn't find one and I automatically threw the paper away. Anyway, I was standing on a heap of rubbish. I can't see the logic of this, how can one litter a rubbish heap?

GUARDIAN OF ORDER: Is that what you think?

YOUTH: You can see for yourself.

GUARDIAN OF ORDER: I don't see any rubbish here. Are you able to explain to me why you are fouling the ground and air of our town just at the moment when the noble pair are about to pass?

YOUTH: (*politely*) My friend, I swear this is a pure accident. Come on, do cheer up, surely we can talk about all this with a smile. Anyway, I'll gladly pick up the paper. (*The* YOUTH *looks at the garbage heap, bends and rummages in the rubbish*)

GUARDIAN OF ORDER: (*shouting*) Don't move! Don't touch anything and stand still!

YOUTH: (*getting up*) Friend, I have really come to like you very much for this matter-of-fact, sad tone of voice. Let us be friends. I never had any evil intent. I love people. I love flowers. In my heart I am not capable of killing even a fly.

GUARDIAN OF ORDER: Let me see your documents.

(The YOUTH *pulls the flower out of his buttonhole and smilingly hands it over to the* POLICEMAN. *The* GUARDIAN OF ORDER *steps back.)*

YOUTH: (*stretches out the hand with the flower*) Please, do take it.

GUARDIAN OF ORDER: What is it!? (*Moves back in terror*)

YOUTH: A flower. (*He takes a step towards the* POLICEMAN) Please don't be afraid.

(The GUARDIAN OF ORDER, *gazing at the* YOUTH'S *face, slowly reaches for his truncheon.)*

YOUTH: *(takes another step)* It's for you, I wish to offer you a flower in memory of this funny misunderstanding.

(The GUARDIAN OF ORDER *draws back, pulls the truncheon. The* YOUTH's *face grows serious and still. It is now veiled in sadness while a smile appears on the* POLICEMAN's *face, or maybe it is only twisted in a grimace. The* YOUTH *drops the hand with the flower.)*

VOICE OF THE OLD WOMAN: Sonny, Sonny! Where are you? Don't hide from your old mother, Sonny!

(The lights flash on and off, on and off, while the stage empties slowly.)

Sonny, Sonny! Where are you?

(The OLD WOMAN *mounts the rubbish heap, she looks round, searches, ferreting round all the rubbish bins, holes, looks under the tables and chairs. She knocks on the wall and listens.)*

Sonny, do answer me. Don't frighten me.

The OLD WOMAN's *movements are alternately slow and feverish. As she searches she loses her numerous headgears, false hair, jewellery, bracelets, necklaces, stockings, shoes. She now digs in the rubbish with a stick she has found. Suddenly she stops utterly still. She throws away the stick and kneels. She digs into the rubbish faster and faster, fiercely. She is tearing the earth with her claws. She is panting heavily. She leans over the hole she has dug out. She keeps repeating an inarticulate word.*

The curtain suddenly cuts off the action and the performance. The curtain falls very quickly and does not go up again. This is the end of the performance and the end of the play. The curtain could be made of heavy metal. It falls like a sword and cuts the actors off from the spectators. It cuts the performance off from the auditorium. The actors do not appear on the stage nor do they come in front of the curtain. They do not bow. They do not hold hands. They do not smile at the audience. They do not accept flowers, etc. The curtain cuts the actors off from the audience, the auditorium from the performance. The curtain suddenly cuts the performance and the play's action.

February 1968

BIRTH RATE

The biography of a stage play

31 October 1966. Today I'm on the verge of surrender. I've lost the will and the necessary energy; I don't believe in the need to bring this play to life.

Over the last few weeks, work on this theatre piece has been nothing but dilemmas and departures. The quantities of notes, cuttings, drafts and scenes, the sheer number of its individual elements, grow endlessly. Today, however, I have been confronting the greatest block of all. I'm not talking about technical difficulties, it's something absolutely basic: I feel that the 'times', 'the spirit of the times' (I believe in this famous phantom, to we dramatic poets it's as real, stubborn and vengeful as 'the ghost of Hamlet's father') ... I feel that the 'spirit of the times' now demands drama (maybe tragedy) but not comedy. Suddenly all my comic ideas seem sinful; the very act of writing comedy an act of treason and a waste of time. Since this morning, I and this work of mine – which is already alive, has been growing in me, in my imagination, for years – have been going through some difficult hours. The last day of October 1966. Cold, dark. Tomorrow is All Saints' Day, Wednesday is All Souls'. November. And I, an inhabitant of the most massive cemetery in human history, am supposed to carry on writing a 'comedy' called *Birth Rate*. I spelled the title out again last night, in black letters. I keep telling myself I am 'a man of letters' and therefore that I'm entitled to write not only drama but comedies, and comic sketches too.

For forms to exist and develop, they must have free space around them. It can be silence. This play *Birth Rate* deals with a living growing human mass which, because that space is lacking, destroys all forms and pours 'from emptiness into the void'. In the third Act, the walls burst open and a flood of people pours in through the cracks. The action is this very process of cracking, the crumbling of the walls. Voices and words have no connection with the action.

It must be the first time since I started writing 'plays for the stage' that I've experienced such an overwhelming need to talk to the director, designer, composer, actors . . . to the entire theatre. But (here and now) I am alone. I feel I need direct contact with these people already, during the writing process. In fact, I could start the rehearsals now. I could jettison the full literary text and opt for a scenario. But I am on my own and I am forced to write a work of literature, to describe what would be more easily *expressed* through direct contact with living human beings. I don't have 'my own' theatre or director. Perhaps in a few years, an accidental director will turn up who'll run the play through his own workshop, and I'll receive an invitation to a 'world première'. I've resisted writing this play for a long time. I began it in 1958, almost at the same time as *The Card Index.* Actually, it wasn't 'resistance', but I couldn't bring myself to write up and describe something which already existed in my imagination in a fluid but realistic shape. Something which was growing in all directions. I couldn't resolve to grasp the shears-pen, get down to trimming the ideas and images, to begin the pathetic activity of describing the spectacle (pathetic and slightly tedious). I kept interrupting my multiple attempts to write, discouraged by the gnawing thought that it would be better to improvise the whole thing with a company. Only when I realized that I had been condemned solely to write things down did I start writing this play. (I wonder should I limit myself to the playtext, or describe the 'history' of this piece, its biography?)

At the very beginning, the play was to be set in an arbitrary train or tram compartment into which more and more people crowded. The interior would be furnished like a train compartment. When the curtain rises, the compartment is empty. A young man enters, sits down casually, he might even stretch out across the seats. Next a young woman enters. They start up a conversation which turns into flirting, mutual attraction. During the play, more and more people enter. Individually or in couples. At first civilized forms are maintained. Forms exist. Space permits forms or civilized (polite) relations to survive. But the numbers of people are steadily growing. There's no more room on the seats. People sit shoulder to shoulder. More and more. Old people, women with children. Sportsmen, pregnant women. People clamber into the luggage racks. Cram the aisles. They still apologize, however, get indignant, hold the children up above the crowd. Nonetheless the forms are changing. Before our eyes they undergo a terrifying metamorphosis generated by lack of space. First, all those sitting inside try to shut the door. A majestic High Priest strides into the compartment. He utters a few platitudes, gives his blessing, pats children's heads; he is pushed to the floor and then tossed in the luggage rack, but he keeps rambling sanctimoniously about the dignity of motherhood, the sinfulness of contraception, about the 'rhythm method'. Pregnant women tell of their marital problems, others are off to a spa for treatment, despairing of their infertility. Meanwhile the pressure's growing from outside, the walls bend in. The living mass is so squeezed into the closed space that it begins to boil. There are two, three explosions, one after another. Movement mixes with screams. Finally everything goes still. Out from the mass, the young couple emerge in silence and start to flirt, attract each other. Their voices are like pigeons cooing in the silence.

It was a vision of a play based exclusively on movement, on the growth of the living mass. Dialogue would only come in at certain moments and create specific phases of a process taking place inside a closed space.

Over the years I collected press cuttings, made notes from brochures and books, corresponded with a demographics expert, a friend from secondary school who'd become a world authority in the field.

The development of this theatre piece was a two-way process. On the one hand my imagination constantly created and compiled new 'images'; on the other — the 'documentation' — the pile of information kept growing. Over the years, ever since I first had the idea, some images have departed or simply vanished unrecorded without trace. Similarly with the cuttings and notes — some disappeared, some are lying amongst layers of papers, and only some have survived until today, until the moment of realization. Of course, in the realm of art (drama) a work develops from one image to another, but these images grew on a heap of notes and news, the journalistic and statistical manure from which the images drew their juices (information).

One article was entitled '5000 Babies per Hour'. It appeared several years ago in the English journal *Forward* and was based on data from the *United Nations Demographic Yearbook*. Of course, I translated the data for theatrical use — I sketched images. Babies are arranged on a tiered trolley like loaves in a bakery. Nurses push the trolleys or circle round with their baby load, circling faster and faster. This grew from the images of a production line and a conveyor belt down a mine, as well as from some paintings representing Heaven and Hell in the imagination of 15th and 16th-century artists — where angels and devils transport whole armfuls of redeemed or damned souls to their destinations.

Another image I was going to introduce was a cellar containing women-vessels. I imagined a scientist's laboratory shaped like a cellar, with women-vessels arranged in rows, shaped like jugs, amphorae . . . . The scientist would go from one vessel to the next, peer in . . . . This journey would be broken up by monologues and dialogues. Living women would be speaking vessels. For instance one 'vessel' would say to the Scientist-Hermit:

> hit me
> with your cane
> touch me
> stick your rod
> in this hornet's nest
> let life gush out.

But I still had all the data about the birth rate, it had got under my skin. A scene in a 'chastity-belt' workshop, the 'cell' scene and the 'hermitage' scene — these were simply intended to prepare the atmosphere for the explosion of the 'population' bomb, the central, essential scene of the whole piece. A conversation between the scientist (a pseudo-schizophrenic) and a pseudo-male-nurse takes place in isolation from the external world. But there is a feeling that beyond the 'cell' walls that world is growing, seething, multiplying — a feeling that clearly penetrates into the isolated 'cell'.

Somehow within the piece, issues of celibacy, virginity, the pill, the 'rhythm method' all had to be taken into consideration. The reading list was vast, and it's hard now to name all the books I 'consumed' while collecting my material. So there are quotations from St Jerome which were to be used in conversations between the hermit and the women (vessels of sin), there are popular pamphlets from the Family Planning Association, there are scientific handbooks, diaries, instruction manuals for newly-weds, etc, etc. One of the first drafts of *Birth Rate* began with 'The Ballad of the Vessel'. Of course, it was about woman (vessel of sin). The quotations from Church Patriarchs stem from that period. They arranged themselves into a pattern which would eventually take the form of 'The Ballad of the Vessel'.

> how long have we borne the treasure
> in clay vessels
> (I have no oil)
> take the mill-stone grind the flour
> expose your shame
> show your shins
> wade through the rivers
> god is the belly
> the devil's power lies in the hips
> and strength is in the navel
> painful to relate
> how many virgins fall each day
> over how many nests the proud enemy
> erects his palace
> how many rocks are hollowed by the snake
> that then lives in the crevice . . . .

(For me the image of a Satan-snake boring into virgins/rock and living in the crevices was rich with many meanings.) The issue of 'heat', without which there is no love, was important. Heat generated by intercourse and the friction of bodies. The question of 'heat', which certain aesthetes (humanity's enemies) used to compare to 'cow dung', was (and is) one of the main concerns of the *Birth Rate* play. Now the closed space is getting hotter and hotter. People create heat. The entire human mass seems heated up.

11 January 1967

'But in life, people don't shoot each other all the time, don't hang themselves, don't propose. They don't always talk cleverly. Most of the time they eat, drink, flirt, talk rubbish. So that has to be shown on the stage. Someone must write a play where people would come in, go out, eat dinner, talk about the weather, play cards . . . . Let the stage be as complicated and as simple as life is. People eat dinner, they just eat dinner, and, at that very moment, their happiness is born or their life falls to pieces . . . .'

I'm happy to interpret this remark of Chekhov's to my advantage. I'm looking for an excuse for my own 'comedies' and 'so-called comedies'. I'm wracked by doubts again. I cannot go on writing in this 'tone'. The contemporary comic writer is a fool wading in puddles of blood, rivers of blood that engulf him from every corner of the world. I will not pretend it isn't difficult. For months I've been unable to hack through to the one true shape, to the play's organic form. I'm cutting my tongue and feet on jokes.

> Darkness through the window
> menacing darkness.

Via the radio, strange news is reaching us here from China. I've abandoned art again and thrown myself into reading books and the papers. Finally . . . (but that's irrelevant). I feel I'm taking the thing in the wrong direction. Or perhaps I am being taken, shoved, in the wrong direction by the 'thing'? As I lie in the dark with my eyes open, I have a feeling (I feel) that the very act of writing is the act of dying pointlessly. Why is the original concept – so pure, so clear – becoming covered with fool's bells! The play's organism is becoming riddled with tumours. They devour the bright healthy idea. I'm turning into a tool in the writing process. And I don't want this . . . .

13 January 1967

I could have built this play yesterday. From the morning onwards, I kept escaping into the newspapers. I kept pottering round the room. I read some Chesterton (he's aged horribly), I tried correcting a failed poem, read Porebski's *Cubism*, wrote letters, went to the Wrzosówka Café, listened to the radio: the situation in China, the President's address to the US Congress, the war in Vietnam, the death of Zbigniew Cybulski. In the evening I looked through some illustrated magazines from 1966. I watched *The Cobra* on TV, I felt like sitting with other people downstairs in the 'commu-

nity room'. I went back to the radio. Midnight: a soliloquy. I condemn myself for my poetry-writing habit. I get up. I switch on the
light. I go back to writing the play. I look through the 1966 notes:
a play with 'no end'. I don't want this play to 'end'. Critics can't see
anything. They can't see basic differences: plays by ABCDMYZ,
even plays by Witkacy and Gombrowicz, have an 'end'. My plays
don't have an end. That's one of the fundamental differences. Led
on by producers or directors — and sometimes I let them lead me
— I would add some sort of ending just for the sake of peace and
quiet. Take *The Laocoon Group* or *Spaghetti and the Sword*. Another
concern, the problem that keeps me awake at night. Time. What is
this about infernal dramatic time? The themes of my plays don't
develop in time, so the action doesn't 'develop' either. This is the
problem! It isn't a question of documentary montages, press reports, court transcripts (dramatized?). Forget political treaties, scenes
from life! It's not the Eichmann case, Pius XII, the Rosenbergs,
Oppenheimer, Stalin, Churchill. The latest trials, wars, crises, generals' journals, letters ... all of that will always grab the attention
of producers, reviewers, audiences ... but as far as dramatic principles are concerned they're all secondary. The new drama — post-
Witkacy and post-Beckett — has to tackle the problems of dramatic
technique, not some 'fantastic' subject .... You can expose Julius
Caesar's impotence, or Rudolf Valentino's, you can show the Deputy
wearing carpet slippers on a rocking horse, Bormann playing the
flute, the revolution in a madhouse ... you can glue together the
history of the Dallas assassination and some flimsy 'literary' com-
mentary ... you can do lots of things. But it's all just sterile
journalistic activity. Carrying spectators into miscellaneous real
events has nothing to do with the drama. For me, the issue isn't
the 'beginning', 'middle' and supposed 'end' of a play, but the con-
tinuity of a certain situation. I divide theatre into 'external' (a theatre
where what matters most is action, what happens on the stage;
this is Classical theatre and even Romantic theatre) which extends
until modern theatre, until Dürenmat, Witkacy. It's only with Beckett
that we witness, not merely surface action, but also the disintegration of that action on the stage ... here, the disintegration is the
action. To be precise, the 'external' theatre is already the 'historic'
theatre; a theatre whose process has ended — I'm not talking here
about directorial and critical interpretations. So I divide theatre into

'external' and 'internal'. I am trying to reach the 'internal' theatre by following traces and signs left by Dostoievsky, Chekhov, Conrad . . . . What happens in Chekhov is secondary — it's not the 'plots' or the 'resolutions' we remember but the 'air'; we feel their atmosphere with all our senses, the void between events, the silence between words, the expectation. It is the motionlessness and not the motion that is the essence of the play. How much have they written and said about that gun which, if it hangs on the wall in the first act . . . must fire in the last . . . they've built so many superficial theories on this premise, quoting him all the time . . . . And must it fire in the last act? What if it doesn't? They never stop quoting him about it, why don't they quote some of his less attractive truths? Less attractive but more important both for his plays and possibly for modern drama: 'Most of the time they eat, drink, flirt, talk rubbish . . . eat dinner, they just eat dinner, and at that very moment . . . .'

How often the phrase 'a moment of silence' comes in between the words Chekhov's 'heroes' utter. And what a weight those 'moments of silence' carry. Almost as great for me as that of all the words spoken in the drama. Moments of silence between words, between events . . . often they can build and propel the dramatic 'action'. What's important is what fills those 'moments of silence', how they're filled by the plays' 'heroes', by the author and the spectator-auditors. Over one hundred years have passed since his birth. His moments of silence were filled with the life and expectations of his generation. The moments of silence in our plays, our drama, are and must be filled with different thoughts, different experiences, different memories, different doubts and different hopes. In my plays the silent moments are filled with the thoughts of an anonymous inhabitant of a great city, the metropolis, an anonymous person whose life was spent between a gigantic necropolis and a constantly growing *polis*. The poet and the *polis*? The poet and the necropolis? In the last scene of *The Cherry Orchard* Ania cries, 'Good-bye, old life.' And Trofimov answers, 'Welcome, new life!' And there's the meaning of Chekhov's work, theatre, comedy. And what of our 'heroes'? Think, what do they cry 'good-bye' and 'hello' to, the 'heroes' of Beckett, Dürrenmat, Hochhuth, Weiss, Mrozek, Pinter, Albee? Or the 'heroes' of Witkacy, Ionesco, Gombrowicz? Or the 'heroes' of

Sartre, Camus, Genet, do they have the courage to cry out with a 'pure heart': 'Welcome, new life'?

One of my favourite books from the period of my 'adolescence under Occupation', Conrad's *Lord Jim*, includes a scene which for me is 'the heart of darkness' of that great poem of honour, betrayal, cowardice and love '. . . anyhow, a dog was there, weaving himself in and out amongst people's legs in that mute stealthy way native dogs have, and my companion stumbled over him. The dog leapt away without a sound; the man, raising his voice a little, said with a slow laugh, "Look at that wretched cur," and directly afterwards we became separated by a lot of people pushing in. I stood back for a moment against the wall while the stranger managed to get down the steps and disappeared. I saw Jim spin round. He made a step forward and barred my way. We were alone; he glared at me with an air of stubborn resolution . . . . The dog in the very act of trying to sneak in at the door, sat down hurriedly to hunt for fleas. "Did you speak to me?" asked Jim very low . . . .'

Despite the romantic gesture at the point of death, despite the great struggle, despite the tragic love, for me Jim's true drama took place in a rather sordid, tawdry setting; the noisy courtroom . . . . In the aisle. In the corridor. Somebody sneered at a scabby dog, a genuine scabby stray dog . . . and Jim thought they were calling him. ' "Did you speak to me?" asked Jim very low . . . .' As far as I am concerned this is the most tragic moment in Lord Jim's life. His whole life's drama is encapsulated in it. Here in this scene are the elements of the 'internal' drama that I think and talk of.

THE ORDER SQUAD

The scenario

This play features any number of characters — although the author gives them life, he takes no responsibility for their fate or actions. Their physical presence onstage is probably required. The only constant in this production is the Order Squad. The Order Squad can only be distinguished from the rest of the crowd by the armbands. The Order Squad (probably) has a vision of the whole, knows the plot and the pathways to the so-called end. The Order Squad consistently intervenes in the interests of conventional dramatic development. The Squad is partly invented by the author, partly by his alter ego. Without the Order Squad, the whole thing might degenerate into mere messy reality or some sort of Theatre of the Absurd. Whereas, thanks to the Order Squad, we have drama. The number of persons playing a direct part in the action is (in principle) unlimited. Those who wish to enter the play and participate are allowed in on presentation of a pass. They are required to explain their roles to the Order Squad, to give their personal details and to specify their relationships and connections with every person already onstage.

Only after such explanations can persons auditioning for the play obtain a pass from the Order Squad. There are two kinds of pass: yellow, exclusively permitting speech (soliloquies, dialogue, etc), and black, permitting action (e.g. murder, treason, digestion, torture, wine-drinking, poison-drinking, etc). Some people take advantage of the onstage confusion, as well as of the Squad's inattention, to charge onto the stage individually or in groups and speak lines or even influence the course of the play without permission. The Squad either intervenes at once or listens patiently. Often the Squad is not quite sure whether the person in question has indeed the right to participate in the action; in such cases, the Squad first debates amongst itself and only then does it throw the individual off-stage. As for the participants, some appear only once during the performance, others reappear throughout at five-minute intervals. The Order Squad cuts and destroys all sub-plots which develop a certain degree of vitality. However, the Order Squad does not preclude such dramas from developing alongside the main plot. Even onstage, they may grow outside of the Order Squad's orbit. The people appearing include some who wish to confess their entire lives in public, others who need to explain something, others who long for some emotional human contact, others trying to hide something, and some people who would like to inform on somebody else. There are some who crave revenge. There are some who begin and some who end. And many, many others.

Essentially, the director of this production blows a whistle and directs traffic. The designer should arrange the set so as not to interfere with the actors or block the traffic. The actors should not pay too much attention to themselves or to the others, or to what they act.

THE LITTLE GARDEN OF EDEN

A play in one act

CHARACTERS

MUMMY

FATHER

GRAŻYNKA — *their little* DAUGHTER

WOMAN

MORALIST (*hiding in the wild rose bush*)

The action takes place in a little garden.

MUMMY: (*in a sweet voice*) Grażynka!

GRAŻYNKA: What?

MUMMY: We don't say 'What', darling, we say 'Yes, mummy'.

GRAŻYNKA: Yes, mummy?

MUMMY: Look, your lovely plum's all ripe now, come and pick your lovely plum.

GRAŻYNKA: O, thank you, dearest mummy!

MUMMY: Come, come and pick your lovely plum. It's made itself ripe especially for you. Daddy said it's soft and squidgy now, so you can come and pick your lovely plum, my little love.

GRAŻYNKA: You're right, mummy. It's so soft!

MUMMY: You can eat it, my little love, it's your very own lovely plum!

GRAŻYNKA: My lovely plum from my lovely tree! Tra la la! Tra la!

WOMAN: (*coming close to the gate*) God bless! Morning all, enjoy your fruit, my little luv!

GRAŻYNKA: Mummy, what does that old bag want? (*Sticking out her tongue at the crone*) Filthy pig ... I'm only my Mummy's little love!

FATHER: (*strong authoritative voice*) What's going on in there?

MUMMY: Some old bag's messing with Grażynka! Come and see!

FATHER: (*sternly*) What d'you want here, woman? Can't you see it's a private path, private gate, private little garden, private lovely plum, private little love? I'm calling the police.

WOMAN: I was only saying hello . . . .

MUMMY: She's upset the child. She'll be sick in a minute! Get out, woman!

WOMAN: (*murmuring*) Ought to set Chairman Meeow on this lot, Chairman bloody Meeow . . . .

FATHER: (*pushing the old WOMAN along*) Out! Or I'll set the dog ... out!

(*MUMMY squeezes GRAŻYNKA's head. GRAŻYNKA vomits. FATHER hits the WOMAN on the head with his fist ... the WOMAN falls down on the ground. She breaks her wooden leg, hits her head on the stone. Dies.*)

MUMMY: Omigod. What next? What a disaster! Grażynka, don't look, go to the conservatory and eat your lovely plum . . . .

(*Grażynka runs to the conservatory.*)

FATHER: Someone's got to clear this mess up.

MUMMY: Thank God nobody saw. . . . Look what the old cow's done!

FATHER: Someone's got to clear it up quickly. Bury it. In the ground. Go get the shovel, the rake . . . . Hurry up!

MUMMY: Omigod. What did we do to deserve this? And what was the old bag looking for, hovering round decent people . . . ?

FATHER: Her children must have thrown her out . . . . Quick, the shovel!

(MOTHER and FATHER dig a hole in the garden. FATHER tosses the corpse into the hole. They both bury it. They then sow some herbs and flowers.)

GRAŻYNKA: *(from the conservatory)* Oh! Mummy dear, my lovely plum's so sweet!

METAMORPHOSES

The action takes place on a tram.

Old women, bearded and whiskery, some of them balding —
speaking in gruff voices. Young men in flowery shirts and frills,
very tight trousers, long eyelashes, pretty lips (like cherries) —
waggling their bottoms non-stop, shaking angelic curls. A ticket
inspector — checking everything, even the distance between the
various body parts of the passengers. Midi, maxi, mongoose.

INSPECTOR: (*puts his hand on the shoulder of one whiskery-bearded*
woman and says kindly) Have a seat, Grandad.

1ST WOMAN: (*grumbling through her moustache and beard*) Grandad!
Honestly! What next, peasant? Can't you tell a woman from
a man, you old fart? Don't you recognize me? The Dor-
mouse in *Alice in Wonderland*? Don't you remember when
I got that gold disk with my single — *The Trumpet*?

INSPECTOR: O right, and the other leg's got bells on.

1ST WOMAN: Let me sing it for you! (*She's singing*)
Trumpet blow, terrify the foe!
Trumpet blow, terrify the foe!

2ND WOMAN: (*to the boys*) You sit down, girls. You'll do enough stand-
ing, washing, cleaning, childbearing when you're married.
Sit here with me, arm in arm, eh? Old gran won't hurt you.
(*Sings*) Fun, fun, fun, little fannies!

INSPECTOR: (*pushes the woman's chin*) Let's check your bust. Ho, ho!
Medals! Ribbons!

2ND WOMAN: Buzz off, check your own bust.

INSPECTOR: (*politely*) You know how it goes, madam, you've got a
girl and then suddenly ooops! D'you remember, there was
that case of the woman who won three medals in the shotput,
and then turned into a man. Couldn't do the pole vault, she
grew a beard . . . got her legs tangled up in it or something
and fell over . . . .

1ST WOMAN: (*strokes her beard and turns to the boys*)
Little ruffians
are you lesbians
it's the fashion it appears
blood not water   female beards
a bum is not a bum
a person could get glum
little women   oh!
little conmen   oh!

BOY: (*face like a hen's backside*)
Grandad don't talk stupid
we are a new
tram-based
theatre group   it's
amateur-professional

INSPECTOR: Tickets please, my lovely girls, my little spinsters.

BOY: (*sweet as a meringue*)
This is theatre
so you're the one who needs a ticket

INSPECTOR:
Beardy creeps   beasts in heat
some spooks   oh so neat
some crooks   croaks croaks
some boys   some oaks
some curls   some girls

WOMAN: (*robust as a beetroot with a black beard, pulls out a fiddle*

from her bosom and starts grinding. Squealing)
Fun, fun, fun, little fannies,
Come to granny!

INSPECTOR: Sodomites, hermaphrodites, tickets please!

CROWD: Shall we give him one?

INSPECTOR: (*beats his brows and jumps out of the tram shouting*) Bye-bye! Fuck yourselves, the lot of you!

WHAT YOU GOT HERE

At the recycling centre.

A good-looking young farmhand wearing a black tailcoat and lacquered shoes with Cuban heels, carries a sack over his shoulder. He wipes his face with the lace sleeve of his white shirt. He puts the sack on the scales. The manager of the recycling centre looks at the scales.

MANAGER: What you got here?

RUSTIC: (*kicks the sack with the tip of his shoe*) Nothing much . . . .

MANAGER: I'm not buying a pig in a poke.

RUSTIC: Err . . . a few old bits . . . waste of breath to mention.

MANAGER: Let's see, let's see.

RUSTIC: Nothing to see. You'll just get your hands mucky, sir.

MANAGER: Open the sack. I'll have a look.

RUSTIC: (*grudgingly undoing the sack*) Doubting Thomas you are, sir.

MANAGER: (*peeks inside the sack*) What's that, a hand?

RUSTIC: Err, not really.

MANAGER: I can see very well: it's a human hand. Five fingers!

RUSTIC: Not unusual, every hand's got five fingers.

MANAGER: What's going on here, son? You'd better tell me now or get out . . . .

RUSTIC: But what's all the fuss about, it's only Grandad.

MANAGER: I don't need your grandad. Is he still alive?

RUSTIC: 'Course he's alive, he's just asleep, he got tired with all that travelling. So — are you taking him?

MANAGER: What am I supposed to do with him?

RUSTIC:

> When God rejects the sacrifice,
> The calf come home as a surprise.

(He ties the sack.)

Oh well, if you don't want him, I'll chuck him in the river.

MANAGER: What a son! You need a good flogging.

RUSTIC: I told you I'm not his son. I'm just his grandson.

MANAGER: You should be flayed alive.

RUSTIC: Go fuck yourself.

MANAGER: Have you no fear of God?

RUSTIC: But they said God's dead.

MANAGER: Get out, you unbeliever, you'll bring me bad luck.

RUSTIC: And what am I supposed to do with this old bleeder? He's blind, deaf as a post and he shits himself. Look at the city folk. Aren't they lucky? They can stick 'em in a home or dump 'em in front of a station and then they just bugger off out of it and watch flicks all day.

RUBBING HIS HANDS TOGETHER

A musical comedy

CAST

LADIES, GENTLEMEN, TICKET TOUTS, CRITICS, A COUNTRY WENCH, THE ENTOURAGE OF THE GREAT PIANO MAESTRO, TOWN COUNCILLORS, GROUPIES

The stage, covered with cordovan and red carpets, is invaded by any number of little girls (or old ladies). They curtsy and throw flowers at the entering entourage. The Great Maestro wears a tailcoat with the twin tails held by Pages. The Councillors enter from the other side. The Wench holds a tray with a huge loaf of bread, salt, fly-paper, etc.

The Virtuoso kisses the loaf, cuts the ribbon (with scissors or a sword), sits at his piano. Resounding cheers and applause. The Virtuoso rubs his hands. The ovation billows like a sail. The Virtuoso's hands go limp but he rubs them again. The ovation turns into a storm. The whole room sings 'For he's a jolly good fellow . . . .' Sweating with excitement, a critic pulls a small white dog from his pocket and wipes his face.

The Virtuoso swallows a large quantity of pills, washing them down with water. Perhaps he doesn't feel well. With his left hand, he brushes his long hair off his forehead. More cheers.

The Virtuoso rubs his hands and snaps off his index finger (right hand). The finger falls slowly onto the red carpet. A Page picks up the finger and places it with great reverence on the silver tray beside the bread. (The play's director should secrete a wooden finger in the Virtuoso's coatsleeve.)

The Virtuoso leans over the keyboard. A moment of tension. Dead silence. All one can hear are creaks, coughs, mutters and rumbling stomachs. Yet the Great Maestro is still delaying, rubbing, folding, unfolding his hands. 'Encore, encore' rings out. It becomes an avalanche. Everybody's running towards the stage. They seize his hands, they pull them off, they pick him up and carry him on their shoulders, on and on and on. He's moved, he's floating, he's ours, we love him.

BABYBABBA

Romantic Love Knocks At The Door

HE — 18

SHE — 17

> *A room. Some art reproductions on the walls. Some 'artistic' fabric. Some illustrated magazines. There may also be some music playing on the radio or a record player. From time to time, he chews gum. It allows the actor to experiment a bit.*

SHE: we're gonna have a babba man

HE: what's a babba man

SHE: a baby man

HE: what baby man

SHE: an itsy one

HE: itsy?

SHE: yeah itsy bitsy witsy

> *(HE stops chewing and sticks the gum onto the wall or some furniture.)*

SHE: a bitsy-witsy babba with ickle dimply cheeks

HE: spit it out get to it whassa babba

SHE: a babba's a baby

HE: babybabba babbababy can't you talk human man

SHE: can't you guess man

HE: (*sticking his gum to the sole of his shoe*) you're talking like some

SHE: (*provocatively*) like what like what

   (*HE chews gum.*)

SHE: it'll have hazel ickle eyes

HE: eyes?

SHE: ok then blue

HE: (*chewing gum*) blue?

SHE: like two lovely flowers a nose like a little potato and your little pigly ears I'll kiss him day and night tickle his legs ears and fingers you know that kinda baby's lots of fun he'll be good and quiet first he'll drink milk from my breast and then from the bottle

HE: bottle breast first you gotta getta breast

SHE: idiot getta breast getta breast you go breast yourself

HE: why can't you say what you really mean speak like a man like when you talk about money slippers dresses

SHE: ok then you are going to become a father

HE: a father me?

SHE: well it can't be me

HE: listen man

SHE: yeah

HE: say it again

SHE: you're a daddy

HE: (*takes out a bottle of beer opens it and drinks*) daddy daddy what'll you come up with next man

SHE: the daddy of our baby

HE: you're just trying to freak me out

SHE: but it's cool up to now you've been a little squirt and now
you're a daddy wait a year and our baby will be calling you
papa you'll be a sweet papa

HE: (*chewing gum*) daddypapa are you cracy

SHE: he'll have the softest hair it'll turn into black curls

    (*HE chews in silence.*)

SHE: aren't you happy

HE: man!

SHE: yeah?

HE: listen what you putting on me man?

SHE: darling I'm so happy I can share it with you

HE: share what?

SHE: that our babba's already in my tummy

HE: don't try freaking me out man

SHE: you'll see how sweet he'll be

HE: won't see

SHE: what d'you mean

HE: I mean I won't see

SHE: see what

HE: the baby

SHE: what do you know! O! he'll be tiny and plump he'll have a
head like an angel

HE: he'll have two heads

SHE: he'll have silky hair

HE: bald head red thin greasy hair square head

SHE: a lovely navel like a little button

HE: one foot long and it'll keep coming undone

SHE: he'll gurgle so sweetly

HE: he won't talk till he's eighteen and then he'll just mumble

SHE: stop it

HE: he'll have stick eyes tiny like the tips of polyps up somebody's nose bent feet harelip he'll be a coprophiliac sodomitic
hermaphrodite idiot sadist

SHE: (*smiling*) give me your hand darling come sit with me no
better lie down but please keep your clothes on don't get
undressed don't take your shoes or socks off hold me tight
look in my eyes and tell me you love me now and forever
that you'll love me till you die that no-one can ever part us
don't speak my darling

HE: don't try freaking me out man

SHE: it shall be the fruit of our love

HE: don't pretend you've gone mad love story

SHE: you my beloved husband and father my master Tristan

HE: has that loony Professor Coogle Moogle got inside your head?
has he whisked your languages up?

SHE: Coogle Moogle? in my head? you know not what you're
saying my beloved

HE: that romantic love quack the one who invented the machine
for squeezing tears out from empty heads like yours

SHE: (*choking with tears*) o! woe is me!

HE: (*blowing a bubble that grows in his mouth till it bursts*) how can
you say 'o! woe is me!'? can't you understand one phrase like
that destroys everything destroys you me and this drama
this work of art

SHE: what art you buffoon you embryo you pathetic little actor

HE: you're ruining it all again you're supposed to be using the
language of a seventies' teenager and you keep talking like
your aunt try to get it into your head you're smashing up the
entire internal structure of this play which is not based on
some moronic conflict but the word! Get it into your head!
Lady Bracknell can't come on wailing like Antigone

SHE: and why's that?

HE: because everything will fall apart not only as far as
playwrighting's concerned but also life that is sociology

politology putting it concisely the whole state of Denmark will collapse with a big bang

SHE: you're having me on man every sentence that we utter is true a new reality

HE: get it into your head! if a waiter starts speaking like Chaucer or Yeats they'll lock him in the nuthouse

SHE: why? it would be extremely intriguing and droll

HE: all right and what if a general starts babbling like a granny or a wet nurse with a newborn baby or a toddler coochy-coochy-coo rock-a-bye-baby blahblahblah then every pact and every GHQ turns itself into a creche ... do you get it lovebird? It's a very fine line ... a general like that would end up in coo-coo land within 24 hours that's it! language is the glue the cement the polyfilla that sticks it all together ....

SHE: it seems to me that everybody in Shakespeare speaks Shakespearean language whether it's the fool the king the friar or the whore. The same imagery the same tendency to metaphor pathos exaggeration proverbs clotted words similarly in Brecht and Beckett or Wyspiański and Witkacy that sodding Zakopanian genius.

HE: well ok! agreed! But I'm not talking about Shakespeare but about a play called *Babybabba* and in this play we change the linguistic convention and we're screwed! Total death. Premeditated murder. Anyway it's too late. It's done.

SHE: I couldn't listen to myself talk anymore and that's why I changed towards the end ....

HE: 'o! woe is me!' the moment you said that everything fell apart and turned into an monstrosity unclassifiable .

SHE: it is a remarkably interesting theory it explains the pathological condition of contemporary drama not to mention its so-called crisis but I cannot quite be sure how many guys in this country are even conscious of this problem ...? Three possibly .... Man.

DOPPELGÄNGER

A room. A POET sits at a table covered in papers. He's writing. The OTHER enters. He goes to the open window, shuts it and sticks black paper all over it. He sits opposite the writer, whose face is almost touching the papers.

OTHER: What are you doing

POET: Writing

OTHER: I asked what you are doing

          (POET stops writing.)

OTHER: Give me your pen

POET: No no I must I can't yet just now

          (OTHER opens his palm. POET places his pen in the other's palm. OTHER breaks the pen and puts it in the rubbish bin.)

POET: How will I write now

OTHER: You won't

POET: But I

OTHER: You don't have to write

POET: Have I committed some crime some mistake

OTHER: Ask yourself not me

POET: Maybe writing was my crime

OTHER: I don't know

POET: In Warsaw alone there are several hundred registered professional —

OTHER: Think about yourself now don't look round

POET: What should I do with myself

OTHER: It's up to you

POET: No I won't do this

OTHER: Do what

POET: You know

OTHER: Still want to write poems do you

POET: I still feel I can I was wrong poetry didn't die it's healthy as

OTHER: You weren't wrong

(The telephone rings. The POET *picks up the receiver. A girl-bird* VOICE *chirps in the receiver-nest: 'our school class fan club would like to invite you very cordially to a poetry festival competition reading season spring autumn summer.')*

POET: I am a stone I am as if I were not

(The receiver resounds with chatter and laughter 'oh please we're so keen . . . .')

POET: What can a stone do at a poetry reading

VOICE IN THE RECEIVER:
           The children want to see you touch you ask they're very curious

POET:
           It's all pure nonsense
           New little poems
           In my mouth the tongue loiters
           Plays with the molars

POET: *(puts down the receiver. Looks at the* OTHER*)* Have I done the right thing?

OTHER: *(nods his head)* Yes. But you aren't a stone

*(*POET *moves his finger on paper as if writing.)*

OTHER: Give me the paper

(POET covers the sheet with his hand.)

OTHER: You won't need it anymore

POET: Can't you leave me two or three sheets?

OTHER: No

POET: One sheet half a sheet

OTHER: It's a lot you won't know what to do with it

POET: I want to make a will like the others

OTHER: You'll live another fifty years

POET: I can write with my finger

OTHER: As you like *(gives him a piece of paper)*

POET: *(moves his finger on paper and says)* Let the stone that was the corner-stone rejected by know-it-alls philosophers doctors postdoctorates impotents be thrown into the water and let the circles growing and disappearing on the water testify that here is the grave of poetry

OTHER: *(bursts out laughing)* You little fool priest buffoon pack your books now

POET: The ones on the table

OTHER: First shut the open ones then those from the floor walls and ceiling

POET: All of them

OTHER: Yes you won't need them

POET: I've been reading for forty five years these books have read me I know every spine origin I know where the bookmarks are at least let me keep three

OTHER: Give me their titles

POET: Can I have the old Westa edition of Adam Mickiewicz's works published in Brody 1911 the *New Testament of our Lord Jesus Christ* and one more ... perhaps *The Natural World* by Daykowski

OTHER: If you can justify your choice you will receive the selected volumes

POET: I consume these books I grow out of them I breathe through them the words from these books become my body

OTHER: You've said nothing do you wish to add anything

POET: No whatever I touch turns into a meaningless phrase . . . what's happening in the room next door what's happening in there?

OTHER: They're removing the boxes of books they're nailing them down

POET: (*reads*) 'Therefore take heed lest the light inside thee turn to darkness. For if all thy body keepeth bright with no shade of darkness then all things shall be light, and thou shalt see truth as a flash of lightning . . . .' What are those footsteps?

OTHER: They're taking away the boxes of books and the pictures down from the walls they're bleaching the colours

POET: (*opens the next book*)
'So in the night the wise men lit their lamps
And honed and sharpened their minds on their books,
As cold and hard as steel swords. With a crowd
Of blind disciples they all fished for God.
But treason in the forefront onward strode
And led them down the straight but fatal road . . . .'

OTHER: These paintings can stay they just have to be covered with tar put the books away prepare for the journey

POET: Am I being punished for the prizes? But worse people than me got wreaths ribbons crosses awards monuments palms from presidents kings princes

OTHER: Worse?

POET: I'm sorry

OTHER: Give me your belt braces tie knife shoelaces

POET: Can I say good-bye to my friend

OTHER: Your friend's your enemy

POET: Can I touch the hand of another human being

OTHER: You have cut off your hands

POET: Let me still open the third book (*reads*) 'Spring returns, its warm breath melting the earth's snow cover and bringing life to the shoots hidden beneath. The fields have changed their appearance . . . .'

OTHER: You've half an hour

POET: What shall I do

OTHER: Up to you

POET: I'm going out

VOICE: Will you be back for dinner

POET: I'm leaving for ever

VOICE: Will you be going past the post office

POET: Yes

VOICE: Can you mail the letters

POET: OK

He takes a hammer and nails from the table. He nails planks over the door.

A DISCORDANT DRAMA

'Now, dear reader, I want you to know
that you are reading a tragic history and
not some tall tale so swap your slippers
for cothurni.'

The READER *(in a suit) sits in an elegant but uncomfortable
chair. He reads the play from the beginning to the so-called
end. Actors perform their moves according to the text, but sometimes there is a delay between the words and the actions, or
they pronounce the words too late to match the gesture or even
the events. The actors repeat their lines after the* READER — *though
not always: sometimes they listen in silence. However the* READER
*not only reads the dialogue but also the thoughts of the people
who appear on the stage.*

Scene 1

READER: (*reading*) It is night. People are asleep or busy with bliss or
creating new people. The bedroom which I have selected is
dark. Two heads are silhouetted on a pillow. But only one
person is sleeping, the other lies with his eyes open, thinking. He is thinking the time has come.

MALE VOICE: The time has come, I'll put on a demon's mask, roar, and wake her up; she'll die from a heart attack, and I shall gallop away to my little Betty whose breasts are tiny and sweet as the apples of paradise. Or else I'll pack my case and run away. To the moon! This old hag has whiskers and a beard. I'll shave them off and slice her into pieces.

READER: (*reading*) The man gets up, gets dressed, knocks over a chair. The woman wakes. She asks in a sleepy voice.

FEMALE VOICE: Has my pussy woken up, has he got a horrid tummy?

READER: (*reading*) Before the man can reply, someone knocks loudly on the door. After a while there is a voice: 'Open the door! In the name of King Philus! Or we must break it down!' The man lights a candle, he wears a jacket and long-johns. He goes to the door.

MAN: (*putting his ear to the door*) You can fuck yourself (*he says to himself, making an appropriate gesture*).

VOICE BEHIND THE DOOR: Don Filip, we know you're home. Open the door!

(*The* MAN *puts down the candle, kneels, peeps through the key-hole.*)

VOICE BEHIND THE DOOR: Citizen Centurion! I spy a blue eye on the far side. The colour tallies with the official description, it's him!

MAN: (*in a child's voice*) Daddy's not at home, sir.

READER: (*reading*) The death squad confer on the other side. There are three of them. In black uniforms and ancient Greek helmets. After a while a voice rings out.

VOICE: Who's that on the far side of the door?

MAN: (*with a child's voice*) Daddy's little girl.

ASSASSIN: Open the door, my child. I'll give you a sweetie.

MAN: (*in a child's voice*) Are you assassins sent by King Philus?

ASSASSINS: Yes! We drag citizens from their beds and murder them.

MAN: (*in his own voice*) Idiots! Don't you listen to the radio?! Only an hour ago the King was shot by Colonel Atticus, the Junta has taken over. Amen.

READER: (*reading*) The death squad confer amongst themselves. Terror and confusion overwhelm them. They stand with their mouths agape. They sheath their swords.

CENTURION: Are you telling the truth, little girl?

MAN: They'll string you up by your balls, you scoundrels! Don't you know I'm Colonel Atticus' son-in-law?

CENTURION: Ah! In that case we apologize. Perhaps we could be of some assistance in the future! Sleep tight.

FEMALE VOICE: What's all that racket in the middle of the night? Is it the diarrhea?

MAN: King Atticus sent his death squad for me, but it turns out that the King has been shot by Colonel Philus . . . .

FEMALE VOICE: Haven't you mixed the names up?

MAN: I don't know. Let's go to sleep.

READER: (*reading*) See how our private lusts and murderous designs are intertwined inseparably with public events. For the time being the wicked husband has abandoned his homicidal scheme. But what is this?! The second he closes his eyes, there is a hammering at the door.

VOICE BEHIND THE DOOR: Open up! Colonel Atticus has been shot by the King's loyal guard Philippus, who was hiding behind a curtain. Open in the name of the law, or we shall break the door down!!! And stop pretending you're your own daughter, you old wretch, because you revealed yourself prematurely and carelessly.

MAN: (*with a child's voice*) I was only pretending to be Daddy, to scare you away, you baddies. Peek-a-boo!

READER: As one man the death squad break open the door and tumble into the bedroom waving their swords.

(*At this moment the phone rings. The* WOMAN *[an ample white arm] picks up the receiver.*)

CENTURION: (*loudly*) Get dressed, get out of bed, you've three minutes to say good-bye to your children! I have orders to shoot all the inhabitants of this house. Long live Philippus the Regent!!!

(The SOLDIERS raise their swords and go 'Hail!' three times.)

WOMAN: Shut up you idiots! Atticus' aide-de-camp is on the line. Philippus has abdicated and fled to Crete with his retinue. Here you are, idiot, you can hear it for yourself!

(She hands the receiver to the CENTURION, he listens for a moment, then kneels and starts begging for mercy).

CENTURION: I'm losing my mind in all this mess. I refuse to obey orders. Soldiers! I command you to go on strike! On hunger strike! Lay down your arms!

READER: *(reading)* The confused soldiers abandon their weaponry. The man and the woman go back to sleep. At that moment a military march resounds.

Scene 2

A history lesson at the primary school for Aristotelians. The lecturer is Arthur Vincent Corinth. One year after the events.

CORINTH: In the last years of King Philus' reign the oppression was so great that nobody knew what day it was. Philus' death squad used to wake citizens and drag them out into streets which ran with blood. At that point the officers of the guard under the leadership of Atticus the Centurion determined to depose the King, and hatched a plot. Warned by his friends, Philus crushed the plot in the bud and issued new emergency decrees abolishing the constitution and parliament. And so began the reign of terror. Cows began to give black milk, hens laid triangular eggs. Now children, your homework for tomorrow. You will write an essay on 'The Everyday Life of Ordinary People During the Decline of the Kingdom of Philus and His Successors.'

(Through the window, the sound of a military march.)

WHAT'S MORE WHAT'S LESS

In a park

HE: You've noticed haven't you there's more and more everything but less and less us?

I: you mean less people? just look around!

HE: it's not the birth rate I'm talking about it's the individuals . . . .

I: spring's coming the days are getting longer there's something optimistic something joyous about it!

HE: there's less me. Less hair less teeth less calcium in the bones less sperm less hate less love less friends . . . .

I: less silence Sam!

HE: more awards reviews letters invitations untangled godawful problems lying around like old black shoelaces.

I: but you've had another 'success'? You're caked with prizes.

HE: there's less and less me! Even my death's decreasing. Less smiles and more dog crap on the lawns the pavements

I: you're not an animal lover?

HE: animals don't figure in the human family the more love for animals the less for thy neighbour the more affection for a wuff wuff cheep cheep squirrel the more indifference towards another human being only fools can still believe a good man loves animals a good man loves people.

I: what you're saying is inhuman.

HE: arch-human you've noticed haven't you there's more dog crap on the squares the lawns by the walls? someone should dole out scoops to the owners to clean up after their darling four-legged chums one day they must be forced to they can't expect the state the church to do it for them . . . .

I: do you still write Sam?

HE: in one of my stories the hero keeps his finger stuck up his arse.

I: can heroes keep their fingers up their arses?

HE: not on a monument . . . just in life . . . .

I: you've noticed haven't you Sam your problems are at death's door disintegrating the hero's dying not waving a banner but with a finger up his arse . . . .

HE: when I'm cycling all the problems become condensed into the need to maintain balance when I write I am simply between two walls.

I: your hero pees in a flower pot of blooming red geraniums full of life and joy the flowers wither some sort of metaphor is it?

HE: no no he feels a pressure on his bladder and then a great relief because he's closed I don't know maybe he kills flies they distract his thinking . . . .

I: I still love animals when I see some bint in an animal's skin or fur I begin to doubt whose skin it is . . . .

HE: I don't distinguish between genders my individuals just talk stay silent and stink they shrink
flies are very small animals
Dandruff fell on the velvet collar of his sacque
like snow on an antique horse-drawn
cheap hearse
in the cages birds of prey dragged their broken wings
frayed brooms white with droppings
in the fishtank two pikes of equal size posed snout to snout
motionless tooth for tooth eye for eye
There is less and less afterlife more and more packaging and
books

there is less of the word more words
there is less man more flesh

er liebt bushes and boulders und er haßt birds und butterflies

I: who? who hates who blinds birds who squashes butterflies

HE: he puts his tongue covered thickly with dung in my mouth

I: have you ever been to Radomsko or will you never see
Radomsko before the end

HE: I was born in a grave there's less and less of me in Paris